COUNTY WEXFORD
IN THE RARE OLD TIMES

County Wexford in the Rare Old Times 1880-1980
by Nicholas Furlong

Editorial and Production Management
Michael Freeman, Editor, MF Media.

Consultants
Bernard Browne
James B. Curtis
Mairead Furlong
Hilary Murphy
Celestine Rafferty

Photographic Management
Peter McDonald

Design
Sinéad McKenna, Sin É Design

Printing
Printed in Ireland by Naas Printing ltd., Naas, Co. Kildare

Distillery Press wishes to acknowledge the generous support and encouragement given by Wexford County Council towards the publication of this work.

Since 1995, many photograph donations have been made to us. We have endeavoured to trace holders of copyright materials. In a number of instances we have been unable to contact the specific photographer while some of our donors are now deceased. We ask that those who can help us in source or identification would write to the publishers.

ISBN- 978-0-9555574-1-5

Distillery Press, Kellystown, Drinagh, Wexford, Ireland.
Web: www.nicholasfurlong.com Email:info@nicholasfurlong.com
Copyright © Nicholas Furlong. 2010.

All rights reserved. No part of this publication may be reproduced, stored in a retrieval system, or transmitted, in any form or by any means, electronic, mechanical, photocopying, recording or otherwise without the prior permission of the publishers.

County WEXFORD
in the Rare Old Times
1880–1980

Nicholas Furlong

Distillery Press, Kellystown,
Drinagh, Wexford, Ireland.

Overleaf: 1930s Wexford from
Johnny Hughes' land. Mulgannon,
currently occupied by the residence of
Councillor Padge Reck. Colfer's land
in foreground with thatched cow
house. The Byrne family occupied the
slated house next door.
*Lawrence Collection,
National Library of Ireland.*

*To the photographers and those
who preserved their work*

Opposite: Violet Elgee with her mother.
Photograph by Charles Vize, c.1910.

CONTENTS

Introduction	10	
List of Photographs	14	
1 People of the Land	21	
2 Arts	41	
3 Politics	71	
4 God's Acre	89	
5 Families	107	
6 Memories of 1798	119	
7 Characters	123	
8 Presidential	131	
9 Sights and Scenes – A Miscellany	137	
10 People of the Sea	149	
11 Transport	157	
12 Sport	167	
13 Education	187	
14 Armies and War	197	

INTRODUCTION

The evidence of photography, particularly early photography, is vulnerable. Age, neglect and indifference have resulted in loss of much which in later ages would have become important.

The motivation for initiating this series in 1985 was the search, the collection and restoration for publication of the first images made of County Wexford in the dawn of the photographic era. We continue to stay on this course particularly where the collected photographs are of substantial importance to County Wexford's history. It is still surprising, but challenging that important photographs of Wexford life still remain to be gathered and given permanent record for future generations. Without realising it at the time, 1985, we were in fact at the end of an era. Ahead lay another era of change, deep trouble, elation. The developments in the science of photography over the last twenty five years have been extraordinary and that is an understatement. The Wexford world of which we treat in the volume is however a world that is gone. The photographs we have compiled range from the 1880s to the 1980s.

In 1985, following an economic upsurge we were experiencing another recession unexpected by the general public and certainly incredibly by the banks who had distributed credit liberally. The cause of that depression undetected by these agencies' agents in Brussels was that massive over-production in agricultural produce all across Europe meant a devastating collapse in commodity prices with a comprehensive roll-on effect. It signalled the end of the viable small acreage family farm.

Previous: Browne's Castle c 1400 at Browneswood, Enniscorthy. Residence of the Browne's until October 1649 when it was taken by Oliver Cromwell, all the inhabitants perished. Across the River Slaney stands the 18th Century residence of the Hatton family. *Lawrence Collection, National Library of Ireland.*

1985 also produced the first public evidence of the approaching turbulence in Church politics and camouflaged iniquities. One has only to reflect on the enormous changes to realise that most significant developments were taking place before we had time to identify them twenty five years ago. Above all, the development in photography and photographic communication throughout the last quarter of a century has been mesmerising. A gardener, farmer, housewife or merchant illegally burning refuse in the assumed privacy of yard or field is now observed and identified clearly by satellite.

We have collected photographs which are of importance beyond our confines because Wexford's geographic position and continuing development render it of more than usual significance. One of the effects from which we hope present and future viewers will derive satisfaction is the realisation that we have survived and overcome times of the greatest difficulty in good heart and with determination.

Nicholas Furlong
December 2nd 2010.

Going to the circus in Rosslare, 1929.

A breath-taking draw with Galway in the All Ireland Senior Hurling semi-final, playing Cork's great stadium in August 1976, goalie John Nolan of the Gers O'Hanrahans makes a spectacular save with Willie Murphy of the Faythe Harriers and Teddy O'Connor, Rathnure, at left making certain that he survives. He did, and Wexford won the replay.

INTRODUCTION | 13

LIST OF PHOTOGRAPHS

PRELIMINARIES

Wexford from Mulgannon	4
Violet Elgee	7
Browne's Castle	8
Circus Rosslare 1929	11
All Ireland 1976	12

1 PEOPLE OF THE LAND

Sacks on knees, Kellystown	20
The Evictions Phase	22
All Stars of 60s	22
New Ross Meat Market	23
Oylegate Farmer	24
Point to Point at Lingstown	24
Self Help at Piercestown	25
Gorey Fair Day	26
Sacks on knees	26
Weather for spraying	27
Cutting corn with a binder	27
Threshing Day	28
Motorised Technology	28
Agricultural Conference	29
Cattle being shot	30
Sheep for slaughter	30
Munitir na Tire	31
World Ploughing 1973	32
Ploughmen's memorial	32
Monageer Macra na Feirme	33
Fethard Macra na Tuaithe	33
Buttles Barley Fed	34
Polder Wexford Harbour	34
Nunns Malsters	35
M.T. Connolly's class	35
IFA gathering	36
Blackstairs vista	36
Joe Rea's Wexford team	37
Women's anger	37
Shelburne Cooperative	38

2 ARTS

William Doyle, *Mikado*	40
Outing to Dunbrody Abbey	42
Séamus O'Dwyer, Jim Liddy	42
James and Margaret O'Keeffe	44
Gorey Band	46
St Michael's Brass Band	46
Band uniform	46
At Gorey Bridge	46
Brass and Reed Band	47
Gorey Pipers at Rathdrum	47
Feis Charman	47
Balfe's *Bohemian Girl*	48
Light Opera aristocrats	49
King of the Pipers	50
Count John McCormack and friends	50
Christian Brothers	51
The Boker's *Pirates of Penzance*	51
Feis Charman	52
The Dublin Wexford dance	54
Wexford Festival Opera	54
Festival first decade	55
Back stage workers	55
Saw Johnny Hoy	56
Voluntary staff	56
Crab Fishing Championships	57
Liam Gaul	57
The Lunatic Fringe	58
Edgar	58
Wexford Festival	59
Stooping to anything…	59
Corpus Christ Procession	60
Bands in Belfield	61
New Ross F.C.A. Pipe Band	61
The Free Press	62
Printers of Anne Street	62
St. Brigid's, Bunclody	63
The Gaul School of Dancing	63

LIST OF PHOTOGRAPHS | 15

Amateur Drama in Enniscorthy	64
C.Y.M.S Christmas Party	64
Gorey Loreto Schools	65
Gorey Deanery Plain Chant Festival	66
Astor Cinema	67
Dungeon Theatre Group	67
Wexford parish drama group	67
1972 Tops of the Town	68
1977 Glorious Bands Era	68
Cómhaltas Ceóltoiri	69

3 POLITICS

Captain Robert Lambert	70
Republican processions	72
The Blueshirts	72
The Clonee Blueshirts	73
Blueshirt Commemoration	74
Monument to Peter Doyle	74
Blueshirts in Killinick	74
O'Duffy's Irish Brigade	76
Seósamh O Cuinneágain	77
General Franco greets Fr. Leander Cleary	77
Home Rule meeting	78
John E Redmond faces	78

Irish American commemoration	78
Interment of Captain William Redmond	79
Redmond Anniversary	79
Éamon de Valera visit	80
Fr. John Butler	81
Mussolini's Rome	81
With hurling trophies	82
Irish College Students	82
Ms Phyllis O'Kelly née Ryan	83
Mussolini's Fascist Youth With Conor Cruise O'Brien	84
County Council Staff	84
Banner at Vinegar Hill	85
German Ambassador visit	85
Fianna Fáil Dinner Dance	86
Blessing of the Shamrock	86
Lemass, Corish, Cosgrave	87

4 GOD'S ACRE

House of Missions	88
Our Lady's Island procession	90
Christian Brothers, Kilmore Quay	91
CBS Primary School	91
First Apostolic Nuncio	92
Theological students	92

Corpus Christi	92
Corpus Christi	92
Corpus Christi Gorey	93
Confirmation Our Lady's Island	93
Remembering Cromwell	94
Twin Churches Centenary	95
Archbishop Levame, Apostolic Nuncio	96
Archbishop John Charles McQuaid	96
The Shepherdess of Lourdes	96
Ferns Pilgrimage to Lourdes	97
Wexford Pilgrims	97
Bishop Donal J. Herlihy	98
Confirming in Taghmon	98
St. Peter's College seminary	99
London Wexford 50s	99
Corpus Christi Bunclody	100
Rev Norman Ruddock	100
Bishop Noel Vincent Willoughby	100
Ferns happy party	101
With little people	101
Bishop Comiskey reaches out	101
Monaghan Support	101
Ordained Comrades	102
Archbishop Dr. Tomás O Fiaích	103

Ecumenical Committee	103
Horeswood Confirmation	103
Bishop Browne's Jubilee	104

5 FAMILIES

Elgee's visit Nan Cogley	106
Robert McClure	108
The Wexford Elgees	108
Richard and Archer Elgee	109
The Sweetmans	109
The Ryans of Tomcoole	110
The Roche sisters of Scar	110
The Rackards of Killanne	111
The Rams of Gorey	111
Mary Christina Casamajor Ram	112
The Friary in Gorey	112
Colfer of Mulgannon	112
Doyle family of Marshalstown	112
The Cloney family Dungulph	113
Miss Biddulp Colclough	114
Philip B. Pierce with wife Nancy, née O'Brien	116
Cullens of Coolafullaun	117

6 MEMORIES OF 1798

On Vinegar Hill	118
McCauley's Hotel, Oulart Village	120
Boolavogue contingent	120
Wexford Pikemen	120
Three Rocks, Barntown	120
Kilmuckridge contingent at Tinahely	120
Mulrankin/Tomhaggard schools	121

7 CHARACTERS OF OUR LAND

Ned Roche and Paddy Roche	122
Tranquilisers at St James Gate	124
"Ba" Swift of Keyser's Lane	125
Jem Hess of Whitemill	125
Ned Roche and beauties	126
Departure of Larry Doyle	126
Lil and Marion Roche	127
Dr. Peadar "Pax" Sinnott	127
Musicians	128
At Muintir na Tíre week	128
Andy Minihan	128

Sergeant Major Wally Doyle	129
Father John Nolan	129

8 PRESIDENTIAL

JFK visits Dunganstown	130
Sunny June of 1963	132
Crowds running	133
At Redmond Square, Wexford	133
President de Valera at Enniscorthy	134
At Crescent Quay	134
Inspecting Local Defence Force	134
President Éamon de Valera and Dr. George Hadden	135
Opening of Irish Agricultural and Folk Museum in Johnstown Castle	135

9 SIGHTS AND SCENES – A MISCELLANY

View near New Ross	136
Ferrycarrig's old road	138
Rosslare	138
Killinick Village	139
Borodale Bridge	139

Kavanagh's Bread van	140
Martin Hayes	140
Wexford's empty industrial estate	140
Wexford's streets lest we forget	142
Oyster Lane	144
Enniscorthy in flood	144
National Social Studies conference	145
Haddens, famous name, famous staff	145
The Reunion of Walkers staff	146
Enniscorthy in snowfall	146
Enniscorthy	147
Smith Engineering's sale of Pierces	147

10 PEOPLE OF THE SEA

Kilmore Quay fisherman	149
Gathering Wore, Bannow	150
Kilmore or Rosslare	150
Rosslare Harbour Bridge	150
The whale at Ballyhealy	151
New Ross from the old bridge	151

Two threemasters on the calm River Barrow at New Ross	152
The barque *Saltee*	152
The brig *Industry*	152
The S.S. *Irish Larch*	152
Staffords of Wexford M.V. *Menapia* in the Atlantic	152
Franz Stor saved by the *Kerlogue*	153
Tony Jacob, Rathdowney	153
Last breach of the Hopelands dam	154
First Kilmore Festival in 1986	155
Building Wexford's New Bridge	155
Christian Brothers on holidays in Kilmore Quay	155

11 TRANSPORT

Rosslare Harbour	156
Replace train at Ballygeary	158
At Colebrook House, Wellingtonbridge	158
Mr Jack Walker	159
Gorey workmen	159
Outside the Bank of Ireland, Gorey	159
A lorry halted in Taghmon	159
Old railway friend	159

Matthew Boggan's bus services	160
Bread deliveries at Phillips	160
The Billy Malone Express	160
Latest 1920s model	160
Men of Steam C.I.E.	161
First cars across Wexford Bridge	162
Bill Whitty	162
Wexford Veteran at Dungarvan	162
Pierces of Wexford	163
Benz car mystery	163
The Dion Bouton	163
Junior traffic wardens	164
Corbett-Wilson monument at Crane	164
James Breen and Bernard Levin	164
Zealous men at Wexford's North Station	165

12 SPORT

One Man and his Dog. Tim Flood of Cloughbawn	166
Football Hurling Street leagues	168
Wexford Cycling Club	168
New Ross Cycling Club	169

Blackwater in All Ireland	169	All-Ireland Champions of 1968	183	Galbally National School of highest standards	192
Tennis with American Naval officers	169	Good Counsel College, Senior Football winners	183	St Louis College, Ramsgrange	193
Sarsfields F.C.	170	All Ireland Camogie Champions	183	Christian Brothers Schools in Feis Ceoil	193
Ballymurn Hurling Team	171	Cycling Club winner	184	Leaving Cert, St. Peter's College, 1946	194
Adamstown tradition	171	Defeating Kilkenny	184	Church of Ireland parish school classes	194
Mulgannon Harriers	172	St Martin's Junior Football	184	Bright children Templeshanbo	195
Aganist Dublin 1924	172	St. Dympna's juniors	185	Begerin Island ancient school	195
Enniscorthy's athletic	173	Galbally United	185		
The legendary O'Rourkes in Billiards	173	Michael Hickey of Garryrichard	185		
St. Iberius Club victories	173	Bree Hunt meet	185		
Carnsore shooting party	174				
Wexford defeat Offaly	174			## 14 ARMIES AND WAR	
The Wexford Uniteds hulers	174			German ambassador reviews F.C.A. guard of honour	196
St John's Volunteers	175			National Foresters Convention	198
Dublin versus Wexford	176	## 13 EDUCATION		United States Naval Air Base	198
National Hurling League 1938-39	177	Templeshanbo National School	186	Civil War at Killurin station	198
The Throw In	178	Tara Hill scholars 1900	189	Taylorstown viaduct	198
New County Jerseys	179	House of schoolmaster Morgan Nolan	190	Robert Brennan	199, 200, 202
All Ireland Senior Hurling	179	Shielbaggan National School	190	Brennan-Whitmore	202
Selskar Young Irelands	180	'The Boker'	191	South Wexford Brigade, Irish Republican Army	202
Respectable jerseys	181	Templeshanbo National School	191	Campile bombed	203
Aganist Laois	181	Greta Irwin teacher	192	Air Raid volunteers	203
St. James Boys National School, Ramsgrange	181	Tara Hill Hedge-school perhaps	192	Enniscorthy L.D.F.	204
Table Tennis of CYMS	182				
All Ireland Final against Cork	182				

First uniforms	204
War Time Garda	205
Enniscorthy's Irish Red Cross	205
Tom O'Keeffe of The Faythe	206
Luftwaffe crash landings	207
New Ross FCA	207
Outside wooden huts	208
Commdt. Rtd. Tom O'Hanlon	208
Pipe Band parade Easter Sunday	208
Albatross Recreation Hall	208
First female soldiers	209
Veterans 1919-1921	209
50th Anniversary of Rising	209
Séamus Rafter commemoration	210
Last surviving eleven	210
Old soldiers	210
Officers of 25th Battalion	210
'Step Together' week	211
An improvised altar at Castle Annagh Camp	211
Skinheads of the 25th	211
Camp Guard awaiting	212
Coast watching unit of the Irish Army	212
Mine sweepers at Baginbun Head	212
Hook Light house	213
The Head Keeper	213
Saint Dubhans Medieval Church	213
Wexford Boy Scouts	213
Golden Jubilee Parade of Easter Rising Enniscorthy	213
Loch Garman Feis: Presentation Convent's entry	214
Castlebridge 1949	220
Harvest-time in the Haggard field, Mulgannon	224

1 PEOPLE OF THE LAND

Agriculture is the art of tilling the soil in order that it may produce the greatest amount of food. That is the time-honoured and textbook definition. It was valid for 6,000 years in County Wexford and Ireland until by 1980 Ireland along with Europe had so vastly overproduced food that prices collapsed catastrophically. The lending agencies had pushed money on borrowers in millions. The so-called domino effect created by the drops in income saw thousands emigrate, businesses closed down, bankruptcies, the end finally of the small acreage family farms as independent viable units.

Although the peril was seen in Brussels, no indication of coming collapse was made clear. Three consecutive years in the early eighties had months of rain downpours. Would a new definition of farming replace the old? To many who survived and had to change outlook drastically it looked as if the word cash income, or money if you will, would replace the word food in the definition of agriculture.

With thanks to Des Waters and the Journal of the Taghmon Historical Society.

THE EVICTIONS PHASE. Armed Constabulary members escorting a bailiff and his assistants to a rural eviction in the 1890s. The cart contains a batterin-ram, scaling ladders and other demolition equipment. Most members of the force had a great dislike for this duty, as many of them were young countrymen and paid the rent on their parents' homes to protect them from eviction. If one looks at the tall man with the cap, at the back between two policemen, one can understand why the devious - looking bailiff and his assistant needed so much protection.

LEADERS. If one were asked to select the farm business all-stars of the sixties to the eighties most if not all of these men and women would have walk-on parts. Which would be picked as the greatest character among a team of characters? We certainly would not dare attempt a choice. Inevitably the group in a cross county selection just happened to find themselves on the committee of that most vibrant of social, trade and business institutions, the County Wexford Show, Enniscorthy. Front row: Phyllis Deacon, Clonmore Hse, Bree, Enniscorthy; Pat Doyle, Ballybrennan, Bree; John Mernagh, Coolamurray, Davidstown; John Daly, Boreen Hill, Enniscorthy; J.J. Bowe, Kiltealy, Enniscorthy; M. T. Connolly, Wigram, Wexford; Mrs Duggan, The Leap, Davidstown. Second row: Billy Stamp, Market Sq. Enniscorthy; Martin Flood, Castleboro, Clonroche; Sam Deacon, Knockmore, Caim, Enniscorthy; Watt Creane, Birchgrove, Ballyhogue, Enniscorthy; Jerome Healy, Vinegar Hill, Enniscorthy; Robert Gainfort, Monglass, Caim; Tom Carty, Galbally, Crossabeg;

With thanks to Tom and Mai Carty.

Seán Eustace, Loughnageer, Foulksmills. Back row: John Nolan, Ballinastraw, Glenbrien; Edward Guest, Garryduff, Boolavogue; Jack Morris, Marshalstown, Enniscorthy; Tom Shannon, Newbawn, New Ross; James Doran, Moneyhore, Davidstown, Enniscorthy.

1886: THE LONG-SERVING NEW ROSS MEAT MARKET seen that year just before the Christmas rush. Sometimes known as the shambles, the victuallers of New Ross had different stalls on which to sell their produce. The building and mighty timber gate survived to the present day.

The shambles at the bottom of Mary Street in New Ross was the site of the town meat market, certainly stretching back into the 1800s and probably earlier. It was still in operation into the 1950s. It was then still an open market (stalls roofed but open in the middle with stalls left and right).

Jim Sutton remembers being sent across Barrack Lane to Martin Travers for meat for the dinner. He was the last butcher operating out of it. The Delaney family were butchers there also, and others, including Foleys and Doyles, had stalls there in the long ago. The stonework in and around the big arched doorway is very old. Willie Ronan had his shop a few doors down on the corner of Mary Street, South Street, opposite the Tholsel, or as locals call it, "The Tonsel". The date on the Tottenham Shambles Keystone reads 1831.

By courtesy of P.J. Browne.

Photograph by Tomás Hayes.

THE OYLEGATE FARMER

The Oylegate farmer 2500 B. C. reappears in 1975. Without warning a shallow bank slid by a sod or two on a farm near Oylegate. Exposed after four thousand, five hundred years were the remains of one who lived and died on the fertile soil. The alert farmer announced the find. Action began. Discovery of grave urn near Oylegate. The farmer's grave. As the 4,500 year old tomb shows, care was taken with the deceased. The shreds of pottery in foreground were part of the vessel in which the body was entombed. The grave urn was broken and the bones fell out. The National Museum was notified. Archaeologists arrived and took the remains and tomb contents away for examination and recording.

1929, The Farmers' Point to Point at Lingstown. Photograph by Nicholas Kelly, Rosslare.

SOCIAL SELF HELP. This brave group of men hail from the sea, quarry-hole and reclaimed land area of Piercestown parish. All great good hearted neighbours who met regularly for cards, amusement, and exchanges of reliable information. A lie never crossed beyond their wind pipes. These were different times. No T.V., poor radio if any, no social life except the pub when money was scarce, so they decided to set up a club, modest premises and rules. It worked very well as they created a nest for their pastimes by themselves alone. In 1928 it was time to sit up, dress up and have a members' photograph. Here are the Drinagh Social Club members of 1928. You are looking at great men. In fact they look as solemn as a board of directors.

Heads behind at back: Willie Hall, Peter Devereux, Syl Cogley, Unidentified, Kevin Cogley, Jim McBride, and John Codd. Standing: John F. Byrne, Mike Cogley, Jimmy Hall, Joe Benson, John Joe Devereux, Paul Devereux, Paddy Kehoe. Second row: (Heads) Aidan Cogley, Philly Cousins, Tim Kirwin, Richie Cousins, Richie Maguire, Jack Cousins, Bob Maguire. Front row: Johnny Cogley, Tom Cogley, Willie Kehoe, Jack Codd, Jack Kelly, Frank Doyle, Bill White and Noel Hall.

CALVES TO THE FAIR: One of collector Michael Fitzpatrick's most atmospheric photographs. It is early on Gorey Fair Day during the Second World War. A simple scene, the creels, the donkey, the farmer, motor car wheels, the dung under foot, all a memory.

JIM DOYLE, Kellystown, at right, in Kellystown and Poulbrean, Drinagh, Wexford, sacks tied on knees with binder twine, weeding mangolds or turnips in early summer, 1940. Alongside him his son Donald, a clever national school pupil in Piercestown, but his father, despite his teacher's plea, thought it better to bring him back to work on the land at 14 years of age. However, he took a leadership role in every cultural and sports activity in the parish. The field was at the 'Old Town', a cluster of 18th century cottages now completely disappeared.

"SUITABLE WEATHER FOR SPRAYING," the man on Radio Éireann said, so the Hemingway family of Tomona sprang into action. They have left us another wonderful period piece. The fine potato crop is being sprayed with the bluestone mix against blight. It is late 1940s. The horse is still a vital presence. The horse sprayer, the cart type, the tackle are all memories. Is

N. Furlong Collection.

there anyone left who could tackle a farm horse? The skilful hands of young master Ken Hemmingway are ensuring the right proportions in the mix while his father grips the reins in case his (possible) male heir should come to any misadventure.

By courtesy of Ken Hemmingway.

VANISHING BREED. Tom Stafford of Ballintlea, Taghmon, cutting corn with a binder. That beautiful little saviour, the Ferguson Tractor, minus today's obligatory safety cab, is pulling the machine 'which saved the backs of thousands' (So it was thought at the time). John Player keeps Tom soothed.

Donor: J. Stott.

THE THRESHING DAY. 1959. Somebody arrived at Luke and Willie Murphy's of Skeeter Park, Murrintown, just as the mid-morning break occurred on threshing day. They had a camera, so the helpers and the refreshments were gathered away from the chaff dust. The neighbours relaxed; not realising they were about to be immortalised or that strangers might think the occasion to be a normal Wexford poteen drench.

The Murphys, Luke and Willie, were conspicuous in their good works and progressive farming. They were Macra na Feirme, Irish Farmers' Association, Muintir na Tíre pioneers. In particular, as pig breeders and exhibitors they amassed a huge number of trophies and awards, national, provincial, south eastern.

Amongst those gathered around the big Fordson tractor are at front, Brendan Duggan, Brian Cloney, Billy Murphy, with the supplies basket. Next row: Jim Furlong, Harry Gregg, Jimmy Gregg, Kieran Breen, Johnny Cloney, Dick Cleary, Willie Breen, The Dirr and Larry Butler. At back is Luke, the senior, Murphy.

MOTORISED TECHNOLOGY. As everyone knows the rapid development from the horse-dominated economy to motorised technology accelerated throughout the 1950s. The first machine to replace the horse was the neat little Ferguson Tractor whose grey and smart appearance suggested that a child could operate it. The County Committee of Agriculture allied to the County Wexford Vocational Committee saw the need and at the end of the forties inaugurated a farm machinery course at the extensive Ramsfort, Gorey premises and lands.

Without the trouble of identifying each individual and without offence to anyone else unable to attend, it can be taken that this is a photograph of County Wexford's most alert and progressive farmers of that and the following decade. It is necessary to pay tribute to two of the principals. At the top row extreme right is P.J. Breathnach, Chief Executive Officer, County Vocational Committee. In the second row at extreme right in soft hat is the Philip Pierce and Company senior machine tester, Tom Tynan.

AGRICULTURAL SCIENCE CONFERENCE 1973. Under the inspired direction of Dr Thomas Walsh, Director of the Agricultural Institute, later Teagasc, the great work and vital research information at Johnstown Castle grounds produced national and international respect.

In Ireland and of course County Wexford where the soils research H.Q. was based, soils sample information to farms was not the only benefit. The congregation of top scientists and local soils researchers had a substantial impact on the economy and soils education. Dr Thomas Walsh, an incomparable and brilliant soils scientist, was a native of Piercestown and an established farm production revolutionary before the Agricultural Institute was even inaugurated. Staff scientists were not only issuing vital information to our greatest industry but were invited to speak at study conferences from the Soviet Union to Addis Ababa in Ethiopia and the World Bank.

Our photograph shows a group of 68 taken in Johnstown in 1973 at a conference on Animal Manure, comparative properties and use to the best effect. The importance at the time can be gauged by the fact that Ireland was on the cusp of acceptance by the European Economic Community. Apart from staff, the attendance included members of other institutions and disciplines. We regret that we could not positively identify every one of the 68. Front left to right: 1. A.N. Other, 2. Vincent Dodd (UCD), 3. A.N.Other , 4.Tim Gleeson, 5. Dermot Collins, 6. Liam Gavin, 7.Paddy Power, 8. Andy Stewart (N.I), 9.Ml. Deely, (Meat Co), 10. Hugh Marron, advisor Monaghan, 11. Brendan Cunny, 12 ?, 13.Jim Curry (UCD); 14.K. Hanley, 15. P.F. Ryan, 16.Una Barry. Standing in second row: 17. Hugh Tunney, 18.?, 19?, 20?, 21?, 23?,24. Nicky Furlong, 25. *Cork Examiner* correspondent, 26. Mick Herlihy, 27. Pat Moroney, 29. G. Riordan, 30. Paddy Bergin, 32. Billy Burke, 33. Seán Kelly (side profile).

Third row along back: 34?, 35. M. Murphy, 36?, 37. D. Kelly, 40. D. McGrath, 41, Tommy Ryan, 42, Maurice Le Clerc, 43, B. Coulter, 44. T. Power, 45. M. Murphy, 46. S. Molloy, 47.T. Finch, 48. S. Turner, 49. E. Byrne, 50. P. Hayes, 52. S. McCormick, 53. F. Codd, 55. C. Masterson, 57. Owen Daly, 60. M. Clancy, 61. M. O'Sullivan, 62. Ned Hearne, 63. Kiernan Dunican, UCG., 64. Val Stone, Paul and Vincents, 65. Mal O'Keeffe, 66. A.O'Sullivan, 68. Tom Neville, farmer, I.F.A., Wexford Pig Co-op, Killurin.

Photograph by Vincent Staples. Our thanks to him, Hugh Tunney, John Lee and Austin O'Sullivan.

FOOT AND MOUTH PLAGUE

Foot and Mouth plague. The three terrible photographs from 1940-41 are reminiscent of the Russian front horrors, except it took place on the Wexford Carlow border and it was the cattle and sheep which were involved. The horror nevertheless was terrifying. To live, Wexford and Ireland depended on agriculture.

To add to the peril World War II was in full swing. The waters off our coast were churned by U-Boats across the North American trade routes to Britain. The foot and mouth plague had the potential to wipe out every animal in infected Ireland. The only solution was to slaughter infected herds and flocks and isolate the counties involved. Travel from those counties was strictly restricted. Trivial by comparison but still sorely remembered, several counties were forbidden to take part in the football and hurling championships. Tipperary teams for example had to be withdrawn. Unbelievably, for a small population county our neighbours Carlow, with the best, most stylish team in Leinster and probably Ireland, were compelled to withdraw.

Our snapshot by T.J.Barrett shows firstly the deep trench dug by the army with the cattle being shot in turn.

Our second photograph shows the sheep herded into the trench for slaughter.

The Muintir na Tíre National Conference was held for one week in St. Peter's College, August, 1951. Based firmly on self-help and rural neighbourliness, Muintir na Tíre enjoyed cross community support with spectacular success when founded in the 40s by a modest but mobile parish priest, Fr. Hayes of Bansha in County Tipperary. This 'Rural Week' as it was called, gave promise of a more cosy, happier, more prosperous countryside merely by organising local action of united purpose.

It was a time when rural electrification and rural water schemes for example were non-existent. Fr.Hayes with Muintir na Tíre turned the tide for self help into national help which changed life in rural Ireland forever. Fronting the local, national and international gathering are the founder Fr. Hayes, Bishop James Staunton, Patrick Furlong, chairman, Muintir na Tíre Rural Week, and Fr. Hugh O'Byrne, President, St. Peter's College.

WORLD PLOUGHING

World Ploughing Crisis 1973. With enormous effort, diplomacy and political skill, plus the viability of a superb site the National Ploughing Association succeeded in procuring the World Ploughing Championships for County Wexford in 1973. This was a colossal achievement for there was understandably intense competition from much larger countries.

The beautiful site was constituted by the broad acres of the Leigh estate in Rosegarland, Wellingtonbridge, with good soil, suitable infrastructure and glorious vistas. No need to stress the show-piece it was for agri-business, for the great multi-national machinery firms, fuel oil giants, every possible type of farm service and massive requirements of food production. It was covered and promoted by every branch of the media, European and American. The organisation was perfect. As far as one could estimate, nothing could go wrong except the weather.

Nothing except the unexpected that is. The team from Ian Smith's Rhodesia, totally dominated by 250,000 colonial whites, arrived without one member of the 16 million African majority included. Crisis, fright and publicity, was immediate. The first grievous blow arrived when the President of Ireland, His Excellency Erskine Childers, withdrew from the grand opening ceremony and attendance in protest. The protests accumulated but one factor saved the world championships. The project in situ was of itself too huge, too massive in content and too irretrievably compact to be halted. It went ahead, the weather was excellent, and hundreds of thousands over the week arrived. The National Ploughing Championships took place there simultaneously.

There is a unique and lovely ceremony attached to the World Ploughing Championships. Each competing nation brings a stone from the home country on which is inscribed the country's name. These are all set together in a memorial at the world championships site. They can be seen today

Photograph by Christina Jordan.

in the little memorial garden at Rosegarland, Wellingtonbridge. The first world championships were so successful that Rosegarland was chosen again by the World Ploughing Association in 1981. On the 1973 memorial you will see the stone with Rhodesia etched on it. On the 1981 memorial you will read the ancient African name, Zimbabwe.

The exhibition and trade area at Rosegarland, Wellingtonbridge. World and National Ploughing championships, 1973. The memorial garden to two World Championships and individual all-Ireland champions at Rosegarland, Wellingtonbridge. There is a second memorial to the first World Championships there also.

ANOTHER IMPETUS WAS GRABBED BY MACRA NA FEIRME when they entered the world of drama. In this, Monageer Macra na Feirme had great success not only as a group, but in the individual acting talents they developed. Our photograph by courtesy of Mary Walsh was of the Monageer Macra na Feirme group in Drama Festivals of 1959,60,61. Back row: Myles Rath, Mike Walsh, Pat Rath, Pierce Redmond, Nick Walsh, Frank O'Brien, Nick Rath. Middle row: Olive Jeffs, Mrs Kehoe, Helen Rath, Anas Gahan, Eugene Stafford, Catherine Rath, Michael Stafford, Mick Redmond, Ciss Breen. Seated: Jimmy Stafford,

Mrs Walsh, Mrs Rath, Nick Stafford, Paddy Rath, Mrs Stafford, In front: Lar O'Brien and Owen Kehoe, both enthusiastic organisers and promoters of Macra na Feirme in its formative years.

Photograph by Denis O'Connor.

FETHARD MACRA NA TUAITHE, 1973. At back: Anne Hickey, Eileen Flanagan, Eileen Gleeson, Iris Chapman, Pete Rowe, Michael Colfer, Seán Power, Linda Stebbings, John Kelly, Eamonn Tubritt, John Stebbings, Michael Bardon, Tom Murphy, Johnny Colfer, Angela Stebbings,

Front: Ann B. Foley, Mary Colfer, Josephine Finn, Mark Flanagan, Matty Colfer, Fr. Richard Hayes, Eamon Power, Anne Rowe, Alison Flanagan, Kathleen Ryan, Debbie Molloy, Eric Molloy, Betsy Hickey, Kiernan Tubritt, Richard Molloy.

For this bright photograph from Fethard-on-Sea, we thank Eileen Cloney Kehoe, Liam Ryan and the team members, Eamon Power, Willie Gleeson and Dominic Power who collected and produced a volume of photographs from The Hook in the old and not so old days. It was a very valuable exercise.

FARM BUSINESS thrives before recession. Buttles Barley Fed Bacon. The phrase had a ring to it. It was a household word in the south east. Its business had tradition and was managed by Colman Leigh Doyle.

Our photograph shows one of the most dynamic ministers for agriculture, Ray Mac Sharry, visiting Buttles during the first Haughey administration. Mac Sharry knew County Wexford well. He recounted bringing lorry loads of Polly blacks down to County Wexford purchasers as a youth for his father. The group at Buttles are inter-county hurler Harry O'Connor, Lorcan Allen, T.D., Rory Murphy, M.C.C, Patrick Leigh-Doyle, Ray Mac Sharry, M.D. Colman Leigh-Doyle, Michael Sinnott, M.C.C., Seán Browne, T.D. and Gus Byrne M.C.C.

THE SOUTH SLOB, or polder, in Wexford Harbour was reclaimed from the sea in early 1850 with great difficulty. It took several years to consolidate. The extent of the adventure and the risk in putting these lands ten feet below high water level into food production can be gauged against the small 'Upland' fields in the distance.

The canal system appears as a bright road near the whitish field at middle right. The Rosslare Harbour railway runs across the photograph right to left and across the coal channel, the route taken by flat-bottomed cargo boats from Wexford, to the little port of Ballybrennan, top right hand corner, before the reclamation. It is now fresh water. The prospect today would be different because of maturing forest plantations.

Our photograph was taken looking south over half a century ago for a geographical survey for Teagasc. The statute acreage banked out by the dam in the South Harbour is approximately 3000.

Photograph by Denis O'Connor. Eamon Doyle Collection.

NUNNS MALSTERS (W.B. Nunn and Company) were one of the most dominant grain merchants and exporters of quality malting barley for which County Wexford's Clonroche series soils are productive. Their head office staff members were widely known.

At the company annual dinner 1969 in the Talbot Hotel, Wexford, are found standing: Matt Roche, Paddy Ryan, Oliver Hickey, Tommy Ryan, Pat Ffrench, Eamon Doyle, William Collopy. Seated are: John Tyghe, Ms May Kearney; Mrs T. Redmond, J.L. Nunn, Mrs W. Bradish, Lt. Col. W.B. Bradish and Thomas Redmond, manager.

AGRICULTURAL EDUCATION went forward from strength to strength in every area of the county under the enlightened and industrious Chief Agricultural Officer, Michael T. Connolly, M.Agr.Sc., to whom the families on the poorly- treated lands of Wexford owe an enormous debt.

Courtesy of Teagasc. Denis O'Connor photograph.

Our photograph is of one such class in New Ross 1976-1977. We do recognise the well known agricultural movers and shakers seated, advisor Bill Kehoe, the great Michael T. Connolly, Michael Harte, Chairman, County Committee of Agriculture, Kieran Maloney, adviser, and Pat Carroll, adviser.

Amongst those we identify at the 1976 to 1977 class held under the EEC Directive Agricultural course 161 based in Ramsgrange were: front row: Bill Kehoe, Michael T. Connolly, Michael Hart, Kieran Maloney, Pat Carroll. 2nd row: Brian Nuttall, Esther Power, James Boyd. William Auld. A.N. Other. 3rd row: Michael Finn, Robert Kelly, A.N.Other, Aidan Hickey, Bernard Wallace, Eamonn Power. John Doyle. 4th row: A.N.Other, Michael Murphy, Robert Young, Piery Fardy, Vincent Rowe. A.N.Other, Noel O'Connor. Back row: A.N. Other, Matt Carty. Séamus O'Keeffe, Jim Whelan, Matt Larkin, Martin Foley, Michael Cummins, A.N Other, J. J. Murphy, John Cummins.

'WE WILL NOT BE RATED as good land when it is bad land'. Grim overflow attendance at a County IFA gathering at the Farm Centre, Enniscorthy, about the rateable valuations of land even though two found something to smile at.

1963 THE BLACKSTAIRS MOUNTAINS looking northwest. A beautiful vista where the fields seem to radiate from a central farmstead approached by a tree-lined avenue. Note the perfect domestic double-ringed rath or earthworks by the roadside in centre foreground. The whole scene proclaims rich Clonroche soil type land and substantial occupants.

Courtesy of Michael Freeman

THE 1980s SEVERE SLUMP in farm commodity prices led to bankruptcies, loss of hope, loss of collateral, loss of health and home as well as the end of the viable small acreage family farm. The vast over production shock concerned all of Western Europe. In Germany, big areas of good land were flooded and turned over to water sports. The Dutch abandoned the imminent project to reclaim another huge polder.

Ireland's best agri-business brains in Brussels informed us that farming Ireland was so heavily borrowed that an all round 10% commodity price increase would not save us, "and we see no light at the end of the tunnel". They, the Irish experts, urged the adoption of "alternative crops and enterprises - most especially forestry". There was recourse to protest in fury at home. County Wexford followed a leader with Wexford blood, Joe Rea.

Our photograph shows Joe when he was IFA President presenting the rates case written submissions at Government buildings with Richard Donovan of Ballymore, Terence McCann of Camolin and George Gahan of Ferns.

Courtesy of Michael Freeman

WOMEN TAKE THE LEAD IN EXPRESSION OF ANGER.

From Simon W. Kennedy Collection.

THE SHELBURNE COOPERATIVE. The cooperative movement escalated in the early part of the 20th century. For farmers it was felt to be the one system which would raise them above the commercial interests that decided and dominated prices for farm inputs as well as payment for farm produce. In simplified theory, farmers could join together in a group or area to form a body of cooperation which would enjoy legal protection from the State. In that situation they could buy all needed commodities by themselves for themselves and purchase farm produce from each other under joint committee management.

One of the biggest and most successful cooperative movements in Ireland evolved from the first World War period and the War of Independence in the barony of Shelburne, South West County Wexford. The grouping attracted the best farm and farm business minds from the area, an area of fertile soils and a large number of small and big acreage farms. It was an area of the so-called 'Land Wars', evictions with deep bitterness from the 1860s to the 1890s.

The effective grouping of men to set up their own cooperative movement took place in the spring of 1919. On May 19th 1919 it was legally inaugurated. Our photograph presents us with an intractable puzzle. It may have been taken at the opening of the Cooperative Creamery for milk producers in Campile or on the occasion of a branch opening later. The photographer was the famed pioneer of commercial photography, Poole of Waterford.

There is one identity which creates a big surprise as well as putting a date on the photograph. The young priest seated in the front row was as famous at the time as Christy Ring, Nicky Rackard or Henry Shefflin in later years. He was Fr. Edmund Wheeler of Killurin, then curate in nearby Cushinstown parish, winner of four successive All-Ireland senior football medals with adventures better than those devised by Arthur Conan Doyle. He is seated to the right of the Chairman, Shelburne Co-op, Michael Cloney, Dungulph Castle. The gentleman with the hat and moustache in the doorway, centre, is the later General Manager, Simon Murphy.

We regret we cannot be positive about individual identities even if we know they must be included. The first General Manager was Martin Howlett, Dunbrody. Branches were opened in the next few years, Old Ross, 1928; New Ross, 1928; Foulksmills, 1929; Haggard, 1930; Boro, 1935; Ballywilliam, 1936. The 1919 Management Committee included Michael Cloney, Dungulph; Chairman; Simon Murphy, Ballykelly; Michael J. Doyle, Houselands; Patrick O'Brien, Dungulph; Philip Rice, Whitehall; Nicholas Howlett, Ramsgrange; Samuel Warren, Whitechurch; John Griffin, Ballykelly.

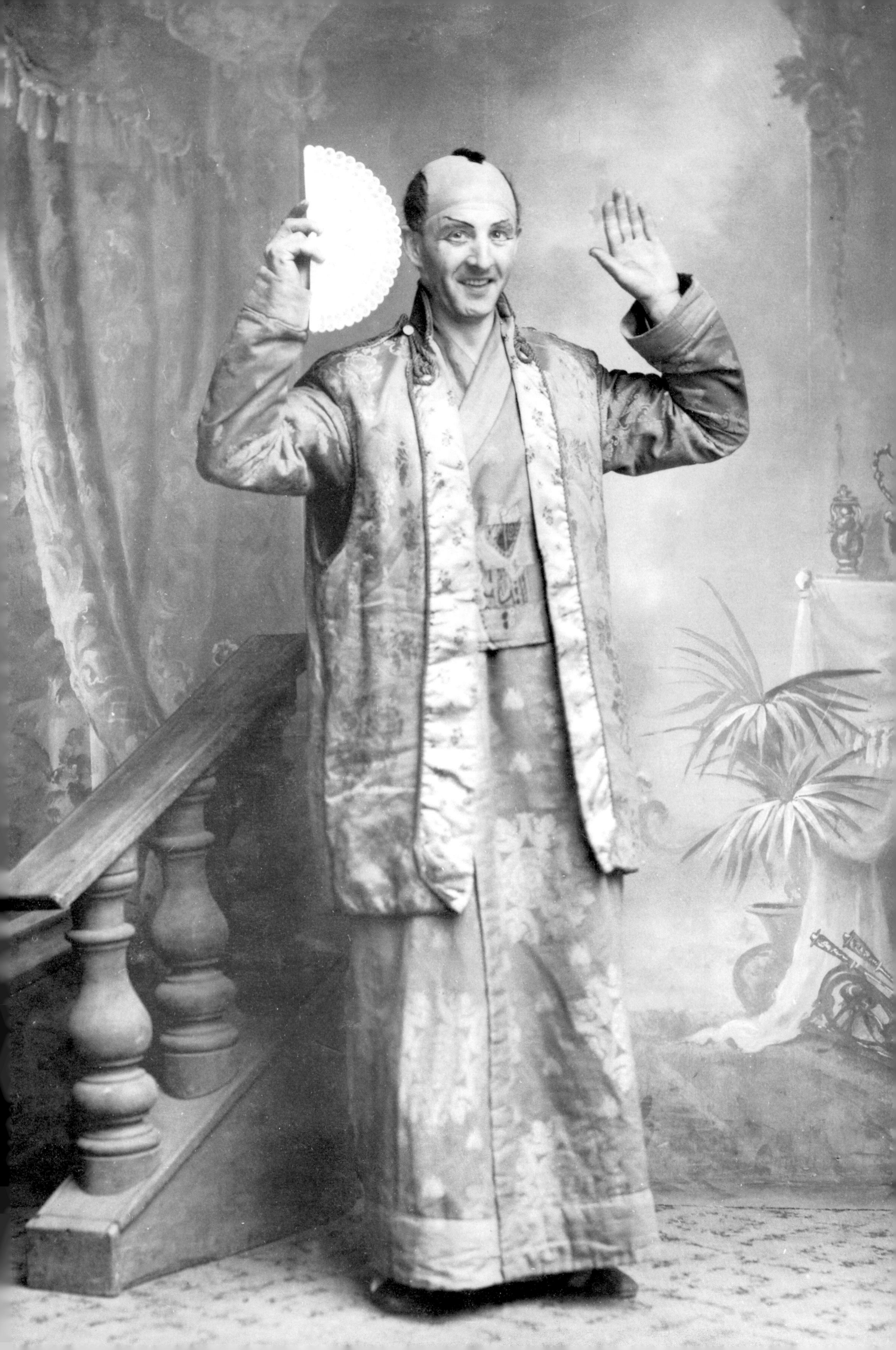

2 ARTS

Art in general was the plaything of the elite. That is until within the last half-century. Its constituency has now broadened to include everything from lilting to Mozart, from mumming to the Swan Lake ballet, straight theatre, ballad and Donizetti opera to Seán Nós, whistling, oil painting, composing, sculpture; the scope is massive.

The important thing is that so many did not realise that their lightly-regarded choice of amusement or entertainment qualified for inclusion in the exotic world of the arts. A citizen of any kind would need to be a remote island recluse not to see that the arts embrace everybody today in a role that is urgently required for self expression and sanity. Thankfully, County Wexford has enjoyed a long lead over the centuries. The arts are alive on every one of our statute acres and municipalities.

Our donor Eamon Doyle's father, in the Gilbert and Sullivan Mikado by the Wexford Light Opera, in the Theatre Royal, Wexford, 1940.

Photograph by Charles Vize.

*Séamus O'Dwyer and
Dr. Jim Liddy.*

SÉAMUS O'DWYER

Postman Impresario

Séamus O'Dwyer was one of the few individuals in Wexford during the 1940s who was not just an opera lover. He was an unobtrusive opera zealot. His knowledge of voices, operas, roles, talents in that art zone was prodigious. It hardly needs to be said that he was a friend of that other zealot, Dr. Tom Walsh, founder of the Wexford Opera Festival. On one fixed night in alternate weeks one would attend the other's home and lapse into a delirium with music and voices from their favourite operas. Again it hardly needs emphasising that Séamus O'Dwyer was a lionhearted, close collaborator of Dr. Tom's in the years of the audacious foundation of the Opera Festival from 1951.

Séamus O'Dwyer was a postman working out of Wexford's General Post Office. His expertise intrigued critics and visiting journalists as if a postman had not a right to be so richly endowed, not that that's a reflection on postmen. The photographic portrait of Séamus hangs with the other founders in the Opera House Founders' Room. He reached an almost incomparable pinnacle in his career in 1955 when Dr. Tom was unable to undertake the auditions abroad for the great tenor role of des Grieux in Puccini's Manon Lescaut. He deputised Séamus O'Dwyer to undertake this task.

To be brief, Séamus left, auditioned, heard several and later engaged an operatic champion in Italy, Salvatore Puma, whose powerful voice, acting and passion left audiences and critics overwhelmed with admiration. Dr. Tom made certain that his marvellous protégé basked in appropriate honours.

Séamus died suddenly at work in the G.P.O. 4th October, 1977. He was 54.

Mystery Outing to Dunbrody Abbey, c. 1880. The big size of the group, the fashions and very formal posed attire suggest no other but the annual expedition of the Royal Society of Antiquaries of Ireland, Dublin based but with nationwide adherents.

Dunbrody Abbey.

THE ART OF JAMES O'KEEFFE

Well over half a century ago at an auction in Paris a wood carving expert and collector declared in astonishment a work of wood carving art as a masterpiece. Its origin was unknown, the master craftsman's identity was unknown, but whoever he or she was became a *cause celebre* among connoisseurs and art publications.

He was James O'Keeffe of the Moor, Mulrankin. He died in February 1923 aged 73. He probably did not know of his new-found fame abroad but his fame was already thoroughly celebrated and realised in rural south Wexford. He was by profession a builder. His legacy: In brick and mortar to-day are the County Council cottages dotted

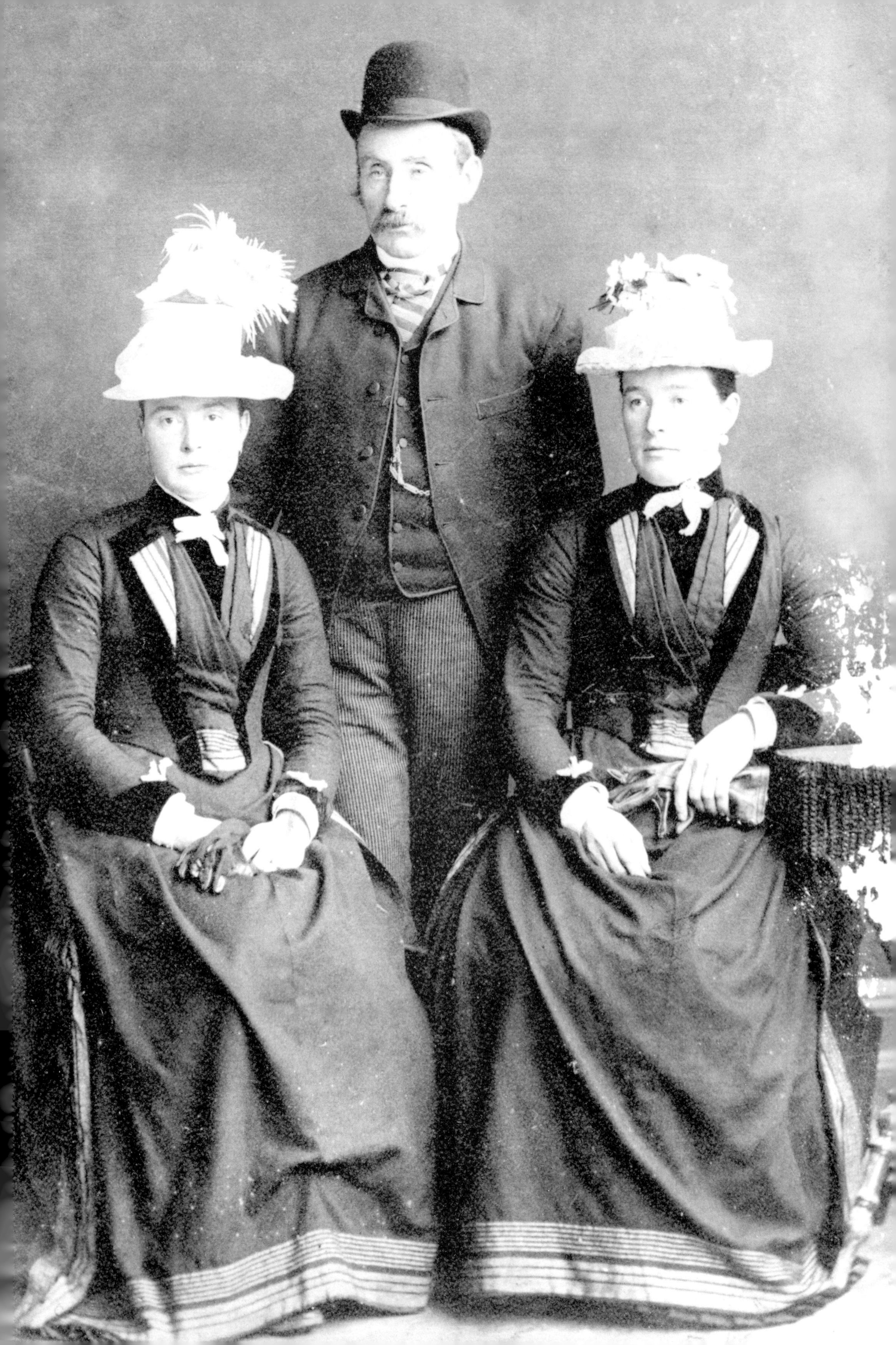

around the south Wexford area. He was a skilled wood cutter who could transform bare oak into elaborate furniture with intricate designs.

As a carpenter of the highest order, he had a ready market for his product. They were sold to people in neighbouring townlands of Mulrankin, Bridgetown, and Kilmore and farther afield who furnished their homes with James O'Keeffe's work. There is an understandable reluctance to boast of the possession of any of his carved works in his home area.

An editor, Michael Heverin, contributed a tribute to him in the Kilmore Journal:'His pieces of furniture are as much his legacy as the cottages. But unlike the cottages, they have not always been attributed to him and their true value not always realised.'

There are many superb examples of his work. Perhaps the reader would like a list of owners and addresses? Our lips are sealed. Some of the more striking are in sitting rooms, for example sideboards and over-mantles. Their feature is the ornate intricate carving. Serpents and leaves abound in the design work and there have been suggestions that they bear some relationship to either French or Italian work of the time.

James O'Keeffe was a most versatile craftsman and there still remains a wooden table with ornate design; a fresco-like depiction of the Sacred Heart and carved doors made of plaster in just one home. The revival of interest in his accomplishments came about following an exhibition of furniture in the Arts Centre. During the exhibition, a number of pieces attracted a lot of attention.

Immediately a search was on to find more of his work. The Irish Country Furniture Society became involved. The Society confirmed that the work was unique and was confined to this part of Ireland. They were also very anxious that it would not be sold off and it would remain in its own area.

James O'Keeffe's handiworks became famous in a matter of weeks, even to the extent that during Wexford Opera Festival, visitors were taken on a tour of the south Wexford area to study his work. When his parents died, he designed and made a magnificent monument over their grave in Kilmannon cemetery. When he himself died, he was buried under that same monument. His grave memorial is now further evidence of his craft. Several pieces of James O'Keeffe's craft are now on display in the National Museum of Ireland and in the Irish Agricultural Museum, Johnstown Castle, Wexford.

Wedding Photograph, 1889. James and Margaret O'Keeffe (née Cullen). Margaret is the lady on the left. The bridesmaid is Eleanor Cullen on right. The best man Thomas Bolger was unavoidably absent.

This James O'Keefe treasure is the front of a home altar which is on exhibition in the National Museum of Ireland.

Courtesy of Séamus O'Keeffe.

GOREY BANDS

THE GOREY BAND, 1872. Photograph taken at the old Penny School House to the back of Anne St., Gorey, which was in use as a school pre-1842. Centre front is retired ex-sergeant major William Walker, Bridge St. (now Esmonde St.) Unfortunately we are not sure of the complete band personnel. Back row, l to r.: Garry Doyle, A.N. Other, Wm. Savidge with beard, William Dixon, Gorey's ace cornet player at that time.

Also in photograph is John Redmond, Bridge St., who was married to Annie Williams – grandparent of the Redmond family, Gorey Bridge 1987. Patrick Madden on Bass Drum and William Murphy from Tara Hill. Also in the band was Marge (Murphy) Leacy, Eire St. Mr. Tom Davis, Main St. was also a band member and a noted musician who played in the 'Gorey Orchestra'.

ST MICHAEL'S BRASS BAND, 1940, at Gorey Vocational School. Front row, l. to r.: Patsy Kinsella, Tommie Curran, Joe Forde, Ted Clince, Bill Egan, Tom Murphy Snr., Simon Sheehan, Patsy Madden. Centre row, l. to r.: Tom Lawlor, Percy Furlong, Nicholas Byrne, Paddy Swords, Ml. Breen, Ml. Noctor, Billy Murphy, Ml. Nolan, Jackie Spencer, Peter Maddock. Back row l. to r.: Tom Travers, J. Guering, Wm. Kenny, Martin Hosey, Thos. Donohoe, Tom Murphy Jnr., Tim Byrne, Jimmy Murphy. Missing from photograph is Bandsman Paddy Sheil.

BAND SPORTING THEIR FIRST UNIFORM taken at the Gorey Courthouse 1952.

Front row, l. to r.: Tommy Curran, Jn. Byrne, Paddy Keogh, Peter Waddock, John Kane – Band Master, Jimmy Murphy, Ted Clince, Paddy Sheil.

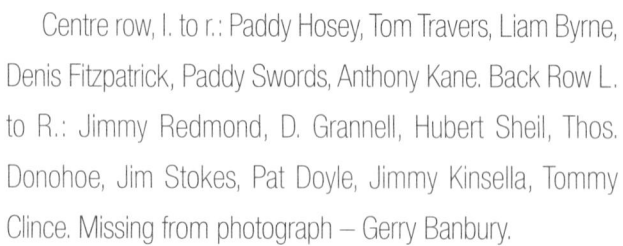

Centre row, l. to r.: Paddy Hosey, Tom Travers, Liam Byrne, Denis Fitzpatrick, Paddy Swords, Anthony Kane. Back Row L. to R.: Jimmy Redmond, D. Grannell, Hubert Sheil, Thos. Donohoe, Jim Stokes, Pat Doyle, Jimmy Kinsella, Tommy Clince. Missing from photograph – Gerry Banbury.

GOREY BRIDGE, C. 1950. Mr Peter Maddock, leading St Michael's Brass Band. With grateful appreciation to Michael Fitzpatrick, Cluainin, Gorey, for permission to reproduce from his Gorey Collection.

GOREY BRASS AND REED BAND 1925. Reorganised in 1915. Twenty six people attended the first practice including four former members, band master, Mr Bennett and later Mr. Daniel Donohoe. Front row, l. to r.: Tom Doyle, Jim Kinch – Bass Drum, Michael Kenna, Daniel Donohoe, Billie Dempsey, Tom Murphy, Michael Brown, Pk. Kinsella – Side Drum. Centre row, l. to r.: Mattie McDonagh, Jack Hogan, Ted Clince, Tom Waddock, Charlie Hobbs, Michael Hogan, Paddy Hogan, Tommy A. Spencer. Back row, l. to r.: Ned Jackman, Dan Kinsella, T. Murphy, Paddy Redmond.

Ml. Fitzpatrick Collection.

THE GOREY PIPERS TAKEN AT RATHDRUM 1944. Drum major, Seán McGrath. Front row l. to r.: Pipe Major – Jn. Leacy, Séamus Dooley, Ml, Leacy, John Redmond. Second row, l. to r.: Andy Somers, A.N. Other, Billy Dempsey. Third row, l. to r.: Jimmy Rooney, Paddy Lancaster, Fourth row, l. to r.: Matt Byrne, Jackie Furlong – Bass Drum, Paddy Dunne, Fifth Row, l. to r.: Ml. Dooley and Mylie Donohoe.

Courtesy of Michael Fitzpatrick.

THE FEIS CHARMAN OF 1931 was at middle point of the Feis Golden Age. There was a fever for Irish culture and advance even exploiting industrial exhibitions of County Wexford production, agricultural machinery especially. Our photograph shows the prize-winning champions of their sector, the Enniscorthy Branch of the Gaelic League. We cannot vouch for all the identities so we considered it better to observe 'Ciúineas'.

P.A. Crane Collection. Courtesy of Ibar Carthy.

THE SINGERS AND ACTORS, photographed by Charles Vize may be forgotten now but they dominated the concert platforms, the theatres, the musicals and the church choirs from 1920, or earlier, up to the 1950s. It's suggested that the opera may have been Balfe's *The Bohemian Girl*. Seated in front is the large and powerful baritone John Kirwin of Mary Street, Wexford, who was a big cattleman and dealer, farming at Killiane, Drinagh.

Seated next is the wealthy Eva Cousins of St Peter's Square (Wexford Mineral Waters Co.) a soprano of professional standard in leading roles for decades. She simply had no vocal rival. She married Dr Tom Walsh, founder of Wexford Opera Festival and had a huge influence in the Festival's early years. At her back is Miss Gaul of South Main Street, one of the family which owned the great hardware and undertaking premises now occupied by Penneys department store. The uniformed actor is Patrick Horan. The lady at left is unidentified.

ONE OF WEXFORD LIGHT OPERA'S GATHERING OF ARISTOCRATS, 1938-1939 in Gilbert and Sullivan's *Iolanthe*, Theatre Royal, Wexford. In this Charles Vize study, we see standing, William Doyle, Con Macken, Dom Sinnott, Michael Lane, A.N. Other and Nick Swords. Lane and Sinnott carried on singing for decades. George Ross filled a huge niche for himself in traditional music.

Opposite:
Eamon Doyle Collection.

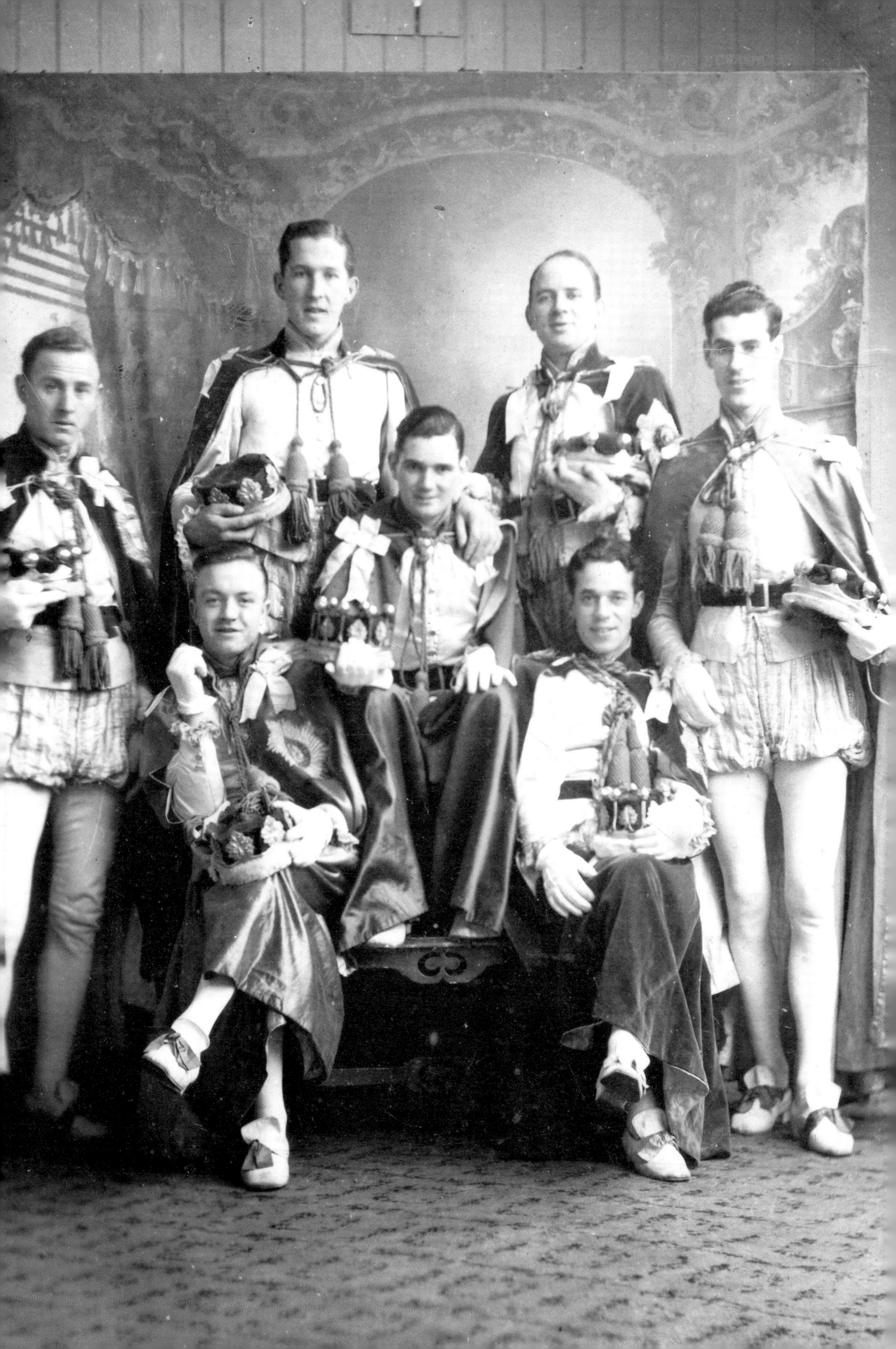

Tom Williams Collection.

Rí na bPíobairí (King of the Pipers) Leo Rowsome who married Helena Williams of the Taghmon bakery family is pictured left at back. His son Leon who carried on the playing and making of the pipes tradition is on right. Twin daughters Helena Grimes née Rowsome and Olivia Grimes née Rowsome are standing either side of Leo's niece, Ann Williams of Taghmon. Leo Rowsome was the first Irish musician to appear on B.B.C. television. He was an incomparable music teacher with many future music celebrities as pupils, for example Paddy Moloney of the Chieftains.

Michael Fitzpatrick's zeal for collecting has meant a substantial saving of Gorey's history and records of which this is a fitting trophy. It shows the greatest tenor in the world of his day. Count John McCormack in his later years attending the first Holy Communion of his friends, Deirdre Boland, now Mrs David Bolger of Millmount, Gorey, and her brother Raymond.

WE ARE NONPLUSSED. We do not know whether this last-supper-like gathering should be in the religious, cultural, social or political section. It seems to be a farewell to a distinguished teacher and Superior of the Christian Brothers Schools in Wexford, Brother Kelleher.

There are several notable links with past days. The reception took place in the old and atmospheric County Hotel in Anne Street, Wexford. At the top table are 1916 veteran Tom Byrne, St. Patrick's Square; Fergal Cardiff, Irish traditional culture promoter; Brother Kelleher, Fr. M.J. O'Neill, Adm. Wexford, (later P.P. Kilanerin) who had an industrious C.V. in the Gaelic League, chairman of the Wexford Opera Festival, Vocational Education, Anthony Perry memorial at Inch, Legion of Mary, Dun Mhuire Theatre; Michael Kehoe, N.T. Glynn, President of the G.A.A., historian, writer, teacher; Séamus Gallagher, county secretary, Conradh na Gaelighe.

Standing, Ms. Other, Ms. Other, Ms. Other (possibly teachers), N. Cleary, B.E., Mrs Séamus Gallagher, Muiris Moynihan, District Court Clerk; Bean Ui Cléirigh, Eugene Curtin, N.T., Mary Wall, Bunclody, Patrick Kinsella, English's Printing; Mrs S Reynolds, Brendan Barry and Ms. Other.

Patrick Kinsella Collection Photograph by Denis O'Connor.

THE TRIUMPHANT *PIRATES OF PENZANCE* heroically performed by the undaunted scholars of the Christian Brothers Schools, The Boker, Wexford, in war-torn 1944.

Eamon Doyle Collection.

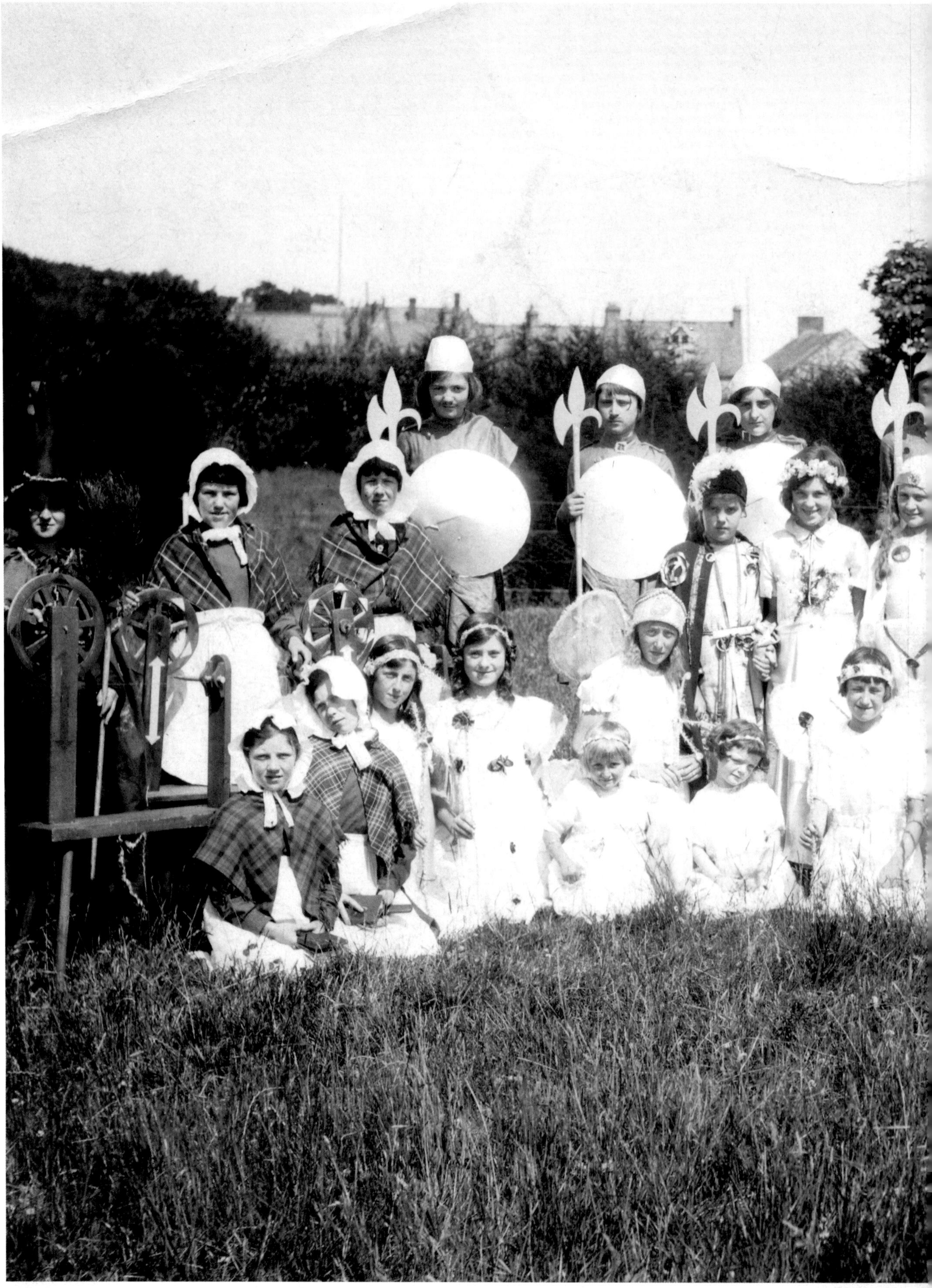

THE PRESENTATION CONVENT, FEIS CHARMAN 1930S ENTRY. The photograph included choral, concert and future festival greats. It was taken at the rear of Doyle's old foundry, Redmond Road, Wexford.

THIS EXCITING AND UNEXPECTED DONATION come to us with a self-explanatory letter from which we quote: "The Dublin Wexford dance at the Ormond Hotel 1935 -1936 season and a grand crowd they were. Perhaps you can use this for your old photograph collection which is very interesting. I am not going to give you my name. I have too many nieces and nephews, and grand ones as well. I would never hear the end of it."

WEXFORD FESTIVAL

Eugene McCarthy, member of the Festival council, Dr. J. Liddy, member of council, Dr. Des French, member of council, Elvina Ramella, Italian soprano, Nicola Monti Italian singer, Gino Vanelli, Italian baritone and Peter Ebert, producer. 1952.

Although the spirit, standard and enthusiasm were generated by the Wexford Festival from the start, the second Opera Festival in 1952 set it on an irreversible course forward. It was the explosive performance of Donizetti's L'Elisir D'Amore, chosen, and previously little-performed, by Dr. Tom Walsh with inspired selectivity.

The major story or remembered words were those of the world celebrated baritone, Vanelli, who was giving his farewell performance in the role of Belcore. When he was introduced to the tiny theatre, the stage and primitive facilities he allegedly wept and said, "Has Vanelli come to this?" By the Festival's end however he was converted to the quality, laughter and enjoyment.

Wexford Festival Opera, back stage voluntary workers. Ear and eye witnesses of the perambulations of Wexford Festival Opera's ghost, Johnny Hoy, are collected on stage to be recorded as reliable witnesses.

The photograph from the first decade of the Opera Festival is undoubtedly a treasure. At back: Nick Hayes, Jimmy Doherty, Billy Stafford, Bill Hartigan, Ms A.N.Other and Anna Lambert. Middle row: June Dandridge, Mai McElroy, Peggy Meyler, Breda Broaders. Seated: Jim Roche, Jimmy O'Neill, Kevin O'Mahoney, Nicky Cleary, Michael Gaddren, Billy Cadogan and Sheila Bergin.

Wexford Festival Opera's back stage voluntary workers, 1950s.Sheila Bergin Walsh; Kathleen Saunders; Peggy Meyler; Breda Broaders; Mai McElroy.

Kneeling: Elizabeth Drury.

The noted art teacher and artist Mai McElroy was one of the many who had experience of the THEATRE ROYAL ghost's presence, Johnny Hoy who died in the Theatre, c. 1934.

In the second row, insurance chief Conor McElhinny with friend and Mrs McElhinny. In plain clothes, shockingly, a member of the Italian Embassy staff. With glasses and hair swished to right and left, the English conductor Bryan Balkwill. He conducted the orchestra at not less than eight Wexford Festivals, so here he was an audience member.

Behind Balkwill is Mrs. C.J. Doyle née Stafford, Ballytory Castle. To her left is Mrs Vera Young, Horetown House. At Mrs. Doyle's right was E.S. (Ted) Doyle, Bridgetown. Behind Ted Doyle are Canon Hazely, Rector of Wexford, and party. In the same row at extreme left are Nancy Kelly, church organist Nora O'Leary and Bessie O'Connor. The four people behind them are Pádraig O'Connor, B.E., and Mrs. Maisie O'Connor, Liam Ryan, manager of the Talbot Hotel and Mrs Ryan. Next to Mrs. Ryan is a member of the Corcoran family of Mount Henry, - John or Brendan.

For this photograph, we thank Dermot Walsh of Ennis Road, Limerick, formerly Carrigeen.

It's a long-lost picture of the BACKSTAGE VOLUNTARY STAFF in the Festival's first decade. Two professionals only are in the photograph, one of them of opera world fame; yet according to Nellie Walsh one of stage infamy.

"You'd want to get danger money," said she, "to get into a Tony Besch production". Front row: Sheila Bergin, the donor's mother, Peggy Roche, artist Mai McElroy, Kathleen Murphy, Kevin

O'Mahony. Next row of immortals: Pierce Walsh, Billy Cadogan, Nicky Cleary and, believe it or not, Anthony Besch, director, whose set, it is alleged once caused Miss Walsh to break her leg; Dr Tom Walsh amongst the disciples; Michael Gaddren with protective arm on Jimmy O'Neill. Back row: Jim Roche, Dick Whitney, Billy Stafford and Richard Day, professional stage director from Glyndebourne.

Photograph by Dan O'Brien.

There's a funny story about Day. He was told by somebody to be careful in Wexford because they were all I.R.A. men and they carried revolvers around in their pockets. He therefore kept to himself, was both silent and, to all intents and perceptions, a loner. At his second festival he realized his informant was a liar 'putting the wind up him.' As the photograph shows, he became 'one of the lads' himself subsequently.

One of the greatest international attractions of the 1950s Festival was the Crab Fishing Championship. If there is a doubt about its world importance it should be recorded that this competition was always attended by His Excellency the Ambassador of Japan and his children

LIAM GAUL. The photograph was taken by Denis O'Connor for display in a photographic exhibition by the Wexford Camera Club during Wexford Opera Festival 1957. The photographs were exhibited to the public at the Legion of Mary meeting room over the present Dun Mhuire Theatre. The photograph was titled, 'Nimble Fingers'.

Liam was a pupil of the famous Wexford accordionist, George Ross from The Faythe, and went on to win the Junior All-Ireland Button Accordion Championship at Fleadh Cheoil na hÉireann at Dungarvan in 1957. This success was followed by the Intermediate All-Ireland Championship at Fleadh Ceoil na hÉireann at Longford in 1958. The same year he won first prize in the Senior Button Accordion competition at Oireachtas na Gaeilge in the Mansion House, Dublin. Switching to the piano accordion, he gained the Senior All-Ireland Championship on that instrument at Fleadh Cheoil na hEireann in Thurles in 1965.

Denis O'Connor Photographic Archive.

THE LUNATIC FRINGE

The Long Room, Whites Hotel, Sept. 1966.

A rehearsal for *The Lunatic Fringe*, The Wexford Opera Festival 1966 production by Nicholas Furlong, directed by Tomás Mac Anna, contracted by the Wexford Chamber of Commerce. Actors rehearsing are Joan Duggan, New Ross, Des Waters, Taghmon, Michael Doran, Gorey and Tony Stacey, New Ross. The production received national U.K. and U.S. publicity.

Des Waters Collection.

The story involved a bogus Franciscan Friar which the Wexford Franciscan Superior, Fr. Mel, found offensive. The production was denounced from the altar resulting in full houses in the Dun Mhuire Theatre, wit, notoriety and temporary fame for the author plus the accolade of a first appearance on Gay Byrne's Late Late T.V. Show with the ultimate at the time, a press conference before the national, British, and New York Herald Tribune press correspondents in White's Hotel.

EDGAR

Edgar, 1980 Festival, at its most heart-breaking moment. From left to right: Virginia Kerr, Teresa Shaw, Eilish Gaul, Katherine Lyons. Kneeling: Clare Kelly, Mary Carberry, and Rita Harpur, with at back, the professional men's chorus, and Bride Street Boys' Choir, comprising Gerard Lawlor, Chorus Master; Martin Bergin, Stephen Foley, Paul O'Donohue, Martin Crowley, David Healy, Gregory O'Leary, Philip Culleton, Shane Kirwan, John Parle, Michael Doyle, George Lawlor, Michael Roche.

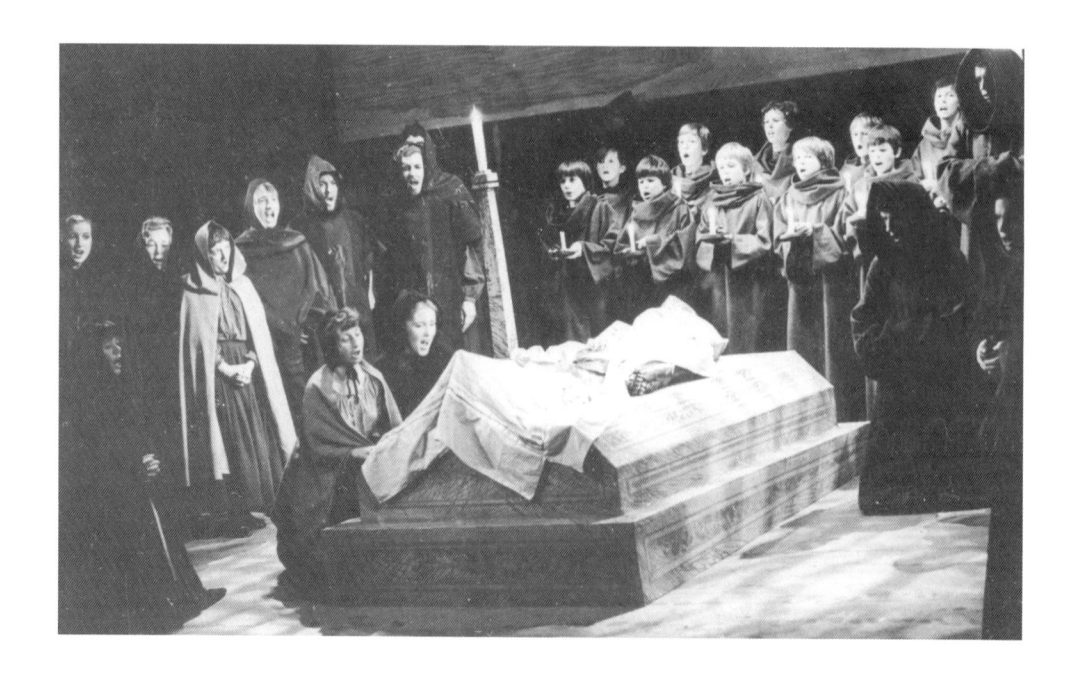

Nico Boer as Edgar; Iris Dell'acqua as Fidelia; Roderick Kennedy as Gualtiero; Terence Sharp as Frank, with the Wexford Festival Chorus in the Wexford Opera Festival production of Puccini's Edgar, 1980.

This beautiful photograph of Wexford Festival 1980 was taken by O'Kennedy-Brindley's master photographer, Brendan Hearne, born in Littlegraigue, Duncormick.

Wexford Ladies Chorus. From left to right: Rita Harpur, Bridie Walsh, Eilish Gaul, Mary Carberry, Katherine Lyons, Marian Finn, Joseph Browne, Margret Gibbon, Betty O'Brien, Nellie Walsh, sister of Dr. Tom Walsh and established contralto in her own right.

STOOPING TO ANYTHING FOR IRELAND and Wexford's sake and certainly for Whites Hotel's Cabaret. This early introduction of Soho-on-Slaney was perpetrated by John Small with the Drag Queen's debut at Wexford Festival Opera thirty years ago.

WEXFORD FESTIVAL SINGERS

A distinguished product of the Opera Festival was the gathering of County Wexford's best and most committed singers who combined to produce a standard in keeping with the international Festival itself. Our photograph from thirty years ago records the singers at a pinnacle of their acknowledged talent. Our donor informs us however that this cropped photograph has unjustly excluded twenty other singers. We are not guilty of this crime so in trepidation and compensation we list the entire Festival Singers of the program. The musical director was Alan Cutts (who remains in County Wexford). The accompanist was Ruth Miller.

Agnes Barry, Bunty Donnelly, Peter Blagden, Kathleen Caffrey, Eileen Campbell, Eamonn Deering, Maureen Considine, Maura Clancy, Father James Doyle, Bernadette Corbett, Helen Doyle, Leslie Dowse, Elizabeth Doyle, Rita Franklin, Evans Dier, Margaret Gibbon, Sandra Haythornthwaite, Cyril Murphy, Avril Harvey, Eileen Humphreys, John Parle, Eileen Herlihy, Evelyne Jordan, David Wagstaff, Catherine Hurley, Eve Kaye, Fintan Whitty, Margaret O'Dowd, Ann Lacey, Father Richard,

OFM., Eithne Scallan, Sr. Regina Lambert, Michael Paget, Mary Wallace, Evelyn Miller, Laura Connolly, Anne Murphy, Cora Kavanagh, Marie O'Reilly, John Browne, Catherine Ruttedge, Mary Parle, Fred Burrell, Irene Haslacher, Selina Scott, Canon Victor Dungan, Charlotte Warham, Kitty Sinnott, John O'Sullivan, Mary Burke, Isolde Fitpatrick, Michael Smyth, Peg Carroll, Helen Ronan, Brendan Kealy, Moya Bolger, Dorothy Owens, Fr. Laurence Murphy, OFM., Eileen Carty, Deirdre Hasset, Jim Maguire, Patricia Davis, Bernie Lloyd, Brian Murphy, Elizabeth Hawkins, Jutta O'Meara, Conal O'Brien, Phyl Lynch, Ann McCarry, Gerard Leahy, Margaret Moriarty, George Stacey, Rita McCormack, Terry McCabe, Patricia McDonald, Betty O'Brien, Evelyn Roche, Lily Trappe, Tissy Wheeler, Eileen Crosbie, Heather Miller.

CORPUS CHRISTI PROCESSION 1954. The feast of Corpus Christi (the body of Christ) is celebrated spectacularly across Europe. Wexford town's procession was no less colourful or comprehensive. Streets vied with one another to put on show the most colourful and devotional display. The Holy Family Confraternity band, the Loch Garman Silver Band and St. Patrick's Fife and Drum band took part.

The Confraternity band led the civic dignitaries headed by the Mayor, Kevin C Morris with the Mace Bearer, William Kehoe. Behind the band on the left are John Byrne, Town Clerk; Dr. Toddy Pierce, Myles Redmond, Thomas F. Byrne, James Gaul, Frank Cullimore, James Sinnott, Nicholas Corish and Brendan Corish, T.D. At left is the municipal legal officer, Fintan M. O'Connor.

The band, one of the best in Ireland on concert platform, field, street or church, contained superb individual musicians. They are first rank, left reading, front to back: Frank O'Donnell, Jas. Gaynor, Séamus O'Neill, Thomas Walsh, Des. McDonald, John Gallagher. Second rank: Des Ruttledge, Risteárd Murphy, Thomas Furlong, Kevin Ruttledge, Thomas Parle, Thomas Byrne. Third rank: James Murphy, Michael Curran, Seán Busher, Richard Roche, Jim Roche, William Rossiter. Fourth rank: Alf. O'Leary, Jack Hayes, Declan Curran, Dan Cunningham, Bryan Furlong, William Power. Fifth rank: Patrick Furlong, Jim Evans, Laurence Doyle, Ed. Busher, Ed. Forristal, Michael Sutherland. In front: Patrick Parle, Bandmaster.

THE MARCHING BAND, two great teams, 1956 in Belfield for the Walsh Cup Final. The thrill of listening to Enniscorthy's Confraternity Band complemented the pageantry which one small boy could not resist. It was an extraordinary game. Half time scores Kilkenny

1-8, Wexford 0-3. Full time score Wexford 2-10, Kilkenny 1-8 still! Unbelievable! The band, one of many which elevated our hearts, paraded as follows: Staff man, T. Bolger, E. Askins, Ml. Doyle Jr., Thomas Askins, Wm. Martin, Ml. Doyle, Patk. Murphy, Lce. Murphy, Brendan Bolger, Seán Walsh, W. O'Connor, J. Hennessy, Jos. O'Connor, Thom. Farrell, Wm. Quirke, P.J. Kelly, Kevin Carthy, M. Kinnaird, Ml. O'Neill, Danl. Murphy, Sonny Murphy. The All-Ireland Champions are lead by Jim English, Nick O'Donnell, Mick Morrissey, Mick O'Hanlon, Ted Morrissey, Tom Ryan, Oliver Gough, Art Foley, Martin Codd, and in the distance, Frank Morris, Nicky Rackard, Harry O' Connor, Tom Dixon, Bobby Rackard, Jim Morrissey.

Dominic Williams Collection.

THE NEW ROSS F.C.A. PIPE BAND relax following the St. Patrick's Day Parade 1982

Courtesy P. Browne. Peter McDonald Collection.

Photograph by John Scanlon. Our thanks to Ger Busher.

A PHOTOGRAPH OF JOLLIFICATION like this should not be of great significance. This one is. It is a tribute to the vitality of a liberal and fearless Wexford newspaper, *The Free Press*, in 1961-62. Chastisement and overbearing interference from the arrogant was treated with scorn by William M. Corcoran of Riversfield, owner and managing director. It was a grievous loss to Wexford county journalism when The Free Press ceased publication at Christmas 1970. Its greatest national moment came when it drew down the full editorial wrath of the Irish Press in the 1940s. Our photograph is that of The Free Press Tops of the Town competition team, several of whom were dispersed in 1970.

Back row: A.N.Other, Tom Mahon, Dermot Kelly, Eddie Busher, Michael Carthy, Joe Maloney, Johnny Roche (not Errol Flynn), Pat Holmes. Middle row: Oliver Hall, Frank Thomas, Declan Kelly, Tony Busher, Fergus Hall, Ms A.N.Other, George Roche, A.N.Other, Ger Busher, Brendan Dowdall. Seated: Mena Scallan, Maura Hayes, Stella Roche, Another lovely A.N.Other, Leo Carthy, young Holmes, Alderman James Sinnott, Nancy Murphy, Ms A.N. Other, Kathleen Giltrap, Nan Kavanagh.

PRINTERS, PUBLISHERS, SINGERS, ACTORS, COMEDIANS of the famed quality printers, Messrs English of Anne Street, Wexford, with the trophy for a scintillating entry in the Tops of the Town Competition 1960. At back, Thomas O'Grady, Séamus Kinsella, Simon Quirke, Cyril Scallan, Eamon Sinnott. Middle row: Manager Shane Sinnott, Peadar Dempsey, Jimmy Hogan, Patrick Kinsella, our photograph donor, Liam Gaul and friend, Con Sinnott, Séan Sinnott and Dom Sinnott, another of the talented Sinnott singing brothers. Seated: Mosie O'Leary, Nick Scallan, Ms. Kelly, Mollie Crean, Ms Kelly, Adrian Sinnott and Fintan O'Leary.

SAINT BRIGID'S
MELODIOUS
CHURCH CHOIR IN
BUNCLODY, 1956.

THE GAUL SCHOOL OF DANCING. The Gaul School of Dancing was brought to nationwide attention when national, provincial and individual awards started to accumulate. Brilliant traditional dancer Maureen Gaul set up her own school based in Wexford town when in her enthusiasm she identified a vacuum in the Irish dancing scene. For decades she and the school enjoyed spectacular success. We cannot state the date or place of this silver gale, nor the name of the adjudicator, but seated and grown up are Claire Gaul, Eileesh Keegan, and school director, Maureen Gaul. We suggest nervously that the date may be plus or minus 1960.

P.A. Crane Photograph. Ibar Carty Collection.

(J.G.) Murphy's photograph.

THE ENDURING AMATEUR DRAMA tradition in Enniscorthy, built for decades and continuing with national as well as provincial top honours was demonstrated in the 1957 production of *The Patsy* in the Athenaeum. The cast members were as follows: Back row, l to r: Ossie Bailey, T. Sweeney, Marty Kinnaird, Jean Foley. Middle Row: Jasper G Tully, J.J. O'Leary, Pauline O'Neill, J.F. Forbes, Molly Ennis, Peggy Sheridan, Kathleen Whelan, Angela Waters, Séamus Dempsey, Dolores Grey, Ann Hanlon. Seated: l to r: Teresa Ennis, J.R. Bennett, Ann Forbes, Harry Ringwood, Teresa Ringwood, Ivan Lynch.

ANOTHER C.Y.M.S. enterprise, the members' children's Christmas Party in 1952. With this cast of thousands we are defeated but some we do recognise. In the centre we see teacher Alderman Nick Corish and alongside him Santa Claus unmasked, Kevin O'Mahoney. At extreme left in mid air is Tom Cullimore. We are reliably informed that there are delegates from the Hayes, Hall and Fortune families, Harry Doyle's girls, Cyril Hogan, Charlotte Gaul and Fr. Brendan O'Rourke – though not yet ordained, - amongst others.

GOREY DEANERY PLAIN CHANT
Gorey Loreto Schools

A wonderful phase of church choral music took place in Gorey and north Wexford district in the 1950s. It was the annual Plain Chant Festival held in Gorey. It brought a whole new breadth of song, competition and the sounds of angels for fifteen years. Then, as many church music-lovers will mourn, Vatican Two's new liturgical arrangements made plain chant somewhat redundant. It has had a glorious risorgimento with best-selling CDs on the world market from several monasteries now, but the best days of Gorey's plain chant festival were over and replaced with, let us say, for peace sake, less archaic airs. We are fortunate to have photographs of several entrants at Gorey from the Irish Press where this writer was once a contributor. Girls in two pictures, boys in another and for gender balance boys and girls in a fourth.

We should point out that despite appeal, Gorey girls would not tell us how long ago it was.

Irish Press.

Irish Press.

Gorey Deanery Plain Chant Festival at Gorey, 1950.

Irish Press.

Gorey Deanery Plain Chant Festival.

Irish Press.

Gorey Deanery Plain Chant Festival.

THE ASTOR CINEMA in Enniscorthy was opened by the Doyle family, film and T.V. business innovators, in October 1938. In 1959 the energetic proprietor, Andy Doyle, held a 21st anniversary week of special films. The great pictorial chronicler, P.A. Crane was on hand to record a new generation of film-goers.

Cinemas were always quite full until the mid 1960s when television became universal. The first broadcast of RTE, then Telefís Éireann, was on 31st December, 1961. The commercial indications were accepted by Andy Doyle. The firm then specialised in television.

THE DUNGEON THEATRE GROUP 1968-69, rehearsing in the little theatre at the lane behind Kelly's Bakery just off Main St. Broadway may have its off-Broadway theatres for rebels. Well this was way-out theatre off the High Street for our radicals.

Scrambled at back are Cyril Hogan, Tom Keeling, Fr. Otto OFM, musician and organist, Thelma Doyle, two visitors and Kathleen Mitten. To the right of Fr. Otto, are Mary Doyle, Larry Murphy, Peggy Doyle and Nuala Lynn. In front, director Kevin O'Mahoney and associate Jimmy O'Neill with Maudlins town's most exquisite wardrobe mistress, Kathleen Murphy.

WEXFORD PARISH DRAMA GROUP Chaplain Fr. Matty Doyle of extensive capabilities. In Roadside, early 1960s.

John Pierce, Donie Murphy (Wexford Post Office), Breda Broaders, Sheila Bergin Walsh, Peggy Meyler Roche, Ms. Martin, Jimmy O'Neill. All were life-long theatre people

Ibar Carty Collection.

Pat Hayes Photograph.

Dermot Walsh Collection.

Photograph by Denis O'Connor, Billy Ringwood Collection.

THE 1972 TOPS OF THE TOWN winners from the County Hall staff. Back row: T.J. Grant, Harry Ringwood, Lorcan Kiernan, Mick Cloake, Padge Kinsella, Eddie Redmond, Kevin Hurley, Adrian Sinnott, Pat Pierce, Seán Dunbar, Ger Griffin, Gerry Forde, Unknown. Row 3: Elva Cardiff, Pat Browne, Anne O'Byrne, Margaret Carley, Mary O'Neill Nancy Byrne, Anne Redmond, Kathleen Curran, Assumpta Doyle, Marie Creane, Carol O'Reilly, Gretta McCarthy, Theresa Codd, Anne Sharkey, Emma Fitzgerald. Row 4: Beryl Kinsella, Vernon Hayden, Nellie Walsh, John Player representative, Jim Morris, Fr. Ned Murphy, Michael Ringwood, Billy Ringwood, Eddie Hopkins, Kathleen Jones, George Furlong. Front row: Theresa Rossiter, Assumpta Byrne, Imelda Byrne, Marie Keating, Mary La Roche, K. Fennell, Jackie Fennell.

Photograph by Ray Flynn. Paddy, Nicky and Rosaleen Cleary.

1977. BANDS' GLORIOUS ERA. The reduction in marching bands has been a musical debacle whatever the reason. They thrilled everyone whether at games, processions, political rallies or concerts. Their loss is deeply felt. At one period between 1940 and 1980 Wexford town enjoyed three marching bands. In this photograph we have the Loch Garman Silver Band comprising talented and well-known musicians even on the showband scene.

At back: Billy O'Neill, Nicky Clancy, Paddy Clancy, Nick Lawlor, Eamon Kehoe, Kevin Roche, Johnny Reck, Davy Hynes, Michael Roche. Second row: Pat Sutherland, Anthony Nolan, J Roche, Tony Hynes, Seán Clancy, John O'Mahony, Derek Thomas, John Fowler, Michael Coughlan, Matt Stafford, Tommy Murphy, Davy Byrne, Bernard Nolan, Joe O'Toole, Tommy Howlin. Front Row: Jimmy Lawlor, Peter Murphy, John Clancy Jr., John Clancy Sr., Tommy O'Neill, John Morris, Frank Tobin. In front: John Walsh and John O'Leary.

THE ALMIGHTY FOURSOME competing in the Cómhaltas Ceóltoiri Éireann county finals at Monageer, c. 1980, - George Rochford, Dick Robinson, George Ross and Gerry Forde.

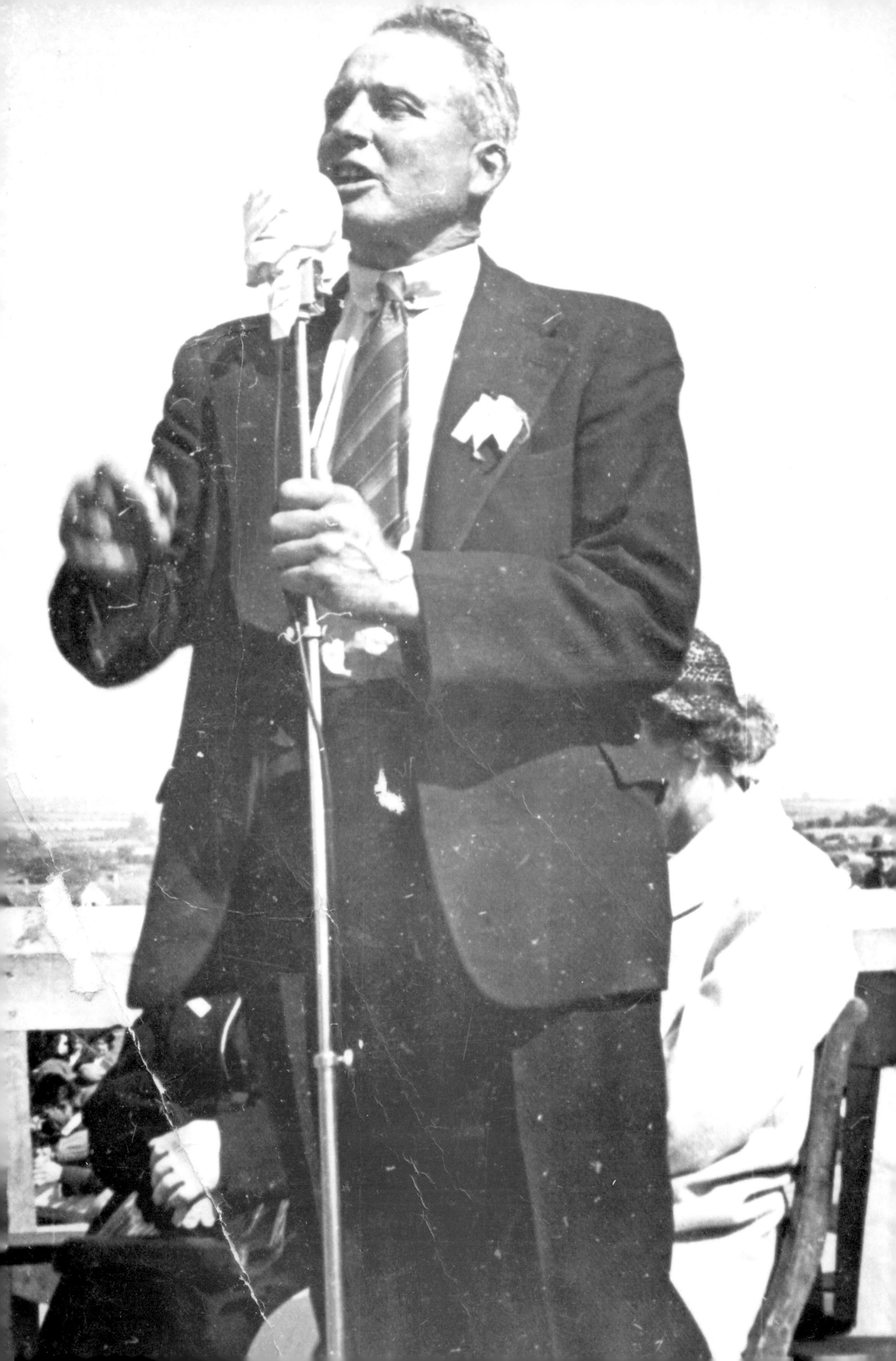

3 POLITICS

Politics in County Wexford, as in Ireland, is still influenced by the Civil War of 1922-23. The strong base of Labour stems from a great tradition inspired by Corish, Larkin, Connolly and the utterly brave hungry revolt of 1911-12. The five seater constituency up to the time of writing gives a near perfect estimation of the situation as it may have existed from the 1923 cease-fire almost ninety years ago. Two seats - pro-Treaty. Two seats - anti-Treaty. One seat- Labour. Youngsters whose parents weren't even born at the time of the Civil War or War of Independence still hold their grandparents' established positions. A question often asked is how Irish politics would have developed had there been no Civil War. Or, was the whole series of developments throughout Ireland a process of evolution?

In this writer's opinion no student in this or succeeding centuries will understand the searing pain or passion on both sides when the Civil War broke out unless they read the published Dail debates on the Treaty itself. They are published by the Government Publications Office.

Opposite: Captain Robert Lambert, commander of the Kyle Flying Squad, speaking at the unveiling of the Parle, Crean and Hogan memorial in Taghmon, summer, 1949. All three were executed during the Civil War by the Free State Army in a phase of reprisal warfare.

Photo by Tomás Williams Collection.

Our thanks to Bernard Nolan, Curracloe road, Enniscorthy.

REPUBLICANS

Republican processions in the late twenties early thirties were huge affairs. They took place as usual on Easter Sunday. The Easter Lilies are on every lapel. The "old" war of Independence IRA still existed, (the anti-Treaty units), so the faces in these interesting photographs were or would be the backbone of Éamon de Valera's new Fianna Fáil plus members of the later illegal IRA of the 30s and 40s.

The photographs were taken from the parapet at the Crosstown terminal of the old Redmond Bridge. The procession was marching to Crosstown cemetery's Republican plot for the commemoration. It is with regret that we cannot identify the Pipe Band in correct uniform.

Another view of the passing Republican parade taken from the Crosstown side of Redmond Bridge, c.1930. The entire bridge, thoroughfare and paths, are packed, all the way back to Carcur.

THE BLUESHIRTS

The Blueshirts. What were they? Who are they? Were they formed to declare a fascist system of government, an elected head with full power, nationalist, a subservient parliament elected from the different and distinctive vocational groups such as electricians, steel workers, farm workers, farm workers, farmers, doctors from the wide medical profession, teachers, industrialists, engineers civil servants so on? The political parties would be abolished.

The system or different shades of the system seemed to be finding support across Europe. Similar exploratory forms to those used in the founding country, Italy, were making appearances in Portugal, Poland, Greece, Germany, Spain. It suggested a reaction to the alleged shambles created by political parties. Fascism, both socialist and nationalist, was in conflict with the socialism known as Communism. Russian Communism was aimed at transnational world communist government on the system developed by Karl Marx and Lenin.

In Ireland the raw hatreds of the Civil War still festered. In fact how democratic Ireland survived the threat of anarchy is something of which the patriot may be proud. As Co. Wexford-born political correspondent of the Irish Times, Deaglán de Breadún, wrote:

"The Fine Gael party was founded with General Eoin O'Duffy as its president and since O'Duffy was not an elected TD, William T. Cosgrave as its leader in the Dail. It was a disturbed and violent time, both internationally and at home.

"Memories of the Civil War, which ended 10 years earlier, were still raw. The Economic War began in 1932 when the Fianna Fáil Government withheld land annuities from the British Exchequer. Farmers were badly hit when Britain imposed duties on Irish agricultural produce in return. Political meetings were marked by violence and thuggery from both sides of the Civil War divide.

Fine Gael was the result of a fusion between three organisations – the old Cuman na nGaedheal party which had set up the Free State; the National Centre Party, a mainly farmer-based organisation whose best-known members were Frank MacDermot and James Dillon; and the O'Duffy-led

National Guard, a quasi-military body otherwise known as the Blueshirts. O'Duffy's past was stormy and controversial. A leading member of the IRA in the War of Independence, he was a close associate of Michael Collins and took the Treaty side in the Civil War. He was appointed Commissioner of the Garda Siochána in 1922, a position he held until February 1933 when he was dismissed by the Fianna Fáil Government under Éamon de Valera. The following July, O'Duffy became leader of the National Guard, previously known as the Army Comrades Association. Ostensibly set up to protect Opposition meetings against supporters of Fianna Fáil and The IRA the organisation's members wore blue shirts and its philosophy had a distinctly fascist flavour. "O'Duffy had met Mussolini while on a pilgrimage to Rome five years earlier. O'Duffy announced a mass march of Blue Shirts to Leinster House on August 13th in imitation, it was thought, of the march on Rome which brought Mussolini to power. O'Duffy backed down when the march was banned by the Government."

In County Wexford the Civil War left a bitter legacy with families divided, brother against brother, sister against sister, old comrades against each other, little wonder it is called in Irish Cogadh na gCaraid, the war of the friends. It is no surprise then to find that the Blueshirts, whatever their grasp of political theory, had been on the Irish Free State side in the Civil War. Their equally zealous opponents were the old Irish Republican Army and the newly elected Fianna Fáil.

The Clonee Blueshirts 1934. Back row: Bill Carton (Clonee), Brian McDonald (Kilbora), Aidan Whelan (Kilbora), John Kelly (Monasootha), Owen Breslin (Ballbuidhe), Denis Kenny (Raheen), Charlie Tompkins (Kilbora), Matt Hayden (Carrigleegan), Matt Mc Donald (Clonee), Tom Lacey (Clonee), Ned Murphy (Coolnaleen), Jack Fitzharris (Clonee), Middle row: Jim Doran (Ballyduff), Art Breen (Tinashrule), Mogue Kenny (Raheen), Dan Doran (Raheen), Din McDonald, Jim Kenny (Raheen), Peter Fortune (Ballyandrew), John Byrne (Monasootha), Art Breen (Tinashrule), Niall Byrne (Monasootha), Pat Kenny (Raheen), Bill Fitzharris (Clonee), A. N.Other. Front row: Jim O'Neill (Bolinaspect), Jim Kelly (Clonee), Paddy O'Toole (Clonee), Jack Shiel (Clonee/Ballybeg), Tom Kehoe (Tinashrule), Johnny O'Toole (Clonee), John Kelly (Clonee), A.N. Other.

Bill and Jack Fitzharris were nephews of the famous "Invincibles" rebel Jim Fitzharris, known as "Skin the Goat".

Photograph by J. Allen.
Courtesy of Pat Codd,
M.C.C.

1934 Blueshirt Commemoration at the grave of Commandant Peter Doyle, Irish Free State Army, assassinated in the grounds of Enniscorthy's Cathedral of Saint Aidan, 10 October 1922. He was a native of Ballinakill, Marshalstown, where he was interred.

Courtesy of Pat Codd,
M.C.C

The monument to Commandant Peter Doyle in Marshalstown graveyard on his anniversary day 1934. Blueshirt ranks and wreath layers with family members stand around the grave.

A group of Blueshirts from south Wexford photographed in Killinick village. It includes the local officers, Dan and Martin Walsh with John and Phil Reilly.

Photograph by courtesy
of Mrs Catherine Walsh.

The Battle of Enniscorthy

Many consider that the last and major battle took place in and around Enniscorthy on 21st June 1798. As we will see from the report of journalist Hilary Murphy an engagement took place, though not of two armies with horse, foot and artillery, on Sunday April 29, 1934.

"A meeting called by the recently formed party, Fine Gael, was arranged for the Market Square. The principal speakers were Commandant Edward Cronin, leader of the Blueshirts and the famed pro-Treaty Minister for Finance, now Senator Ernest Blythe. Before the meeting massed columns of Blueshirts paraded with Commandant Cronin taking the Fascist outstretched right hand salute.

"Contingents were in attendance from Oulart, Blackwater, Ballindaggin, Kiltealy, Clonroche, Wexford, and Enniscorthy and numbering over 800. They formed up in the Abbey Square and headed by a band from Wexford, the parade marched to the golf links, about a mile from town, and escorted Commandant Cronin and Senator Blythe into Enniscorthy.

A huge crowd had assembled at the Market Square and the approaches to the meeting place were jammed. A strong force of Civic Guards, under the command of Chief Superintendent Lynch, kept the situation under control when threatening situations between opposing sides seemed imminent.

In the morning, telegraph wires were cut between Enniscorthy and Ferns. The main road near Scarawalsh was blocked by trees which had been felled the previous night. This was considered the augury for trouble, but the obstructions were removed, and cycling companies of Blueshirts made their way into town.

Once the speakers commenced to address the meeting there was great cheering and counter-cheering, and it became evident that the gathering was a mixed one. A continuous din was kept up, and it was difficult to hear the speakers, while feeling in the assembly became tense. The Gardai did their utmost to cope with the situation and prevent disturbance. Cordons were drawn across the streets leading into the square. Skirmishes took place now and again, and on the outskirts of the crowd, booing was indulged in, and party slogans were shouted.

At one period, when the din was at its highest, Blueshirts charged opposing elements, and batons were freely used. A number of people were knocked down by blows. Crowds rushed for Castle Hill and the Main St. at the other end of the square. The meeting continued to be interrupted from different quarters, and the Gardai exercised every means to preserve the peace and prevent violence.

Just before the end of the meeting a number of men came down Wafer St, armed with sticks and hurleys, and it looked as if a determined onslaught was about to be made. The Gardai, who formed the cordon from the corner of Rafter Street to the Technical School, drew their batons and forced this section back to Lymington Road.

At the end of the meeting other skirmishes took place, and there were a small number of casualties.

More violent scenes took place as Blueshirt contingents were leaving the town for their respective destinations. At the Duffry Gate, the Kiltealy and Ballindaggin contingents were held up by a number of men who hurled stones and bottles at them from Patrick Street.

The situation at this place was very alarming, and a number of Gardai went to the area. Missiles continued to be flung, and it was found impossible to pass the road running at right angles to Patrick Street.

At the opposite end of the town, at Lower Church Street, some Blueshirts belonging to Boolavogue and Oulart contingents were knocked from their bicycles, and received rough treatment. It was stated that one of the assailants attempted to use an iron bar, and was disarmed by a member of the Gardai.

With the arrival of an extra force of Gardai peace was restored in this neighbourhood. Near Drumgoold, two or three Blueshirts from the Blackwater unit were waylaid and the shirts torn off them and burned.

Tension in the town continued until midnight. "Fears were entertained that outbreaks would take place, and that the homes of Blueshirts would be subject to hostile action. Gardai were on duty all night. But no major disturbance took place".

General Eoin O'Duffy, once a major and dependable leader in the War of Independence, became more unpredictable. A founder member of Fine Gael, he was eventually becoming an embarrassment to his party colleagues. He was forced to resign in September 1934, just a year after Fine Gael was founded. He subsequently led a crusade to Spain to fight on Franco's side in Spain's Civil War. Politically a burnt-out case, he died on November 30th 1944. In a show of magnanimity, de Valera gave him a State Funeral.'

The photograph came back with one of Wexford's volunteers in the Spanish Civil War. Photographed are three civilians and two of Franco's soldiers in capes.

THE SPANISH CIVIL WAR

A number of Wexford men joined Eoin O'Duffy's Irish Brigade on the side of General Franco against the Communist Republican forces in the Spanish Civil War which began in 1936.

Three from the Killinick district were Sergeant-Major Seán O'Reilly, Corporal Daniel Walsh and Private Nicholas Potts. They were reported to be looking fit and bronzed when they arrived home in June, 1937, after seven months of active service in Spain.

Nicholas Potts gave the impressions of a young volunteer in O'Duffy's Brigade.

"Having undergone six week's training at Caceras in full kit, the Brigade went into action losing a Spanish Lieutenant, an Irish Lieutenant and an Irish Legionnaire.

"The Brigade advanced on a village on March 13. They were under heavy shellfire practically all the time. In the advance, one man was killed and six wounded. Four others died from wounds. The brigade was jubilant over the blowing up of the army train, killing between 25 and 30 Reds. Caps were thrown into the air while the men cheered.

Conditions at Campozuelos were much the same as that at Caceras. The churches were wrecked. Priests and nuns were killed, and the images in the churches had their eyes picked out by rifle fire and every place showed signs of Red savagery.

Generalissimo Franco visited the Brigade several times and gave them a most cordial welcome."

Ferns reception

An enthusiastic welcome home also greeted seven volunteers from the Ferns district. They were: James Kearns, Clologue; William Conway and Luke O'Rourke, Ferns; Nicholas Walsh, Effernogue; Aidan Kehoe, Tincurry; E. Murphy, Marshalstown, and Dermot Jordan, Clonjordan.

Commdt. W.J. Brennan-Whitmore also spoke in glowing terms of the men who had risked their lives in the cause of God and Christianity. Other volunteers who returned from the war were J. Kelly and J. Radford, Taghmon and Peter Kavanagh, Coolishal, Gorey. (Reports by courtesy of Hilary Murphy)

The former Enniscorthy solicitor, Seósamh O Cuinneagáin, in the uniform of Eoin O'Duffy's Irish Brigade, which aided Franco's forces in the Spanish Civil War.

Dan Walsh, Assaly, Killinick, appointed Deputy Director of the Wexford Blueshirts by General Eoin O'Duffy, fought for General Franco in the Spanish Civil War.

General Franco greets Fr. Leander Cleary, OFM., who served in the Spanish Civil War, during a commemoration in Madrid. Fr. Leander served for several years in Wexford Friary.

JOHN E. REDMOND

HOME RULE MEETING, Abbey Square, Enniscorthy. Identifications are difficult but the number of hard hats on the platform indicates solid "citizen merchant" support. Taken probably around 1910.

The support remnant of a one time Wexford and nationalist Ireland leader at Westminster, John Edward Redmond, M.P. The voice, his brilliant oratory, still rang through the political havoc.

THE REDMOND MEMORIAL COMMITTEE of the late twenties contains a few familiar faces. Seated are Alderman Richard Corish, Mayor of Wexford; Fr. John Sinnott, Adm., probably Ald. Thomas Rossitter. Standing beside the Franciscan may be James J. Stafford of Cromwellsfort. The youth behind Fr. Sinnott is Pat Lambert, Anne St. Bakers; the third head to his right, peering, is Pat Curran, Abbey St, Wexford.

IRISH AMERICAN COMMEMORATION at the John Edward Redmond family vault, c.1929.
Photograph M.O'Keeffe.

THE INTERMENT OF CAPTAIN WILLIAM REDMOND T.D., St John's Churchyard, Wexford in 1932. Numerous Wexford faces can be identified including Herbert Coffey, Fr George Murphy, R.C.A., Alderman Dick Corish and most likely, the Mayor of Waterford. A World War I regimental flag is held near the vault.

Yet another John Edward Redmond anniversary gathering at his tomb in Saint John's Churchyard, c. 1928.

ÉAMON DE VALERA came to power in March 1932. He visited the thriving farm machinery industry in Wexford. The group, photographed outside Pierce's head office includes from left: Denis Allen, Fianna Fáil T.D. for Wexford; Frank Aiken T.D., Minister for Defence; Éamon de Valera, President of the Free State's Executive Council; William White, general manager of Pierce's; Philip Pierce, managing director; and Dr James Ryan T.D., Minister for Agriculture.

FR. JOHN BUTLER IN PONTIFICAL AND MUSSOLINI'S ROME

The 1930 decade on mainland Europe is still a much misunderstood place in its totality. Apart from the national population displacements consolidated by the victory's Treaty of Versailles it saw the anchoring of new political systems of government, Bolshevik Communism in the Russian landmass, Fascism in Italy, Germany, Portugal and several other states. Today the terms Fascism and Communism instigate loathing. In early 1930, proponents of both opposing socialist systems (as each defined itself) considered them worth a try.

While Hitler's and Stalin's regimes leave an unequalled legacy of mass slaughter with vicious and permanent hatreds, a peculiar anomaly attaches to Mussolini. Though initially his diktats improved Italy substantially, it was he, not Hitler, who was the creator of Fascism. It was he who blatantly invaded countries to which Italy had no right, shared culture or language such as Ethiopia, Albania, Greece. Mussolini and Hitler shared one quality. They were both amongst the greatest mesmeric mass orators in history. In their days of rapid accomplishment both were regarded by their own people with fanatical devotion.

Millions of books, films, newsreels, records exist about the period. What is often overlooked is that hundreds of Irish students had a ringside seat at the dramatic events as they unfolded on mainland Europe and in particular Italy.

The Irish College in Rome was packed with Church students throughout the period. A few Ferns Church students were educated in theology and philosophy in other Irish colleges, for example

THE PHILOSOPHERS' CLASS, 2nd year, Irish College, Rome 1937-1939. Fr. John Butler is kneeling at left, front row. The student fourth from left standing is Domnic Conway who eventually became Rector of the Irish College in Rome and later Bishop of Elphin.

MUSSOLINI'S ROME. Mussolini speaks to the Romans from the Pallazzo Venezia. Fr. John Butler Collection.

Fr. Matthew Doyle, Adm. Wexford, later P.P. Camolin, in Salamanca, Spain. The most impressive eyewitness to speak to this writer about all he experienced of historical and world occasions in Rome was Fr. John Butler of Newbawn. He arrived in the Irish College, Rome, as Mussolini completed the takeover of Ethiopia and declared King Victor Emmanuel III of Italy, Emperor of Ethiopia. From then on crisis followed crisis in Europe.

Fr. John Butler, himself a scientific hurler, Dean of Discipline, with trainer Ned Power and Fr. Joe Dooley, all St. Peter's College teaching staff, with the first senior hurling colleges Leinster and All-Ireland trophies won by the Slaney side institution ever, 1962.

He attended many of Mussolini's speeches and theatrical appearances from the Palazzo Venezia. He was there in the crowd as Mussolini declared war in 1940. He informed me that Mussolini was able in his grandiose oratory 'to turn the Romans mad'. University students filled with imperial ambitions frequently demonstrated in Rome for the return to Italy of 'Tunis. Corsica, Savoy, Nice!' When in their days of sensational triumph Adolph Hitler made a reciprocal state visit to Rome in 1938 and 1942 the student John Butler was on hand to soak up the atmosphere. The Dúce and the Führer went through the crowds in open vehicles without any protection. John Butler was 'so close to both of them, no more than six feet, and he estimated that he'could have shaken hands with them.'

John Butler was ordained priest in the Basilica of St. John Lateran in March 1942. He had some difficulty getting home. He travelled through Vichy, France, neutral Spain and Portugal where after patient daily visits to the Lisbon docks he eventually boarded an Irish ship for home. This writer first met him as a teacher and Dean of Discipline in St. Peter's College in late 1943. He never wrote about and, unless asked, rarely spoke about his war-time experiences.

I hope I do not do him an injustice but he gave me the impression that he regarded his student experiences as somewhat less than earth-shattering. "They could have happened to anyone who happened to be in Rome at the time!"

In the days of slow travel, it is doubtful if the visits of Adolf Hitler to Rome were as exciting as the visit to the Irish College students of An Taoiseach, Éamon de Valera in 1939. The snapshots are eloquent. John Butler is second from right. Dominic Conway is third from right at back. There are no dates on the photograph but the occasion must have been the ceremonies of inauguration following the election of Pope Pius XII in 1939.

From the Pope Pius XII inauguration occasion, John Butler's camera friend took another photograph involving a Wexford connection, Mrs Phyllis O'Kelly, née Ryan of Tomcoole, with her husband, Tánaiste and Minister for Finance, Seán T. O'Kelly (later President of Ireland - 1945 -1959) in the Irish College gardens.

IN 1976 during the Liam Cosgrave-Brendan Corish Government, Wexford celebrated some would say the miraculous survival of the Wexford Opera Festival to reach its silver jubilee. Special events were inaugurated.

One such event was a postage stamp exhibition in the Talbot Hotel, Wexford with full participation by the Irish Post Office and commercial firms. Special Opera postmarks on all posted material from Wexford showed a different design for each opera on its performance day. The exhibition was opened by the intellectual lion of Irish politics and academia, Conor Cruise O'Brien, Minister for Post and Telegraphs. Thorough preparations were made to greet and entertain the great man (in some trepidation- the right wines, appropriate menu, peer dinner guests and so on.)

In the middle of his elegant speech a messenger was seen to struggle to get up to the Minister but was held back by security. The instant he stopped, the messenger broke through to him and whispered into his ear. Shock registered. He turned without a word of explanation and literally fled. His state car with Garda outriders screamed off toward Wexford Bridge. The amiable and most distinguished President of Ireland, Cearbhall Uasal O Dálaigh, had abruptly and in rightful anger abdicated, following a gratuitous and bellicose diminishment of his office at an Irish Army function of which he was the head. The President's assailant was his Minister for Defence, Patrick Donegan, T.D., of Co. Louth.

The photograph was taken as the Minister, Conor Cruise O'Brien, prepared to speak. With him is the Opera Festival's Hon. Treasurer F.X. Butler and the Opera Festival's Hon. Press Officer, Nicholas Furlong.

Photograph by Brendan Hearne.

THE COUNTY COUNCIL Staff, 1947 at Jail Road entrance. The photograph was taken at a macabre location. In 1867 the last public hanging of a murderer would have taken place above these beauties and handsome men's heads. With bicycle at left, Peggy O'Connor, later Mrs M.T. Connolly and an unquenchable social services volunteer.

Next is Bridie Doyle, Rosslare; Seán Dunbar, Gorey; Cathleen Sinnott; Lorcan Kiernan, Enniscorthy; the girl in front of him is Eileen Hearne, later married to Frank Cullimore, Wexford Corporation, (parents of Séamus T.D.); Margaret Mitchell, Ursula Kelly, T.D. Sinnott's trusted personal assistant; Alice Walsh, later Mrs John Daly, Enniscorthy, C.A.O. (Horticulture), Maura O'Rafferty, Coolgreaney (later Mrs Eamonn Sinnott); Peggy Doyle, Rosslare, later Mrs Tony Cronin; and Mal Donohoe.

Photograph by courtesy of Bill Creedon.

ACROSS THE WESTERN HEMISPHERE, May the First is the celebration and feast day of the working man and woman. From Paris to Moscow and from Rome to Vinegar Hill, the banners are hoisted while it is to be fervently hoped, the workers of the world unite. Wexford was not behind Moscow or Paris. Our photograph shows the banner carriers on May 1, 1978 with Ireland's Labour leader, Brendan Corish T.D. who until the changing of the guard in 1977 had been Tánaiste and Cabinet Minister in the Cosgrave-Corish administration, leading the vanguard.

From left, Steven Martin, James Carthy, John Flaherty, Jimmy Goodison, Philly Maguire and Tommy Carr, Brendan Corish, John Howlin, Padge Reck, Michael 'Sykie'Savage of legend, Kevin Kehoe and Laurence Carley. Of some significance, sometimes overlooked, is the presence in the honest worker ranks of card-carrying members of Fianna Fáil, lending consolidation to a later Fianna Fáil Taoiseach's declaration that he too 'was a socialist'. The absence of worker sympathisers from other parties raises questions. It is not for us to provide answers. It was a wet day anyhow.

AT THE RECEPTION for the visit of the German Ambassador, with the German Embassy Secretary, to Wexford County's industrial and commercial businesses, c. 1980. The ambassador was accorded a civic reception in the Municipal Buildings. Seated are the Embassy Secretary, the Ambassador, the Mayor of Wexford, Peter Roche; Edward Breen, Town Clerk; Noel Dillon, County Manager.

Standing are William Creedon, County Secretary; Ald. Thomas F. Byrne, Councillor Thomas Carr, Town Sergeant Matt Stafford, James Mahony, Councillors Avril Doyle and Gus Byrne.

Courtesy of E. Breen.

Photograph P.A. Crane.
Ibar Carty Collection.

1952 FIANNA FÁIL DINNER DANCE

BLESSING OF THE SHAMROCK and distribution on St. Patrick's Day, Wexford in the reign of Alderman James Mahony, Mayor; Rev. Fr. Aidan Kavanagh, Administrator and Rev. Canon Eddie Grant, Rector. The year was 1980. The rapidly growing parade, industrial and cultural, was about to take off.

THE TAOISEACH, Mr. Seán Lemass (right), the Fine Gael leader, Mr Liam Cosgrave (centre), and the Labour leader, Mr. Brendan Corish, before their departure from Dublin for New York to attend the visit of Pope Paul VI to the United Nations in New York. It was the first occasion when a Pope addressed the world body. October 1965.

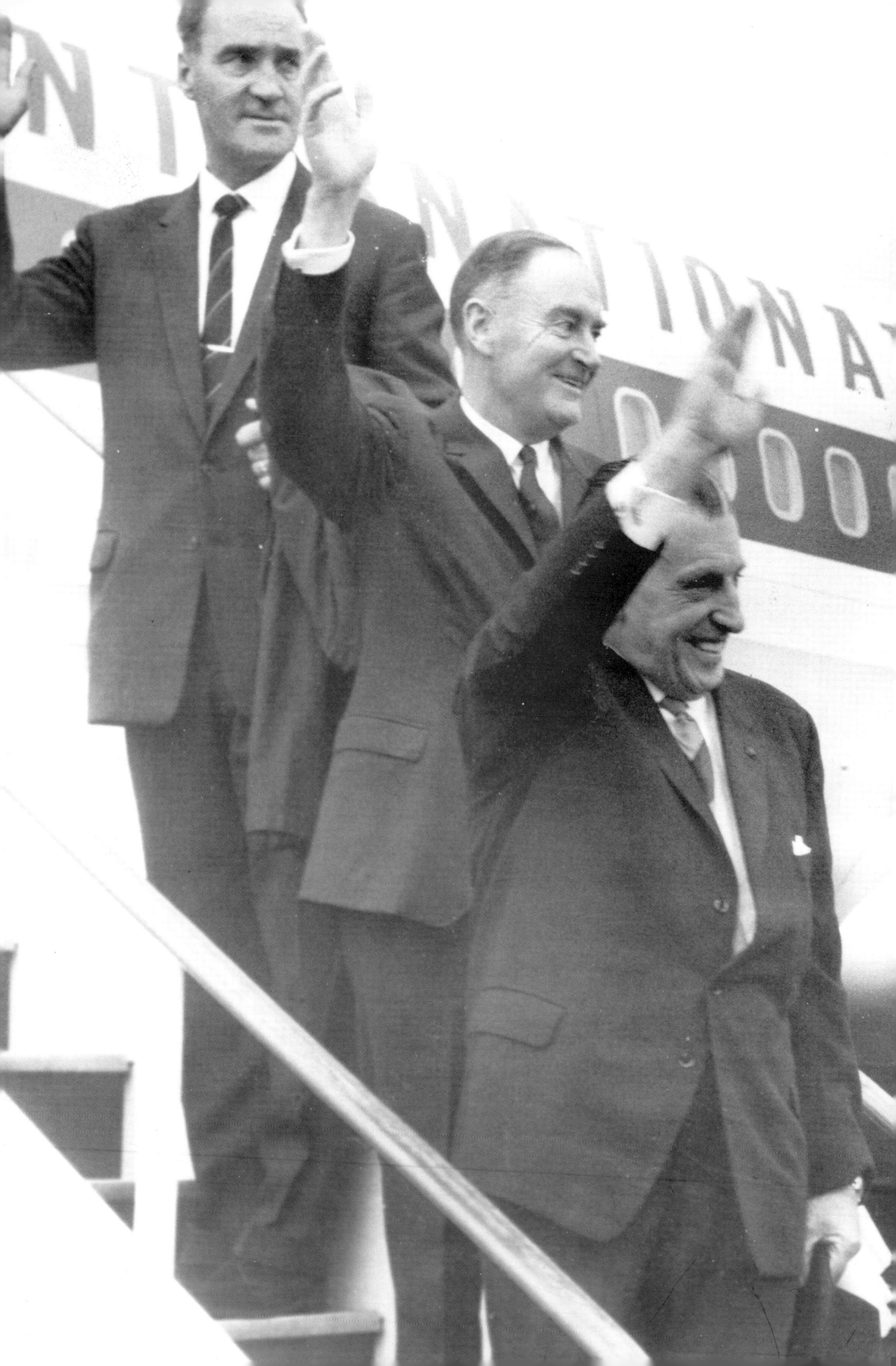

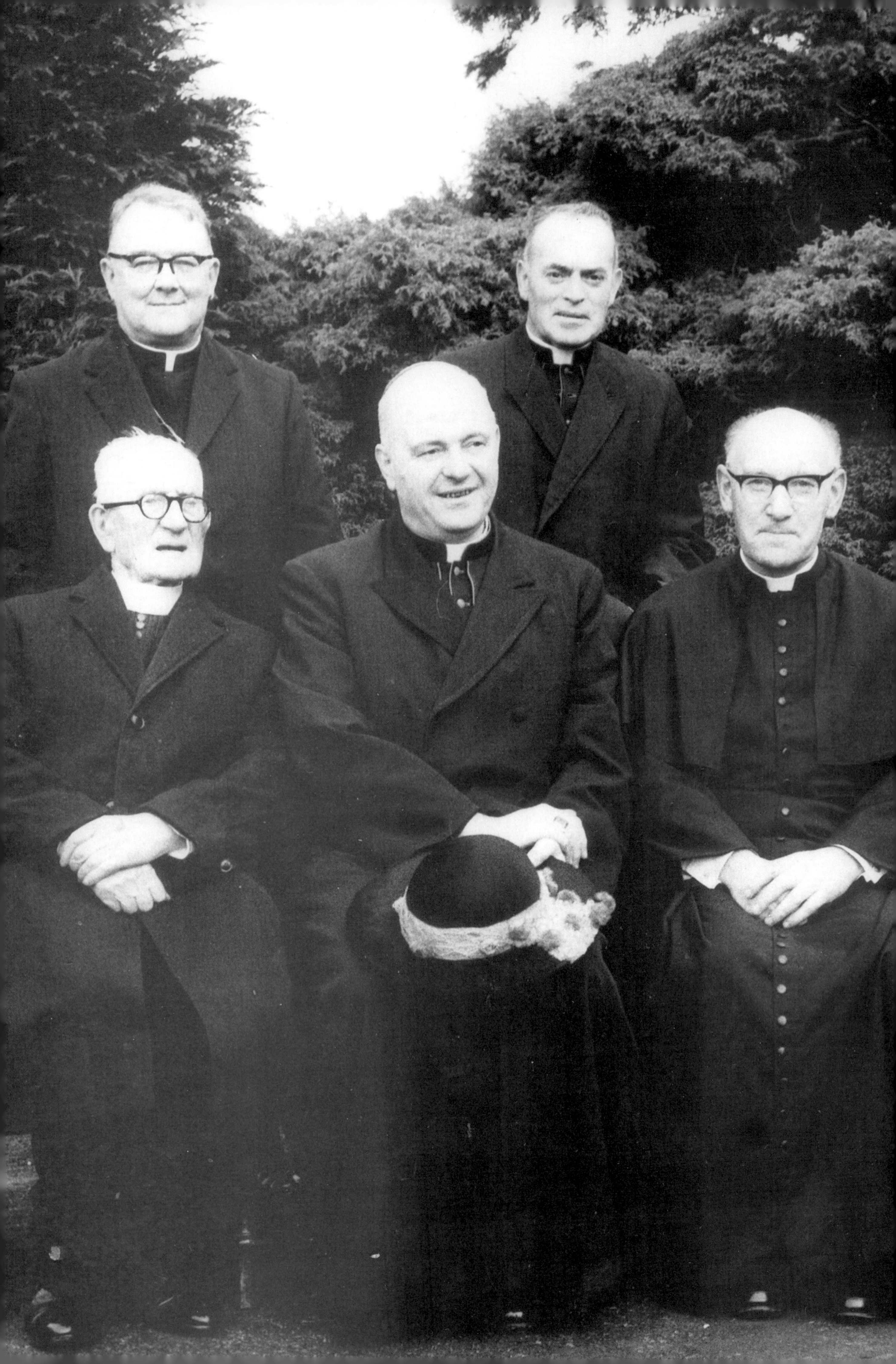

4 GOD'S ACRE

Belief in a universe-creating, intelligent all powerful being called God, is written in the origin legends of all mankind since the ages deep in antiquity.

Different interpretations create many customs from one God to several.

Christian Ireland has from the 5th Century given homage to the one God, though in this century, cynicism and rejection has thrived, whether scientific in origin or in fury over clerical transgressions, moral or political.

We may be on the cusp of great change today, but no one in the past age we portray here anticipated drastic alterations from their established norms.

Priests with a facility in preaching were established in a society of mission fathers by Bishop Thomas Furlong in 1866. From a Diocese of Ferns project based at Templeshannon, they conducted retreats and missions throughout Ireland and the English speaking world.

Of special significance were their retreats and missions to the Irish diaspora in Britain. At celebrations marking the centenary of the House of Missions in 1966 were, seated, the oldest surviving missionary, Rev. Patrick Canon Murphy, P.P. Glynn, William Cardinal Conway, Archbishop of Armagh, Primate of all Ireland; Fr. Joseph Flynn, Superior, House of Missions. At back, Archbishop Dwyer of Birmingham and Bishop Donal J. Herlihy, Bishop of Ferns (1964-1983).

Oileán Mhuire.

Our Lady's Island is not on the Ryan Air or Aer Arann schedules but it has been a place of special and persistent attention for 1,500 years, almost certainly longer. Today buses arrive sometimes unannounced and sometimes off season from as far away as Donegal.

The south-east corner of Ireland, Carnesore, has for plainly logical reasons, been a museum of the remote past since human beings arrived in Ireland over 9,000 years ago. Whatever divine worship they used before Christ's identity and message arrived, it is clear that major activity of a religious nature obtained there. Carnsore of the death inviting seas, currents and rocks is the nearest point to Wales, Britain, France or Spain. Groups of people from remote cultures landed to what was regarded as the last place, 'almost at the end of the world.' (Papal Records. CPL III 565. Mandate to the Bishop of Ferns, January 1355).

The point of Carnsore, where on many days the water of the Irish Sea can be clearly seen like a boundary slapping into the Atlantic Ocean, was infamous for thousands of years. The underwater currents, the sudden fierce changes in those currents, the hidden rocks and reefs made it an annual disaster zone on a major scale for shipping. Long before Christianity came to Ireland, Carnesore was known and mapped as far way as Alexandria in Egypt. Ptolemy the map maker made his map of Europe from measurements made from sailors' measurements.

Carnesore Point was known to them in Greek as 'Hieron Akron' which means 'sacred promontory'. The word sacred or holy referred to the pre-Christian priests or druids who were performing rites involving fire to placate the Satanic presence. So awful were the losses it was believed the place was cursed. At the time of the proposed atomic power station at the Point, the Rath of Saint Vauk on Carnesore was archaeologically excavated. Deep below the surface the remnants of intense fires were found.

It was assumed that Our Lady's Island may have been associated with women, priestesses living in community on the sacred island called 'Oilean na mBan' – 'the women's island'.

When the earliest of Christ's missionaries arrived, the two we know as Saint Vauk and Saint Ibar, they succeeded in bringing the community at St. Vauk's Rath on the Point and the one on Our Lady's Island into the Christian family. Oileán na mBan was changed to the name Oileán Mhuire, the particular and only name used by the Irish for Mary, Christ's mother, Our Lady.

So the island, considered especially sacred for thousands of years, has had pilgrimages just as Lough Derg or Croagh Patrick.

In the seventeen hundreds at a time of deprivation and humiliation the people used gather on

Our Lady's Island procession, August 15, 1930, the day of the major pilgrimage. Nan Cogley Collection.

Our Lady's Island procession on the great pilgrimage day August 15th, 1930. The snapshot indicates the Fr. Martin O'Connor camera and his recently developed Confraternity Band.

special feast days or Patron Days (Patterns as we call them) and pilgrimages all over Ireland not just for devotional ceremonies but also to meet, drink and make merry.

Rome was told of 'unseemly scandals'. Pope Benedict the Fourteenth (1740-1758), in a sweeping reform issued a ban on all such locations and meetings. There were two specific, named exclusions because they had existed beyond time and the memory of man, Lough Derg in Donegal and Our Lady's Island, near Carnsore.

THE HOLIDAYING CHRISTIAN BROTHERS making friends with the Kilmore Quay donkey in summer 1939. Who would have guessed at that time that the Christian Brothers were a vanishing species?

C.B.S. PRIMARY SCHOOL CHOIR, 1948. The Christian Brothers Wexford choir in 1948 defied us for 100% identities. The sixty intervening years had a lot to do with it. It is however most important to pay tribute to the only lady present, Miss Mary Codd. Alone she inspired music, voice, choirs, instrument, stage, concert, church and platform for more than four decades. Wexford was well prepared for its international Opera Festival. Those we recognised are: front Liam Walsh, Wilfred Eisenberg; two more unknowns, then one of the Cadogans. Second last is Liam Leahy, 2nd row 4th from left J. O'Keeffe. Second next is Cyril Hogan; second from him are Brother Murphy and Ms. Mary Codd. Skip one and we have a Kehoe of High St., Johnny Doyle, skip another, Michael Horgan. Third row, Nick Duggan, skip four, Barty French, skip one more, then Jimmy Cullen, Eamon Doyle, Des Allen, J. Hayes and Seán Mitten. Wilfred Eisenberg was one of the young German refugees sheltered with Irish families after World War II. Wilfred stayed with the Frank Cullimore family.

Eamon Doyle Collection.

Eamon Doyle Collection.

THE FIRST APOSTOLIC NUNCIO to an independent Ireland since Cardinal Rinucini in 1647 arrived in Wexford to a tumultuous welcome in 1930. The Fr. Martin O'Connor snapshot shows him with Bishop William Codd of Ferns (1918-1938) as the horse-drawn landau provided by Hantons of John Street leaves the grounds of Rowe Street Church. The brave boy scouts formed the guard of honour. The statue of the great builder inspiration of the twin churches stands high in the background of trees. The Papal Nuncio was an American, a Franciscan and a former journalist, Most Rev. Archbishop Paschal Robinson. Franciscans who are ordained bishops have the faculty of wearing dove grey robes rather than the usual purple.

Photograph by Fr. Martin O'Connor.

A GROUP OF THEOLOGICAL STUDENTS. The familiar background of stone walls and window panes are part of the College square. The photograph from St. Peter's College seminary could be from the first decade of the 20th century before the First World War.

CORPUS CHRISTI, 1949. The procession crosses the exact ground where King Dermot McMurrough and his Norman mercenaries laid siege to Norse Wexford in May 1169. In the lead is Bishop Staunton who as secretary to the Irish Hierarchy had a stormy career, notably in the Noel Browne Mother and Child and Fethard-on-Sea's bitter controversies of 1950-1957. On the right is Fr Robert Hickey, President, St. Peter's College.

J.B. Nolan Collection.

CORPUS CHRISTI PROCESSION in South Main St. Wexford, 1950s. The choir section shows some of the finest male voices (and simultaneously characters) in the sacred music area. From left, John Brendan Nolan, Eddie O'Connor, Michael Sutherland, Peter O'Connor, Séamus Roche and heading the Holy Family Confraternity band conductor Paddy Parle.

THE CORPUS CHRISTI PROCESSION, GOREY.

CONFIRMATION DAY in Our Lady's Island c.1950. The well-known teachers were Gerard Hurley and Ita Murphy, later Mrs Michael Cullen, Silverspring, Ballycogley.

GOREY AND TARA HILL school children were confirmed on an important day. It was the first visit of the new Bishop of Ferns, James Staunton, to Gorey shortly after he was consecrated in 1939. Canon William Harpur, P.P. Gorey sits with him and the dozens of girls and boys in the warm background of Augustus Welby Pugin's Church.

REMEMBERING CROMWELL. October 1949 saw a full week of commemoration of Oliver Cromwell and his English republican army's visit to Wexford in the terrible year of 1649. Wexford port, its government, people and Franciscan friars had throughout that decade in what was called the Great Rebellion showed extraordinary peril to England. Loosely organised into the Catholic Confederation of Kilkenny to which Wexford was the main port, Wexford vessels wreaked havoc on English shipping even as far as the Solent. Each vessel operated under its own command but later employed specially designed ships called "Dunkirkers". The whole population showed determined support for Catholic Spain to the extent of flying the familiar Spanish colours of red and gold. A local jingle went, "God bless the King of Spain, if it wasn't for him we'd all be slain".

The Wexford Franciscans from within their own walls conducted a communications system with mainland Europe, most particularly Spain. Two Wexford Franciscans had a direct link with the Royal Spanish Court itself. Cromwell's "blitzkrieg" reached Wexford in October 1649 where an incompetent Wexford garrison collapsed. Cromwell exacted comprehensive retribution, as recorded. The town was stormed, citizens massacred, Franciscans hanged, the Confederate army was overwhelmed, and hundreds were drowned in the terror stricken rush for safety or escape. The aftermath was devastation and desolation for Wexford and Irish Ireland.

Our photograph shows a service of solemn benediction in the Bullring where the most substantial massacre of civilians by Cromwellian troops took place. The Franciscan fathers had a major role to play throughout that commemorative week.

Giving Benediction is Fr. Charles, OFM, the Guardian (Superior) in Wexford Friary. The thurible is manned by Eddie O'Connor. The altar boy behind Bishop James Staunton (in ermine cape) is our photograph donor, Eamon Doyle. In front of Bishop Staunton is

Eamon Doyle Collection.

Fr. Patrick Doyle, Administrator, and later P.P. Kilmore. Fr. John Butler, later P.P. Cushinstown is framed somewhat by a bewildered dog. The national forester in the magnificent uniform is "Farmer" Kehoe. The scout buglers giving the royal salute are Michael Healy (left) and John O'Rourke.

Twin Churches Centenary

1958 saw the commemoration of the Wexford twin churches centenary. The building in 1858 was a Herculean effort in imagination and construction which even today challenges the mind.

The inspiration, the determined religious entrepreneur was Father James Roche, Wexford's parish priest. His brother, "Fr. Johnny" OFM, was sometime Guardian (superior) in the Franciscan Friary. One feels that he too played a role in his brother James' determination. Since 1691, no parish priest, no secular clergy had a parish church or custodial rights to a church in Wexford town. Press photographers were busy for the commemoration. One feels that groups, even the most auspicious, were assembled in haste.

The photograph on the steps of Wexford presbytery shows some peculiar placings. Seated: Phyllis Bean Ui Cheallaigh, the President of Ireland, Seán T Ó Cheallaigh, Bishop James Staunton, Archbishop Levame, Apostolic Nuncio and Monsignor Gerada, Secretary, Papal Nunciature (In 1989 Monsignor Gerada returned to Dublin as Archbishop and Apostolic Nuncio). At the back left, the lonely friar is Fr. Ernest Cronin, personal secretary to Ireland's Franciscan Provincial. Fr Cronin preached in Rowe St. Church at the centenary ceremonies. Next, the President's aide-de-camp; Canon Patrick Murphy, Glynn; Canon Richard Gaul, Bree; Canon John Sinnott, Blackwater; Thomas Broe, County Manager (hidden), Col. O'Sullivan, senior *aide - de - camp* to the President; Rev. Henry Sinnott, Rev. Mathew Berney, Rev. Michael O'Neill, RCA; Rev Mathew Doyle.

In remote background, Brendan Corish, T.D. recently Minister for Social Welfare, with the formidable County Medical Officer of health, Dr. Honoria Aughney, a great administrator kindly remembered for informing a belligerent farming aggressor, "You sir are not fit to be put among horned cattle". Partly hidden, the Dean of Ferns, V. Rev. Canon John Codd. the Mayor of Wexford, John Cullimore; Fr. Edward Murphy, Fr. James B. Curtis, bishop's secretary. Fr. John Butler, Adm.; Fr. James Cummins, Dr James Browne, P.P. V.G. New Ross; John Byrne, Town Clerk; Fr. Martin Clancy.

Irish Press.

Irish Press.

ARCHBISHOP LEVAME, Apostolic Nuncio, addresses the faithful from the north entrance to the church of the Immaculate Conception, Rowe Street, Wexford, after arrival for the 1958 centenary commemorations. He is surrounded by the mayor, Thomas Cullimore, elected city fathers and officials including county manager Broe.

1958 TWIN CHURCHES CENTENARY. His Grace, John Charles McQuaid, Archbishop of Dublin, Primate of Ireland approaches the portals of the Church of the Assumption, Bride Street, Wexford. Scouts and clergy make a guard of honour. Of special memory, however, are the beautiful robes of the Bride Street altar boys.

THE APOSTOLIC NUNCIO, ARCHBISHOP LEVAME with Very Rev. Dean J. Canon Codd, P.P, V.F. Ferns and Very Rev. J. Canon Sinnott, P.P., V.F., Blackwater, entering the church grounds dedicated to the Immaculate Conception during the centenary celebrations 1958.

SCENE FROM THE SHEPHERDESS OF LOURDES staged in the Theatre Royal, Wexford during the twin churches centenary week, by pupils of Convent schools.

THE NEW ROSS AND DISTRICT GROUP that took part in the Ferns Pilgrimage to Lourdes in 1958.

After the lapse of 52 years it was impossible to identify everyone in the group. Those we succeeded in naming were: Mikie and Johnny Greene, Hilary Murphy, Nellie Hanlon, Betty Murray, Miss Fanning, Sally Whelan, Gerald Ward, Nancy Russell, Peggy Hill, Nancy Lacey, Mick Morrissey, Fr Pat Doyle and the then Bishop of Ferns, Most Rev James Staunton.

Hilary Murphy.

"The pilgrimage travelled over land and sea, starting from Rosslare Harbour. The Holy Family Confraternity Band was present to give us a hymnal send-off. On arrival at Fishguard we boarded a train which took us on the long journey to the port of Folkestone in the south-east of England. After crossing the English channel another train was waiting to take us to Paris for a welcome travel-weary overnight stay in a hotel. An early alarm call got us ready for another long train journey to our final destination in Lourdes where we spent a joyful and prayerful number of days. There was another overnight stop in Paris on the return journey and more free time to roam around. It was one of the most memorable events of my life." - Hilary Murphy.

A PILGRIMAGE TO THE GREAT MARIAN SHRINE AT LOURDES once had the duration or logistics of a trek from Cairo to Capetown. A trip to Lourdes today or any place of similar distance would take no more than two hours out of Waterford, Cork or Dublin. We are nevertheless writing about fifty two years ago and we are writing perhaps of numbers approaching a thousand.

1958 was also the year when the great Ferns diocesan pilgrimage to Lourdes was promoted and assembled. It assembled and created interest, atmosphere and excitement. It was undertaken entirely on sea from Rosslare Harbour, land travel across the U.K., on sea again to France and then by rail to Lourdes via Bordeaux in South West France. The expedition included invalids and some very seriously ill.

Our photograph shows the pilgrims processing toward Wexford's North Station at Redmond Square. Following church devotions they were played out by the Confraternity Band. Crowds came also to bid them farewell. Weather conditions would certainly be better in France than in Wexford on that day.

Photograph by Pat Hayes.

BISHOP DONAL J. HERLIHY who became Bishop of Ferns in 1964 had spent most of his life in Rome. He had been Rector of the Irish College. It would not be difficult to prove that he, scriptural scholar and peritus (official advisor) at the Second Vatican Council, would put into effect immediately the liturgical arrangements agreed. The Diocese of Ferns by contrast to the Archdiocese of Dublin first used the vernacular, altered the sanctuary by bringing the altar forward to the people, allowing the priest to face his congregation where hitherto all people saw, save for preaching, was his back. All this caused much controversy at the time.

For the clergy a new development took place. Vatican Two agreed that several priests, where convenient or necessary, could celebrate the Eucharist at the one time in the same ceremony. Before Vatican Two one priest and one priest only was permitted to celebrate one mass individually. Many will remember side altars in every church for individual priests and indeed many more in evidence in ruined abbeys.

The photograph by Pat Hayes, taken in the magnificent Pugin St. Peter's College chapel with Bishop Herlihy's permission, shows a con-celebrated mass in progress. A poignant feature is the array of Roman style, beautifully decorated chasubles, usually crafted in convents, worn when the priest had his back to the congregation. They have since been replaced (regretfully some would say) by Gothic style chasubles.

CONFIRMING IN TAGHMON. Thanks to Mary Goff and the Taghmon Historical Society, we can display the beauty of Taghmon's Confirmation day girls in 1950.

Front row, l. to r. are: Bernadette King, Maureen Delaney, Teresa Delaney, Betty Donnelly, Maura Lambert, Ninie Waters, Mary Anglim. Second row (l to r): Ethel Kehoe, Peg Donohoe, Stella Hanlon, Lily O'Reilly, Eva Cullen. Back row, l to r: Teresa Parle, Ann Boggan, Peggy Ryan, Nuala Anglim, Angela Lambert, Mairéad Carroll.

Lafayette.

ALL, ALL ARE GONE. St. Peter's College seminary had a capacity and individual facilities for not less than eighty students declaring for the priesthood. Practically each year there was a waiting list of aspirants. One famous President learning of some grumbling below decks addressed the student body in these words: "if there are any among you who are discontented or dissatisfied , please leave. There are plenty to take your place".

Our photograph by Lafayette shows the full complement of ecclesiastical students in early 1954. The senior students including those for ordination are in the front seated. Throughout there are several diocese of Ferns faces. The students wore full clerical clothes including the Roman collar from entry. In the background can be seen the Mercy Convent, the Convent National schools, the Mercy Convent Laundry and industrial school of good reputation as well as a beautiful chapel at far left now demolished.

LONDON-WEXFORD: All the indications of a devotional group fit the scene. It is a church, perhaps a cathedral. In the background, the old crucifix and monstrances of other years are displayed as it were in a museum, so it must be a sacristy of note. Enthroned in front, centre, is the solemn Bishop of Ferns, Dr. James Staunton, (1939-1963). Fr. William Shiggins, later P.P., V.G., New Ross, at extreme left, was superior of the House of Missions, Enniscorthy, for two terms 1949-55, but prior to that he was director of the Irish Missions in England.

It is the London Wexford Association, probably in the early fifties.

Photographed by P.J. Fahy.

1950 CORPUS CHRISTI, BUNCLODY. The photograph of the Corpus Christi procession for Bunclody town in 1950 was surviving evidence of a political and penal code where only the Church by law established was allowed to conduct divine service in towns and villages.

For example, Fethard-on-Sea, Carnew, Campile, Tinahely, Clonroche had or have similar peculiarities. Bunclody's "parish church" was not in Bunclody town or Bunclody parish. It was in the parish of Kilrush on the eastern side of the River Slaney. So as our photograph shows the procession proceeded, led by a potentially famous cross bearer, a young student, Rory Deane. He was later an outstanding inter-county footballer, athlete and golfer, retiring as Rt. Rev. Monsignor Rory Deane.

The anomaly in the case of Bunclody was circumvented at the First Vatican Council, 1870, when Bishop Furlong of Ferns wrote from Rome informing Bunclody's parish priest that the townlands containing Bunclody's parish church in Kilrush parish were detached from Kilrush and attached to Bunclody (or Newtownbarry as it was called then) "for the convenience of the people".

JANUARY 1973, THE HISTORIC PARISHES OF KILLANNE AND KILLEGNEY receive a new rector who was to make his mark in the Diocese of Ferns, Rev. Norman Ruddock. Photographed at his institution in those mountain dominated parts is the Bishop of Ferns, Dr. Henry McAdoo, later Archbishop of Dublin. On his left is the Rector of Gorey, Canon William Parker. In the doorway is Canon Frank Shannon, Rector of Carnew, while the youngster at right about to be unleashed among the unshriven is Rev. Norman Ruddock.

CLERGY OF THE DIOCESE OF FERNS assemble for the enthronement of the new Church of Ireland Bishop of Ferns, a native of the diocese, in Ferns Cathedral, 15 June, 1980. He is Bishop Noel Vincent Willoughby, one of the widely connected Willoughby family of Tinahely.

Ruddock Family Collection

Note we are identifying from right to left. Seated: Canon Shannon, Carnew; Edward Grant, rector of Wexford; Archdeacon Parker, Gorey; Bishop Noel Willoughby; Dean Earle of Ferns; Unidentified; the rector of Kilnamanagh. Standing: reading minister, ,Cecil Dier, Canon Patrick E. Doyle, parish priest of Ferns; Canon Boake, Tinahely; Canon Madden, Ardamine; Canon Wilkinson, rector of Enniscorthy and Canon Jackson.

The young biblical figure with the crozier is not showing ambition; he is facilitating the bishop. He became the recently departed rector of Wexford, Chancellor Norman Ruddock. Alongside Norman is Monart rector Samuel Roe; Canon Lloyd, rector of New Ross with Rev. A.N.Other; We regret to say that accurate identifications of those in the back row escape us but we suggest the Presbyterian minister and three lay readers one of whom is a lady.

Bishop Willoughby Collection.

WITH THE BACKDROP OF SAINT CANICE'S CATHEDRAL and round tower, the new Bishop Noel Willoughby and his wife Valerie give a happy party for diocese of Ferns clergy, friends, wives and children. Many faces are familiar but the children are now thirty years older.

Archdeacon Parker of Gorey snaps the snapper. Canon Eddie Grant of Wexford, Trinity Scholar, is in civilian clothes. Canon Wilkinson is there from Enniscorthy and extreme left, Canon Roundtree, New Ross, I think, the Norman medieval scholar Adrian Empey with Enniscorthy leanings, is there with others such as Canon Boake, Tinahely. Cannon Madden of Ardamine and Dean Earle of Ferns.

Bishop Willoughby Collection.

"UNLESS YOU BECOME AS LITTLE CHILDREN..." Bishop Noel with little people and one in front who has a problem about being there in the first place.

FOLLOWING THE INSTALLATION of Dublin's auxiliary bishop, Dr Brendan Comiskey, as Bishop of Ferns, the County Monaghan community in County Wexford gathered to do their highly regarded fellow county man honour in celebration. This great Ulster assembly met in White's Hotel in May 1984, spouses, partners and children included. The photograph includes most except those who had to travel a distance.

Back row: Seán O'Leary, Patrick Kinsella, Séamus Mooney, Stephen Nolan, Dr. Felix Kierans, Frank Corley, James McKenna, Pat Geoghan.

Second row: Paddy Mulligan, Sheila Mulligan, Frank Cullinane. At this stage the recorder of the night had a shaky hand so while asking the reader's indulgence we proceed with the seated row. Mary Nolan, Frances Connor, Ms .Other, Ms Other, Bishop Comiskey, Kay Corley, Eileen and Anne Kinsella, Rose O'Leary, Ms Other and Mrs McKenna. On bended knees, Ms. Other, Colm Connor, Liz Mooney, Micheál Kinsella, Patricia Kinsella, Ann Kierans, Mary Geoghegan.

Others present were Michael Began, Rita Cleary, Mariella Clerkin, Kathleen Donnelly and Niall Mullen.

Thanks to Paddy and Sheila Mulligan.

BISHOP COMISKEY reaches out to children on arrival in Wexford town, 28 May, 1984, for the first time.

Photograph: Denis O'Connor.

ORDAINED COMRADES. They signal the end of one era. No one realised that a new era had begun. This is a happy photograph. It was a reunion of old colleagues, classmates, fellow ordinands of St. Peter's College Seminary. They had gathered from all parts of the world. One of their fellows, St. Peter's student, St. Peter's teacher, ordained by Bishop Staunton with the class of 1948, had been made Cardinal Primate of All Ireland, Archbishop of Armagh, Tomás O Fiaích. A new bishop of Ferns had arrived, a Monaghan man, a Church order member of glowing academic record and most engaging manner. His name was Dr. Brendan Comiskey. He had smiles, camaraderie, stories. There was hope and confidence.

Since the second Vatican Council, there was a liberalisation from stark legislation. To the best of our ability, the names gathered with Herculean effort are, back row: Fathers James Nolan, James B. Curtis, Noel Hartley, Lory Kehoe, Jim Byrne, A.N. Other, Tony Scallan, Paddy O'Reilly, Philip Donohoe, Aidan Kavanagh, Tomás O'Neill, Rory Deane, Tom Briody, John Havelin, Timmy Sullivan, Mick Larkin, Peter Cronin, Tom Cleary, Phil Egan, Walter Forde, Brendan Nolan. Fourth row: Ben Corrigan, Frank Stafford, A.N. Other, Andy Reen, Dick Hayes, Tom McGrath, Jim Gilfinnan, Joe Murphy, Frank Clancy, Jack Sinnott, Joe McConville, Tony Gillespie, Paddy Browne, Brian Broaders, Seán Hyland, David Hanratty, Pat Furlong, Jim Poland, Michael Gannon, A.N.Other, Ray Rafferty. Third row: James O'Reilly, Jimmy Murray, Chris Kennedy, Tom Curtis, A.N. Other, William Byrne, William Anglim, Michael Lenihan, Liam O'Byrne, Tom Doyle, Tom Glynn, Seán Rogan, Dominic Towey, Morgan Rowsome, Tom Flynn, Eamonn Sweeney, Aidan G. Jones, M .J. Nelon, Michael McMahon, Matt Brennan, Ricky Byron, James Doyle, Jim Larkin, Oliver Doyle, Cyril Reilly, Peter Beglan, Paddy O'Dea, Ml. Cunnane, Seán McCarthy, Tom McCormack, Pete Mimnagh, Jack McCabe, Martin Kenny, Donal Gillespie, Paddy Walsh. Second row: John Caulfield, Matt Glynn, Jim Hannigan, Paddy Toher, Pat Jordan, Jim Hammel, Pat Cummins, Matthew Roche, William Gaul, Cardinal Tomás Ó Fiaích, Patrick O'Brien, Bishop Brendan Comiskey, Richard Breen, Tom Buckland, Paddy Higgins, John Butler, Michael Roche, Brendan O'Sullivan. Front row: Pat Foley, Derry McGrath, Michael Joe Cassidy, (Andy Duignan?) Dick Higgins, Frankie Harpur, William Howell, Ger O'Leary, John Fortune, Peter O'Hare, Matt Kelly, Bernard Cushen, Patk. Sinnott, Joe Travers, Lorrie Cleary, Colm Murphy, Donal Collins, Séamus Doyle, Joe Power.

The last great gathering of fellow church students shown in St. Peter's College grounds took place in July 1984. They were one hundred and thirty four in number. It is with appreciation that we thank Fr. Lorenzo Cleary for the feat of identification research.

April 1978. The Archbishop of Armagh, Dr. Tomás O Fiaích, yesterday visited St. Peter's College, Wexford, where he was ordained in 1948. After offering Mass for the students, he had lunch with the college staff. In the afternoon he presented prizes at the annual prize-giving ceremony. Later there was a reception for clergy of the diocese of Ferns and public representatives. He is pictured here with some of the pupils from the school attached to the seminary. *Photograph by Pat Langan*

Gleams of Christian kindness kept the warming ecumenism movement mobile since Pope John the Twenty Third declared that Christians can be agreeable with one another in spite of disagreements. The Joint Ecumenical Committee in these parts shown here consists of Rev. Frank Forbes, Church of Ireland, Fr. Michael Hurley, S.J., Rev. Roy Cooper, Methodist Church; Fr. Aidan Gilbert Jones, P.P.,Bunclody. It is interesting to note that the popular Roy Cooper who resided in Enniscorthy was made President of the Irish Methodist Church in 2007.

Horeswood Confirmation, 1972. Front: Thomas Kent, Ger Boland, Michael Hart, Seán Clancy, Patrick O'Shea, P.J. Doyle, James Howlin, Ted Shalloe, Tommy Lennon, Francis Doyle, Paddy Millea. Second row: John Banville, Eddie Ryan, Michael Walsh, Diarmuid Corish, Fr. Mathew Berney, P.P. (A native of Monaseed, Gorey, he was ordained in Maynooth on June 22nd 1941. He served on the teaching staff in St. Peter's College and was lecturer in Sociology for the Extra-Mural Diploma course of UCD. He became PP in Horeswood on Feb. 7th 1972, and died in Ely Nursing Home on Oct 25th 1972. He was an uncle of the actor Donal McCann.), Bishop Donal Herlihy, Fr Brendan Kehoe, Philip Corish, Séamus Furlong, John Joe Furlong, Maurice O'Shea.

Third row: Michael Dillon, Larry Larkin, Tony Aspel, Eamon Boland, Donal O'Hanlon, Declan Harte, Liam Halligan, James Larkin, Pat Parker, Pat Somers, John Joe Murphy, John Rowe, Andrew Boland, Senan Clancy, Tony Stafford, John Doyle.Back row: Pat Whelan, Tony Wallace, Pete Chapman, Bernard Waters, John Waters, Kevin Dunphy, Alan Parker, Jim Barnwell, Tom Miskella, Eddie Forristal, Seán O'Neill, Eoin O'Neill, Pat Rowe.

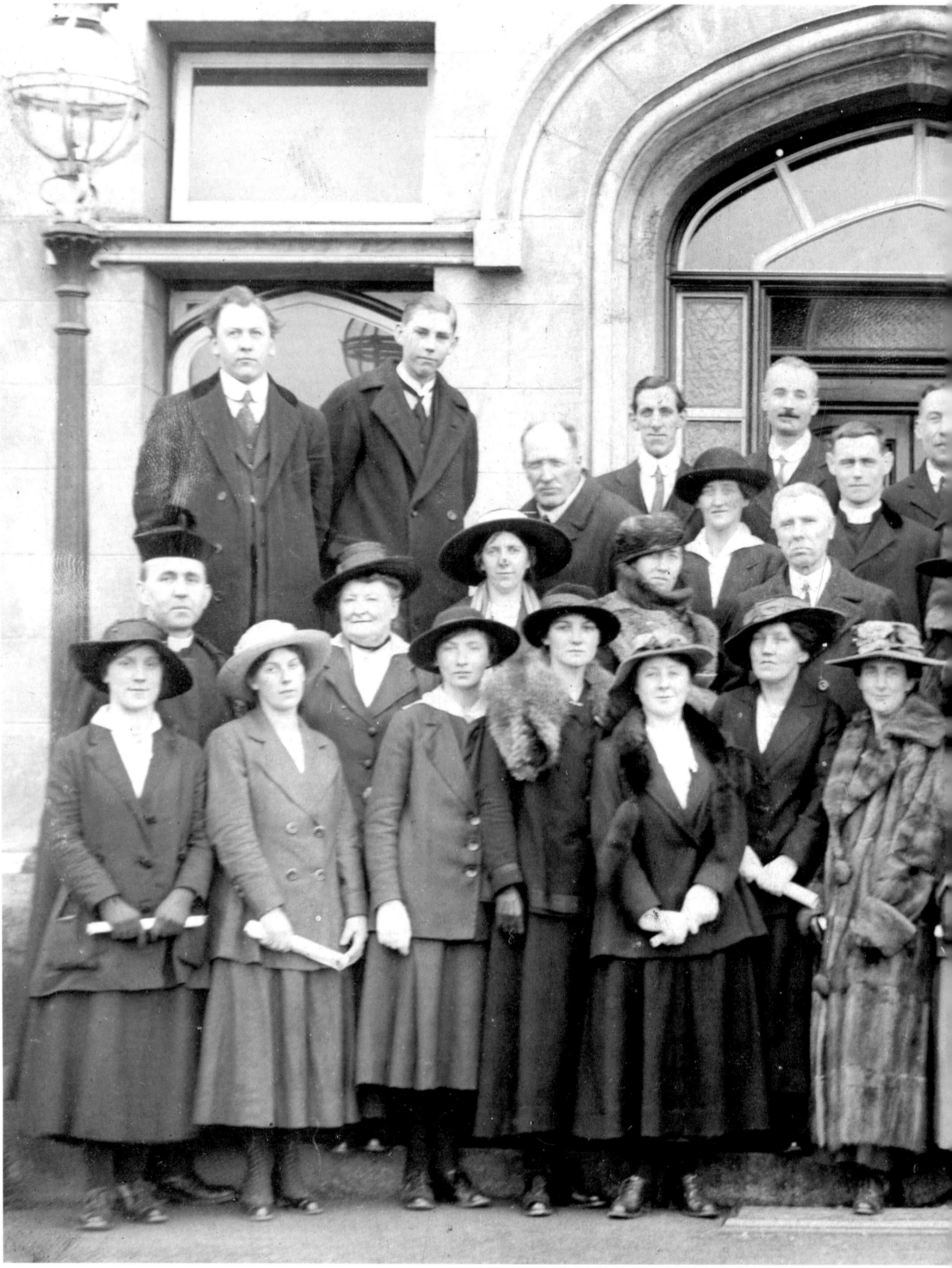

ENNISCORTHY SAINT AIDAN'S CATHEDRAL CHOIR. At the time of Bishop James Browne's Episcopal Silver Jubilee in 1909. The director, musicologist, scholarly historian and composer, Chevalier William W. H. Grattan - Flood is at centre in the second row on the presbytery steps.

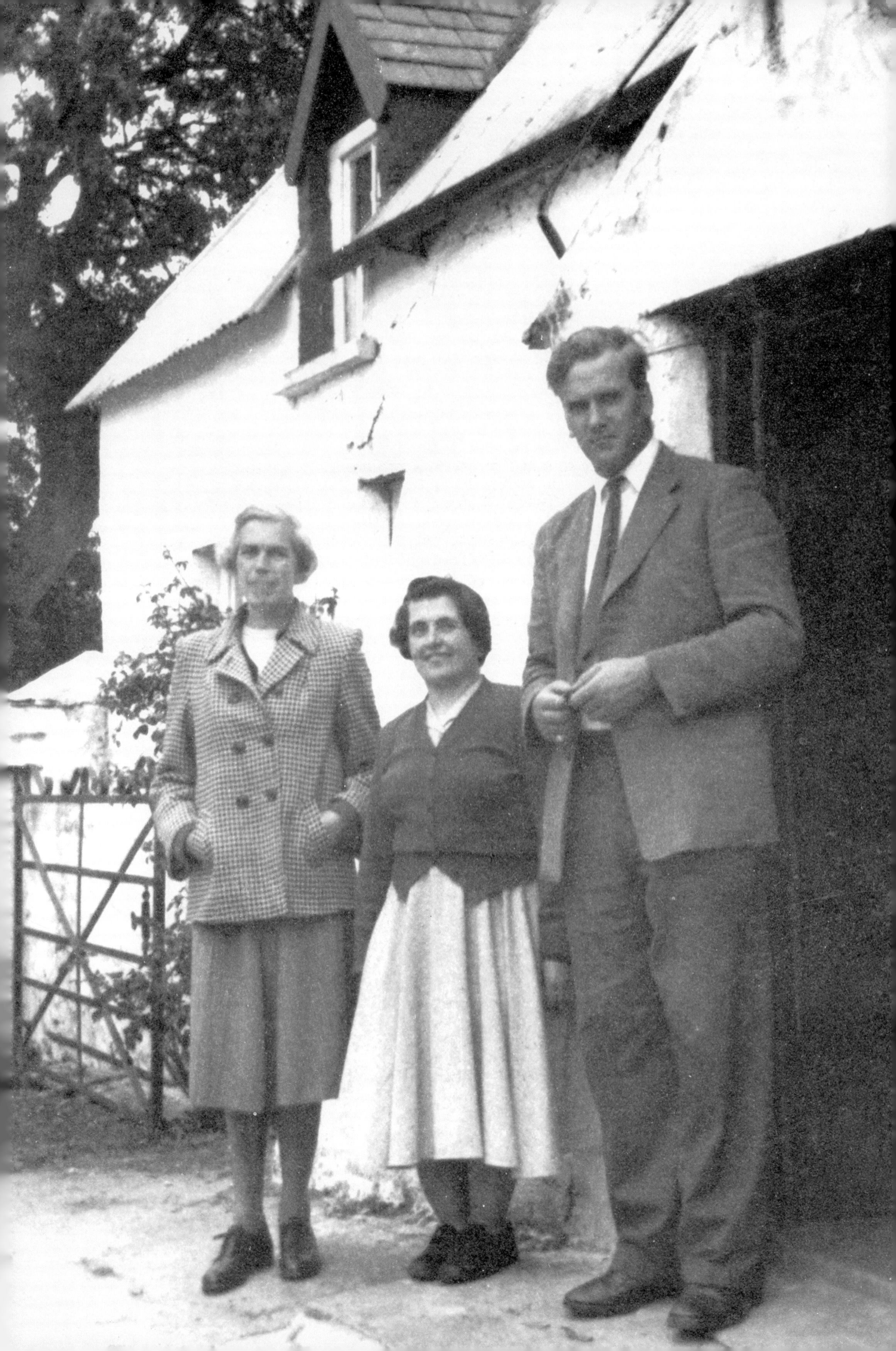

5 FAMILIES

There have been so many prominent families in the south east over the last two hundred years that it would be nearly impossible to declare whose contribution could be considered the most significant. In this work we can only present examples from surviving photographs. Undoubtedly, many more are hidden in drawers or recycled.

DICK AND EDITH ELGEE VISITING MRS NAN COGLEY at Sinnott's House, Mulgannon, 1960s Nan was the Elgee's former housekeeper.

With thanks to the late Nan Cogley, Mulgannon.

The Elgee Family

The Elgee family continue to make waves (no pun intended) down to this very year. Robert McClure, discoverer of the North-West sea passage across Canada's frozen arctic seas has leaped into prominence this very July 2010. His ship H.M.S. *Investigator* has been discovered in a tolerable state of preservation in the Beaufort Sea. Lionised by the Canadian Government, its Minister for the Environment Mr. Prentise said "This is one of the most important shipwrecks in Canadian history because the *Investigator* carried Captain Robert McClure who discovered the North West Passage entry". Robert McClure's mother was an Elgee, daughter of Archdeacon John Elgee, Rector of Wexford in 1780.

Edith Elgee was the last of the name in direct descent from Rev. John Elgee, whose fame involved the repeated heart-break of accompanying respected members of his own congregation to their deaths on Wexford Bridge during and following the rebellion of 1798. His congregation included loyalists as well as leaders in the United Irishmen such as Cornelius Grogan, Captain Matthew Keugh and Bagenal Harvey. The family tradition was service to the Church. Rev. John Elgee's youngest son, Richard Waddy Elgee, also became Rector of Wexford. John Elgee's daughter, Jane Francesca, achieved fame as the fiery nationalist poet "Speranza" of Thomas Davis's newspaper, *The Nation*.

Jane Francesca Elgee's fame took other routes when she married distinguished Dublin physician and antiquarian, Dr. William Wilde, who was knighted by Queen Victoria. Pain filled Jane Lady Wilde's aging days when her world famous son, Oscar Wilde, was disgraced and imprisoned in Reading Goal for homosexual transgressions. The unbearable shock caused Edith Elgee's grandfather to pronounce in their Selskar home, "The name of that abomination is never again to be mentioned in this house".

Edith's father, John Elgee, was a spectacular figure of a man, a feature indeed of Wexford town. He was tall, well-built, and brisk, with a genteel moustache and he wore a formal hard hat except when leisure pursuits urged a tweed cap. He carried a cane and was the epitome of the legal profession's highest standards. He was solicitor to Wexford County Council and Wexford Corporation.

His son, Dick, became the first solicitor to qualify in the Irish language. To achieve that proficiency he spent months in the Kerry Gaeltacht with "Kreuger" Kavanagh in Dunquin. He was seduced into the life-style and, it was said, never emerged from the "Kreuger" stimulation. His love of the sea saw him second-in-command of the Wexford Maritime Inscription, later Slua Muirí, throughout The Emergency. Edith's other brother, William Archer, who also inherited the handsome family features, was tragically drowned.

The Wexford Elgees at Wexford, North Railway Station on 25 August 1947, Archer Elgee, Richard Elgee, Edith Elgee with their Father John Elgee.

By courtesy of Irene Elgee.

Richard and Archer Elgee, Wexford on Mount Leinster, 1940.

The Sweetman Family of Ballycourcy

A happy photograph of a Co. Wexford man with his wife of half a century ago. It is also a photograph of a man and woman who were individually worthy of the closest attention. It is a rare photograph. It is the only photograph of these two distinguished people to survive. It is also the only photograph to survive of an unobtrusive lady who lived in our midst and who would have been in title as well as blood a Royal Princess had Ireland's political development been like, say, that of the Federated Malay States.

She was Mrs Malachi Sweetman of Ballycourcy House, Enniscorthy. She was sister of The O Conor Don. S.J., the legal titled descendant of Ruadrí Ua Conchobhair, Ard Rí na hÉireann (the last clearly recognised High King of All Ireland, Rory Mór O Conor, King of Connaught). She was born in one of Ireland's most stately and most historic homes, since featured twice in an RTE and BBC series, Clonalis

House, Co. Roscommon. She died in Ballycourcy and was laid to rest unobtrusively, even though she was a descendant of the monarch for whom one of the greatest treasures of western civilisation was created, the Cross of Cong.

To the masses of Wexford county, or to the thousands who packed the Market Square, the Bullring, the port of Ross, Bunclody, Gorey, or any one of over ninety churchgates election rallies in any one year in the forties or fifties, the commanding figure, shock of hair and beard of Malachi Sweetman demanded attention, but when that dynamic and unrepentant disciple of De Valera got up to speak, the very valleys and towers of Co. Wexford shook with electrifying fury and roars of excitement. Why he chose to farm and be a forestry pioneer in Ballycourcy instead of entering politics as a career no one will ever explain. He travelled widely, especially Scandinavia, land of his ancient roots. He saw and estimated the mighty potential of timber in this country with its unrivalled growth record. Fools thought him an eccentric, just as fools thought his formidable uncle, Dom Sweetman of Mount St. Benedict to be an eccentric. Their son, Nicholas, informs us that the title, The O Conor Don, was inherited by his cousin, Denis O Conor of Ballybrack, Co. Dublin.

The Ryan's of Tomcoole

Special family occasion at Áras an Uachtaráin gardens in the early 50s. President Seán T. O'Kelly's wife Phyllis, née Ryan, Tomcoole; her brother, Dr. James Ryan, T.D., Government Minister; Mary Frances Lacey, Bolgerstown, and Mrs Molly Ryan, Tomcoole, née Shortle, Castlebridge.

Ryan Collection.

The Roches of Scar

The three lovely Scar born Roche sisters, Annie (Mrs Tommie Williams), Kate (Mrs. Johnny French) and singer, broadcaster Babs (Mrs Dick Egan) just out of school in the twenties.

Tom Williams Collection.

The Rackards of Killanne

The wedding in June 1953 of Mr. Nicholas Rackard, M.R.C.V.S., Killanne, County Wexford, to Miss Ailish Pierce, Tinahely, County Wicklow, who were married in the University Church, Dublin. In the guard of honour of raised camáns are three members of the most famous sporting and inter-county hurling and football dynasty in Ireland. From left, Billy Rackard, Jimmy Rackard, Bobby Rackard on the right, with their friend the Bree M.O.H., Dr Daly.

By courtesy of Dominic Williams and Marion Rackard

The Ram Family of Gorey

The accounts of the Ram family in the foundation and consolidation of Gorey town's core are well documented. Nevertheless, the most dramatic phase was in their last decades, 1850 to 1870. During the so called Oxford Movement, the establishment family Ram left the Established Church en masse.

The progression of the Ram family's conversion to Roman Catholicism led to what a great many regarded as extremes, not an unusual development with converts. Their loudly proclaimed piety and devotive practices were widely discussed in some amazement by Catholics and in some anger by Protestants, aghast that after three centuries of staunch witness and tradition they had, to use an Anglican phrase, 'Poped'.

Shortly after this phase the Ram wealth started to unravel. At the time they owned a "town house" in Paris and another in London. There were however too many Rams pulling from the woolsack. That, and the disappointed antipathy of many Gorey Protestants who felt betrayed led to the decision to leave Gorey, the town the family had practically created, after three hundred years. The Rams vacated Gorey and Ramsfort in 1870.

Our photograph taken by the family's own apparatus was taken in 1858. It includes all resident in Ramsfort on the occasion.

Mary Christina Casamajor Ram, Ramsfort, 1858.
Ram family photograph originals in possession and by courtesy of Ml. Fitzpatrick, Cluainin, Gorey.

THE SITE OF THE OLD FRIARY was once the farm yard of the original Ramsfort House which was destroyed in the Rebellion of 1798. Following their conversion to Catholicism, the Ram family invited Sisters of the Order of St. Clare to Gorey and provided a convent and chapel for them at the farmyard. Five sisters arrived in Gorey on December 7th 1858. Stephen Ram had also petitioned the Minister General of the Franciscans for a foundation of friars on his property with the stipulation that the friars should be spiritual directors to the convent he hoped to establish. Following difficulties the friars duly arrived in Gorey and said their first Mass in December, 1858.

Michael Fitzpatrick.

The Friary flourished in Gorey and the happiest of relations existed between the Irish Franciscan Community at Gorey and the confessional work of the Fathers was very heavy. The then Bishop of Ferns, Dr. Thomas Furlong, gave his consent to the Gorey Franciscan foundation on condition that the friars would not take any collections in their church and the church would be closed on Sundays.

By 1860 the Rams were in financial difficulties and could not keep up their commitments to the friars and the nuns. The friars secured permission from Rome to transfer the community to Killarney and left Gorey in the middle of the night in July 1860 after hundreds of people protested around the friary earlier in the day. The nuns left in 1861 to find another home.

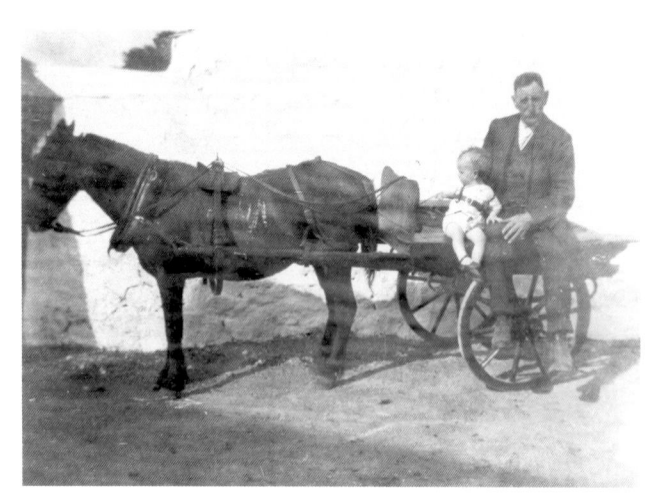

Colfer Family of Mullgannon
Mr Bartholemew Colfer with infant on his sidelace car at his dairy farm, Mulgannon. Bart was a member of the widely-spread Colfer family of Bannow.

The Doyle Family of Marshalstown
When the posed photograph of the Doyle family, their sturdy two-storey slated house and the nearby haggard was taken it was probably looked upon as a nice family record. It may not have been thought of as a superb recording of an era that has passed - a photograph with interesting evidence. The most important element for sustenance, the basic reason for the house and the houses, predecessor site is shown quite rightly in centre foreground. It is the pump of a reliable spring well, the first essential in the selection of any site before the recent community schemes.

It's a photograph of what was known in the last centuries as the house of a strong farmer, pillars of the community in the 1900s. The bicycle and sheep dog are also important acquisitions. The necessary religious and social accolade, a priest in the family, denoted respectability. Young Fr. John Doyle, born in 1894, was ordained in June 1920 and gives evidence of his status at left in soutane, biretta and breviary. He later became parish priest of Rathnure in 1952.

From left: Fr. J.J. Doyle, Joe, Peter Michael, Aidan, Tom. On either side of the door Margaret (Kennedy) and Maria (Codd). Missing on this important day are David and Daniel. We regret we have no record of photographer or donor.

The Cloney Family of Dungulph

One of the most prominent, most publicised, pressurised and agreeable families were the Cloneys of Dungulph Castle, Saltmills, survivors of the euphemistically termed 'Fethard-on-Sea dispute' which assumed the dimensions of a forest fire in the late nineteen fifties.

Seán and Sheila Cloney with grandchildren, Brendan, Jeanie and John.

Cloneys of Dungulph Castle. Seán and Sheila Cloney in Dungulph grounds with Mary and Eileen in September 1959.

The Cloney children, the baby Hazel, Mary and Eileen, at Dungulph Castle, in 1962.

The Colclough Family of Tintern Abbey

Following Henry VIII's confiscation of the monasteries and abbeys along with their lands in 1536, Tintern Abbey was granted to an English knight, Sir Anthony Colclough. He adapted the abbey into a residence in which his family resided until 1959 when the last of the family, Ms. Marie Biddulph Colclough, moved to a more convenient home in Saltmills.

In the folk memory, the record of the Colcloughs was benign, especially in the worst periods of the so called 'Penal Laws'. It was of unexpected good will in a zone which was Irish speaking, particularly by comparison with a racist landlord dynasty nearby. Tintern Abbey has been restored to a great extent by the Office of Public Works and today is a glorious attraction for tourists and scholars. There are guided tours throughout the season.

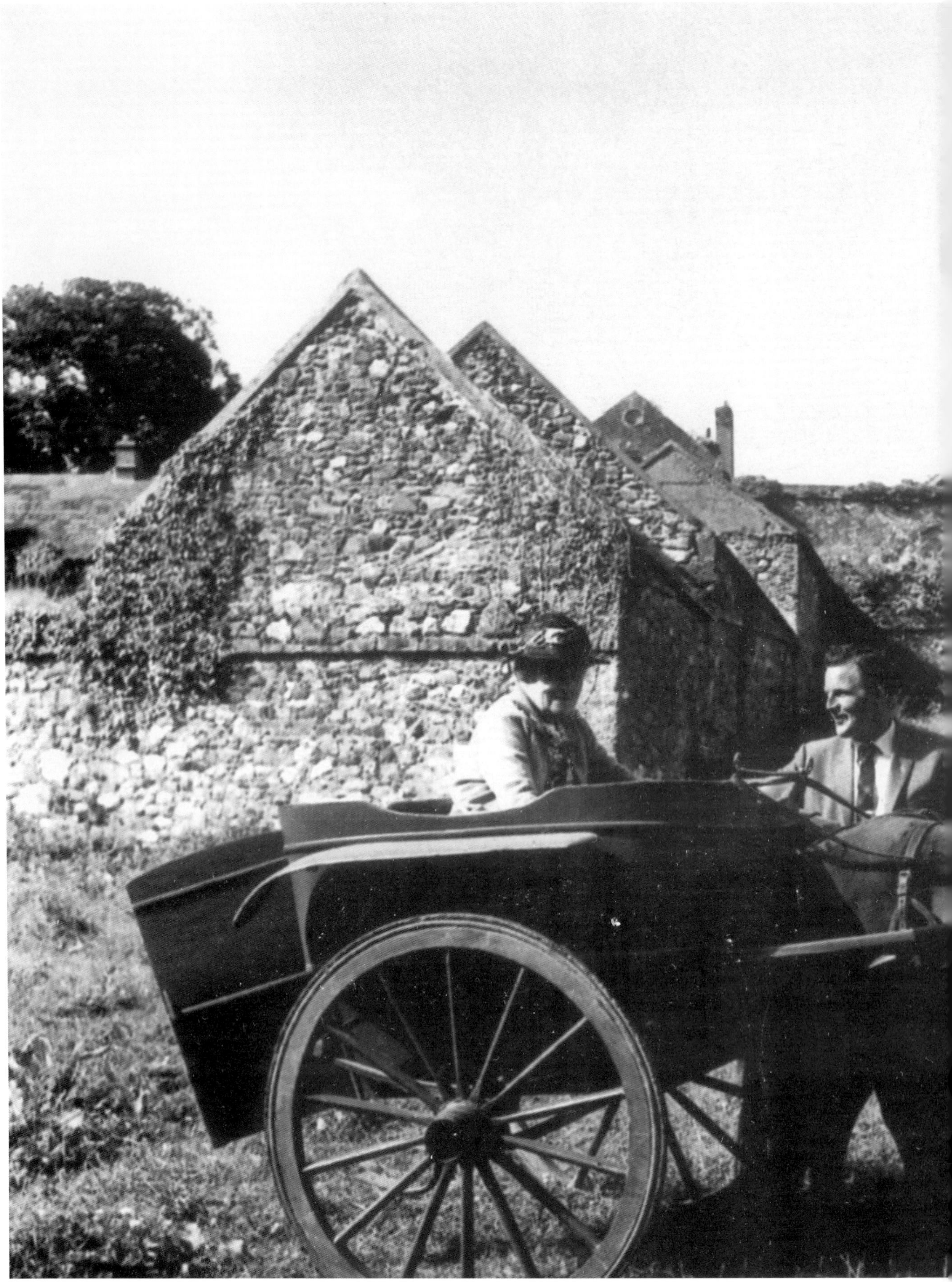

Our photograph shows Miss Biddulph Colclough outside the abbey ruins with Louis Feeley of OPW in 1963. *Photograph by courtesy of the Office of Public Works.*

Philip B. Pierce with his wife Nancy, née O'Brien, in the gardens of their home, Park House, Wexford.
Courtesy of Tomás Williams.

The Pierce Family of Wexford

It is hard to choose an adequate adjective to describe the Pierce family story. They were the personal founders of the Wexford-based farm machinery industry and every subsequent farm machinery development inspiration since moving from Kilmore to the then outskirts of Wexford town in 1839. The founder James Pierce was well observed as possessing distinct talent particularly in building windmills around County Wexford and south Kilkenny.

By the time the firm celebrated its centenary year in 1939, managed by Philip B. Pierce, its market share, laden with national and international honours, had expanded from Argentina to France and Great Britain. The national market was dominated totally by Wexford-manufactured farm machinery. Pierces enjoyed a particular dominance in the Ulster market.

The firm's control passed to Philip B's father, John, in 1907 at a time when Pierces employed 1,000 men. Philip B. succeeded his father in 1926. Philip's twin sister Ethel Geraldine married Jim Harvey of Bargy Castle and died in 1981. She is buried with her mother in Crosstown cemetery.

Philip inaugurated the highly successful edge tool factory in 1928 and saw the Pierce plough win national prominence in county and All-Ireland ploughing championships in the 1930s.

Genealogist Hilary Murphy gives evidence in his Kilmore Journal study (No 18, 1989-90) of what might be described as the idiosyncrasy not unknown in great families. "Though he began life in the Protestant faith of his parents (Church of Ireland) and attended services and Sunday School in St. Selskars, Philip B. Pierce became an ardent Catholic through the influence of his pious maiden aunts who lived in Rocklands House. Like his grandfather, James, and uncle, Philip, he became very attached to the Franciscan Friary. However, in later life he changed his patronage to Barntown church. When Philip B. Pierce died suddenly at his home in Dublin in 1979, aged 85, he was buried with his mother in the Protestant section of Crosstown cemetery, but was reinterred the following year with his uncle Martin in the Catholic section nearby.

Philip married Nancy O'Brien, St. John's Road, Wexford and lived in Park House. His mother, Susan, moved to Killingney, Summerhill, where she resided until her death in March 1944. She requested a private funeral and no mourning. Philip carried out elaborate innovations to the grounds of Park House which he opened to the public.

They had three children – Perpetua Anne Mary, who is called Pam; Philipa Jacinta and one son who was appropriately named Philip and is continuing the long family tradition in the engineering field.

Pierces Foundry, as it was called, was incorporated in Smiths Engineering (Cavan and Dublin) 1964-65. Philip's wife Nancy died in Dublin in May 2010 aged 91. They are both buried in the Pierce family plot in Crosstown, Wexford.

The Cullens of Coolafullaun

At tea in Victorian Dublin. Margaret Cullen née Bambrick, wife to Gerard Cullen of the townland of Coolafullaun, Galbally, co-owner with his brother Robert of a tavern in Dublin in the 1880s, with her sisters-in-law Mary Cullen and Katie Cullen (sisters) of Coolafullaun, who visited her for tea. The era is Victorian. Mary Cullen, centre, married John Freeman of Barmoney, of a family of builders of churches, schools and police barracks and farmers of consequence. Katie remained a spinster to her death at Coolafullaun in the 1950s.

From the Richard and May Reville Collection.

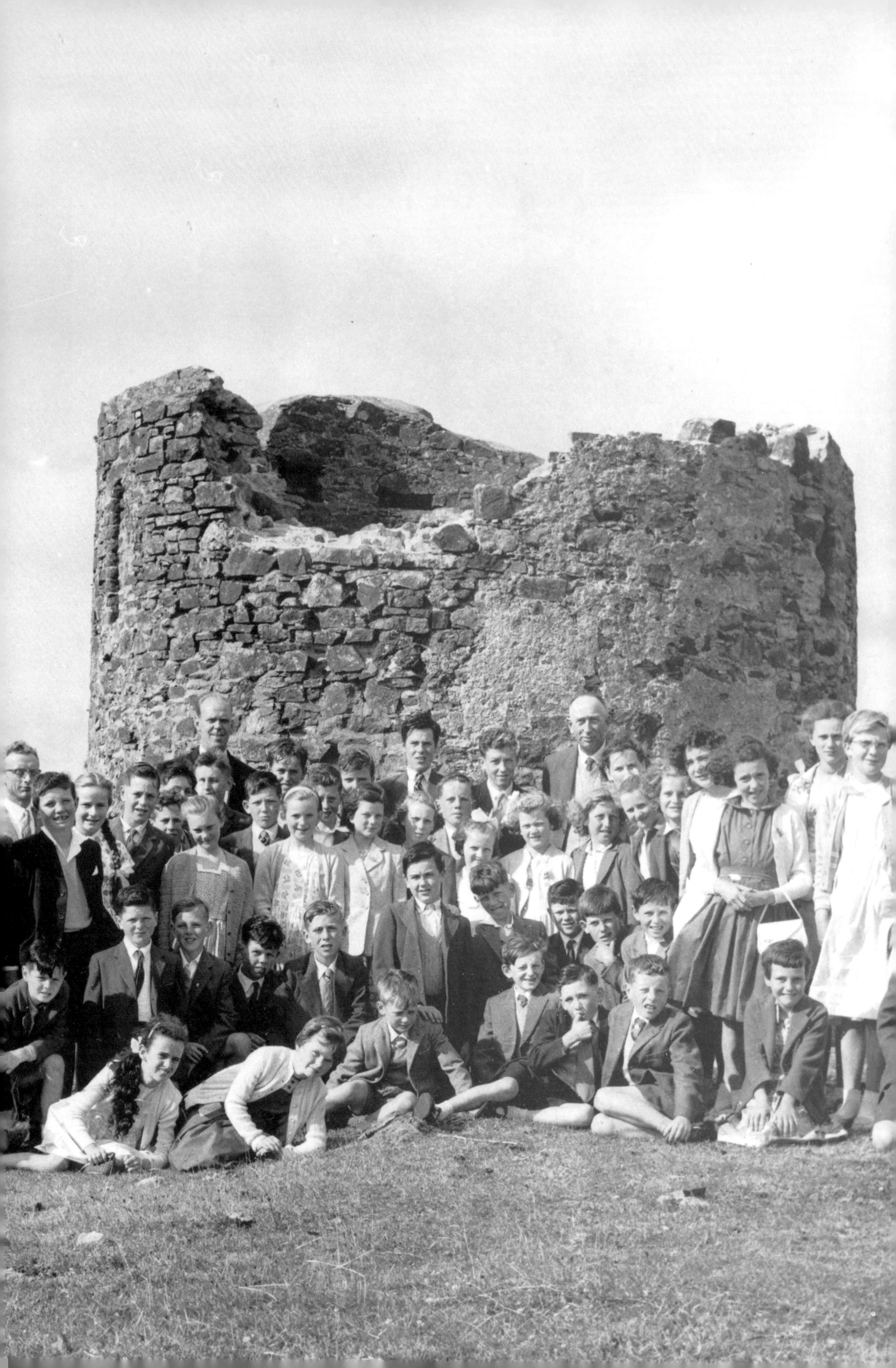

6 MEMORIES OF 1798

As a result of confiscation and penal enactment we have the sorry spectacle of a country governed for generations by a faction and in the sole interest of a minority, the people taxed to maintain a church establishment of that minority, the land alienated for the most part into the hands of that minority and the majority of the people forced to accept, in their own country, the position of unfranchised bondmen.

Dr. Richard Dickson,
The Wexford Rising in 1798, its Causes and Course

The revolt by the United Irishmen against the government and forces of the Crown opened in County Wexford in May, 1798. In ferocity, it was unequalled in Ireland. Men and women of sturdy independence, both Catholic and Established Church, could no longer tolerate the injustice.

Ordinary men and women of the land and towns ignored the Crown's armed might and the stern opposition of their Churches. They fought. They gave up their lives and liberty, fortunes and homesteads. When exhausted in July, their homeland was in ashes. Widows and families mourned, but carried on the battle to survive.

The memory of the dead and their audacious bravery survives to an extraordinary extent in County Wexford. Our few photographs from the commemorations of 1938 and 1948 indicate the place in Wexford hearts where their memory still lives.

McCauley's Hotel, Oulart Village in 1870. McCauley's Hotel, Oulart, prospered when Oulart was an important junction on the horse drawn coach route to Dublin. It was from the upper window of the hotel that Bishop James Caulfield beseeched the crowd which included sworn United Irish revolt-planning insurgents to abandon their thoughts and plans of armed uprising. c. May 23, 1798. He was ignored.

The Boolavogue contingent on Vinegar Hill, June 21, 1948, with their banner and portrait of Fr. John Murphy at their head.
This precious oil painting, now in the custody of the Hall family, Boolavogue, was frequently carried at 1798 commemorations in all weathers.
Courtesy of Joan Kirwan, Vinegar Hill.

Led by Pipers, Wexford Pikemen march from the quays to Barrett's Park for the New Ross '98 celebrations in June 1938.
Irish Press.

1938 Commemorations pageant at the Three Rocks, Barntown.
Photograph by J.W. Whelan M.P.S.I.

The Kilmuckridge contingent led by the Balygarrett Band at Tinahely in 1938. Holding the banner are Willy Cody and Tom Bolger of

Kilmuckridge. Left to right on bagpipes are Jack Hughes of Mangan, Alex Lawless of Monmore (partially hidden by banner), Tom O'Connor of Parkannesley, Bernie Higgins of the Little Crosses, Lar and Matt Cardiff of Monmore, drummers Ted Higgins of Monmore, Matt Casey of Ballyoughna and Pakie Whelan of Kilmuckridge, followed by Bernard Kavanagh of Kilmuckridge, Mike O'Donohoe of Tinacree and Jim Dempsey, Flanders, of Kilmuckridge.

MULRANKIN /TOMHAGGARD SCHOOLS, 1960, under the inspiration of one of County Wexford's most respected teachers, Peadar Byrne, Principal, Mulrankin, made the exciting tour to Vinegar Hill, Enniscorthy. All returned safely.

Back row: Eileen Dillon, Marguerite Kehoe, Trish Kehoe, Jimmy O'Leary, Tom Underwood (teacher, Tomhaggard), Joe Power, Phyllis Delaney, Willie Keating, A.N. Other, Ger Casey, Joe Day, bus driver; Breda Furlong, Matt White, Ollie Newport, Eileen O'Keeffe, John Rowe, Tom Power, Maura Miskella, Bridget Corish, Michael Newport. Tony McBride, Tom Kehoe, Ann Doyle, Nuala Kehoe, Peadar Byrne, N.T., Kate McBride, Patricia Murphy, Cis Kehoe, Patricia Keating, Margaret Power, Frances McCormack. Patricia Doyle, Christine Rowe, Lucy Day, Danny Kenny. Front row: Brian Sarsfield, Michael Hassett, Brian Cardiff, Stephen Corish, Conleth Hassett, Eamonn Miskella, Pat Corish, Liam Kehoe, Johnny Watson, Patsy Kielthy, Pat Howlin, Seán Roche, Tom Miskella, Aidan Lambert, Willie Newport, Martin Murphy, Marty McBride, Ella Keating, Noel White, Michael Hore, Mary Corcoran, Marie Cardiff, Joe Bates.

(Our appreciation to Eileen Berry, née Dillon, for the identities.)

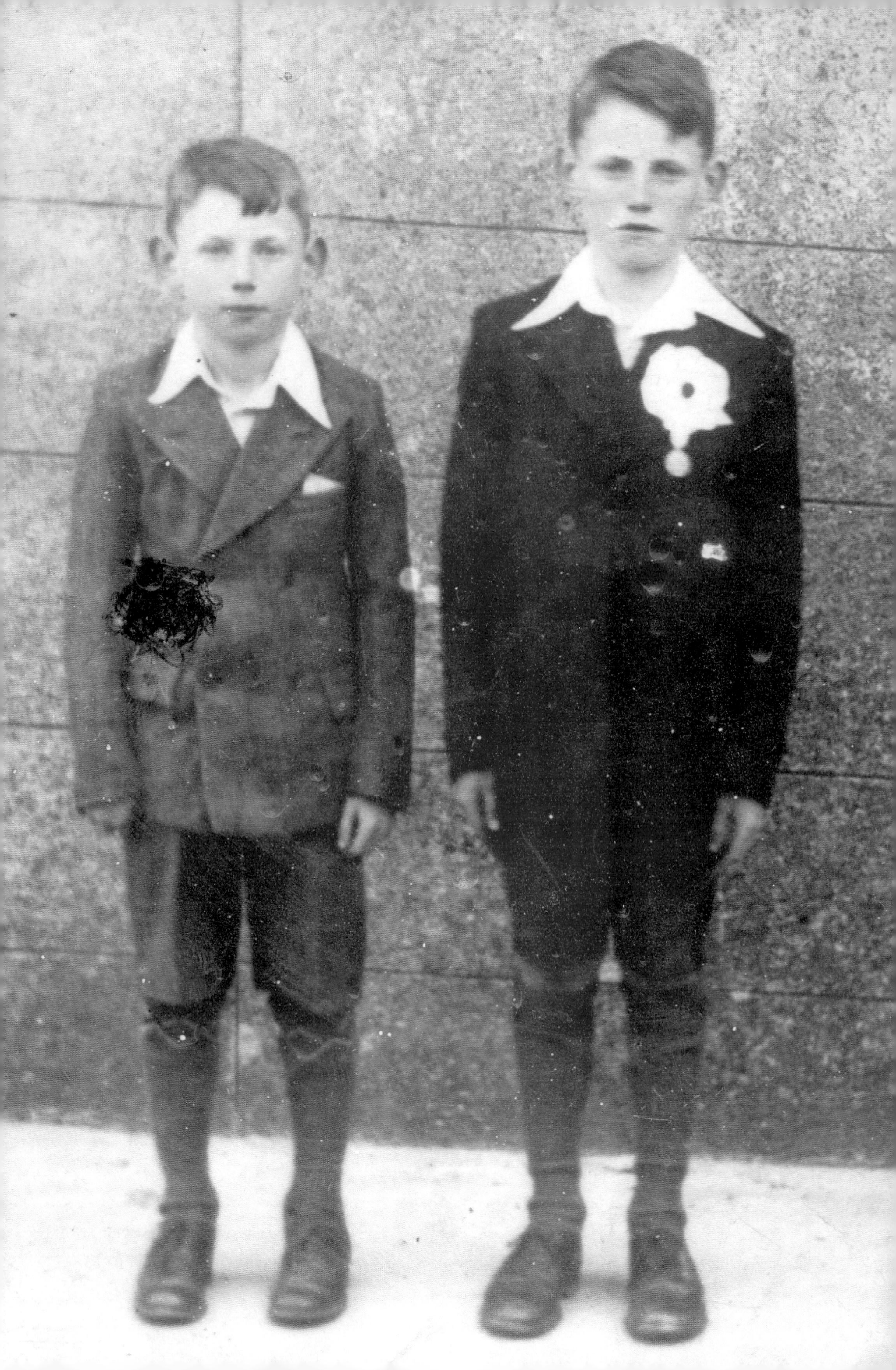

7 CHARACTERS

They say there are no characters anymore. They also say that when one thinks there are no characters one has oneself become a character.
                                                            Thesaurus Mac Gluadóir

A 'character' stands recognisable from the crowd. Whether man or woman, he or she is identified as the life and soul, wit of the club, parish, pub, mart, street or institution. Often such 'characters' do not realise the accolade personally. Or that they distribute such riches in word situations or innocent mischief expressed in the Irish word 'craic', or 'the stave' or 'the term' as it's known in Forth and Bargy, or in that equally misunderstood word ' divilment'.

They are not dying out as a species. They reappear in new guises, in new generations, in all states of life, places and professions. Their contributions to everyday existence have, like the sun's rays, illuminated and nourished all lives in every corner of our homeland.

Our selection is not inclusive. They are the only ones whose photographs have been collected for this work.

Here's to their memory.

A personal present from the good-hearted Ned Roche during the compilation of this edition. Ned is on the left with his brother Paddy. The occasion was their first Holy Communion day, around 1940.

Tranquilisers of Our Land

This photograph was taken by Uncle Arthur Guinness himself on the occasion of a St. James Gate tour. It was given to all the publicans of County Wexford, their wives and their representatives in the early seventies.

If my informant is right, they were all collected by bus, transported to Dublin, given the freedom of St. James' Gate, and smothered in hospitality and the choicest of refreshments. Coming back home that night they sang in such choral harmony with many individual contributions that they would have done credit to the cathedral choir.

That aside, it must be admitted that the photograph contains more genuine well-known characters than hundreds of photographs taken during that period. The older ones are gone and the void is still felt. Many more were stars of football and hurling, some were star backroom politicians, some were prominent on the public scene – but enough. Let's put the focus on them once more.

We are grateful to the scholarly Liam Lahiff for confirming identities. If anyone can put names on those we couldn't identify, we request the editor be informed. Back row: Paddy Travers-Purcell, Tommy Beakey of Pike Corner; the immortal scribe from the Faythe, Eddie O'Keeffe; Mance Mahon, Town Sergeant; Des Walsh of Taghmon; Mrs Eddie Hall, Carrigeen; Mrs Margaret Mathews, née Kelly; and Seán Keating, followed by three unidentified faces and at the end, Paddy Carroll.

Second from back: John Darcy, Tony Meyler, Unidentified, Breda Broaders-Tobin of the Stone Bridge, Fiona Kelly and Mrs Kelly of Monk Street, Mardie Clinch née O'Connor, Mrs Greg O'Brien, Unidentified, Mrs and Mr Tommy Kelly from The Faythe; Eddie Reville, Unidentified, and Jess Purcell.

Third row from back: Patrick Furlong, 72 North Main St., Wexford, Unidentified, Josie Murphy, Liam Roche, James O'Rourke and Mrs. O'Rourke, A.N. Other, Mrs. Johnny Murphy and Johnny Murphy of The Goal Bar; Ann Kelly now married to Tom

O'Leary of the John Street firm; Miss O'Connor of Alvina Brook and (we think) White's Hotel; Unidentified, Phil Gaul, Miss Bailey, Sally Fortune.

Front row: Guinness representative in the South East, Keith Hunt; unidentified, Billy White, Fintan Morris, Mrs Joss Kielthy, John's Gate St; Joss, unidentified, Jack Fane, the most famed Wexford inter-county footballer of the twenties and thirties; Eileen Corish née Meyler; actor and singer Des Corish, former Mayor, unidentified, the Mayor of Wexford, Kevin Morris, Eddie Hall, by a curious coincidence the third Mayor of Wexford in the row; Joe Aherne, Charlotte St., Mrs. O'Leary, Jim Stafford senior of John St; the great think-tank politician Frank Cullimore, father of Séamus; Miss Malone (we think), Tom Heffernan and Mrs Heffernan, the three All-Ireland hurling medals holder, Padge Kehoe of Court St., Enniscorthy and Al Byrne of Arthur Guinness, brother of the RTE great, Gay Byrne.

THIS TINY WHITE-WASHED HOUSE in Keyser's Lane was the home of one of Wexford's most colourful and popular characters "Ba" Swift, actor, singer, stage manager and resident comedian in the Theatre Royal next door.

"BA'S" ANTICS both on and off stage were the stuff of legend in the 1930s, 40s and 50s. The house and "Ba" were local attractions and the house became a regular site on town tours. "Ba" had a convincing stairs painted diagonally on the back wall to cod interlopers.

The great "Ba" Swift, singer, actor, entertainer.

JAMES (JEM) HESS of Whitemill, raconteur, teller of tall tales, delivery transport official Loch Garman Co-op, folklore inventor, the only man to have captured a Whitemill leprechaun only to lose it and the treasure. It was dark and he marked the spot where the treasure was, with a Bookalawn. When he got up in the morning to get the marked treasure, 2000 more Bookalawns had grown up in the night. (The Whitemill Bookalawn is known to botanists as 'senecio jacobea').

NED ROCHE

The undaunted, tireless organiser of beauty competitions, trusted by everybody and a sure guarantee of fair decisions, Ned Roche of Taghmon. In the limelight since the fifties he was very proud of this particular photograph showing "Miss Wexford" herself, Loraine Denton; then little "Miss Easter Bonnet", Danielle Hendrick, Ned himself and "Miss Easter Parade", Gráinne O'Brien.

Patrick Kinsella Collection.

Here we have a photograph of jolly characters, a spur of the moment snap shot. These are the printers and technicians involved in the recognised quality publications of English Printworks, Anne St. Wexford. The occasion on March 9, 1957 was the adventurous departure of Larry Doyle to seek his fortune in America.

The big trunk on the work desk is that subscribed to as a parting gift. Note its size. He could fit his girl friend or his mother in it, maybe both. Those were not the days of 5 hour flights to New York. Those were the days when it took five days or more out of Cobh. Going to New York for the Christmas shopping was unimaginable. You left and you left for a long time if not forever.

Teamed up for the camera click before going home are left to right at back: Mosie O'Leary, Paddy Kinsella, Cyril Scallan, Matt Farrell, Peter Donnelly, Larry Doyle, Larry Donnelly, Paddy Parle, Jim Evans, Peter Dempsey, Jimmy Hogan, Nick Scallan and Tommy Dempsey.

The girls, who had a lot to put up with daily, were Mary Frances Busher, Lily Busher and Marie Byrne, née Reck. Sadly in the same year's winter, Paddy Parle was killed in an explosion during that year's border incursions by the 1950s I.R.A.

LIL AND MARION ROCHE outside their parents' public house in Cornmarket (on Lower John's Gate St.) in 1930. Our donor Eamon Doyle informs us that this building was raided by the Black and Tans more often than any other shop in Wexford with the possible exception of Edward Foley's, burned down during the War of Independence in 1919-1921.

DR PEADAR 'PAX' SINNOTT of Ballygarret and Rocklands House, Wexford with his Duncannon born wife Maureen and an unidentified friend. Both have passed into legend but it is impossible to imagine that a medical doctor, historian, wit and controversialist of his characteristics will ever be experienced again. (1950).

A group of the great troubadours of our time between dotage and childhood. Hard to date, it could be 1960 plus or minus. They may be on stage because the backdrop scene is certainly not Griffins. Standing are Leo Carthy, impresario, the composer John Cousins, and the M.C. is Tom Sinnott, 'contagious' to Ballygeary.

Sinnott Collection.

Irish Press.

New Ross History and Archaeological Society Expedition.

SEATED are traditional violinist Murth Doyle of Roseland, Ballycogley and the shiny nimble-fingered child prodigy Liam Gaul. Despite determined efforts by the late Ibar Murphy, the correct name, Ballygeary, has been marginalised by the name Rosslare Europort.

AN IRISH Press photograph of 60 years ago brings back a breath of those days to an astonishing degree for there are numerous personalities who dominated the scene. We start the identifications from the front. Those in the rear were only possible with a magnifying glass.

Closest for observation are the late Frank Stafford with Mrs Maureen Stafford. Next row we find Mrs. Bridie Roche, St. John's Road, and Mrs May O'Connor, 6 Dempsey's Terrace, Wexford.

Behind them: C.D. Hearn, M.D. Star Iron Works, Pierce Ryan and Vincent Sherwood. Behind those are: Mrs Nan Brennan, sister of Robert Brennan, Ireland's wartime Minister in Washington; Kathy Carr, Selskar; Margaret, Agnes and Lil Harpur, Waterloo Road; Pat Cunningham, Auburn Terrace and Murty Meyler, Jr., of Laurel Hill, Clonard. It was probably taken at the Muintir na Tíre Rural Week in St. Peter's College, August, 1951.

THE PATRIARCH OF NEW ROSS, Andy Minihan leads a variety of followers like the pied piper of Hamelin into monastic Roscrea.

LIKE STOUT CORTEZ on a peak in Darien stands the veteran and retired Sergeant Major Wally Doyle, marshal of parades, town guide, philosopher and informed critic on ethics, military and civil, at home with marching troops or the civilian population. It's Saint Patrick's Day we know not when, but everything is certainly under control.

WHILE THIS IS A FINE STUDY of characters in Macra na Feirme, Ramsgrange, forty years ago, including the teacher and historian, Thomas P. Walsh of Duncannon seated at right, our character focus is on the fine presence, the parish priest, Father John Nolan. Every Catholic National school boy or girl, in every class up to primary certificate knew this shy man because certainly in the 1940s and for 15 years he was the Ferns diocesan Catechism Inspector of Schools. He was the man for whom everyone had to appear spick and span.

Photograph by Pat O'Connor

Teachers were relied upon to teach the pupils their catechism, questions and answers off by heart or Satan might have them all by the leg. He was a quiet pastor who always gave the impression that he would die rather than be thought a grand inquisitor.

The occasion was a Macra na Feirme reunion c.1960 in Reid's Hotel, Duncannon. Timmy O'Connor, Frank Cosgrave, John Joe Kehoe, Terry McDonald, John McDonald, Ger O'Connor, Pat Costello. Front: Andy Knox, Mary Costello, Michael Donovan (former manager of St. Louis Convent), V. Rev John Nolan, P.P. Ramsgrange, and Thomas P. Walsh, N.T. Ramsgrange.

Photo by Edward Prendergast, Campile. Peter McDonald Collection.

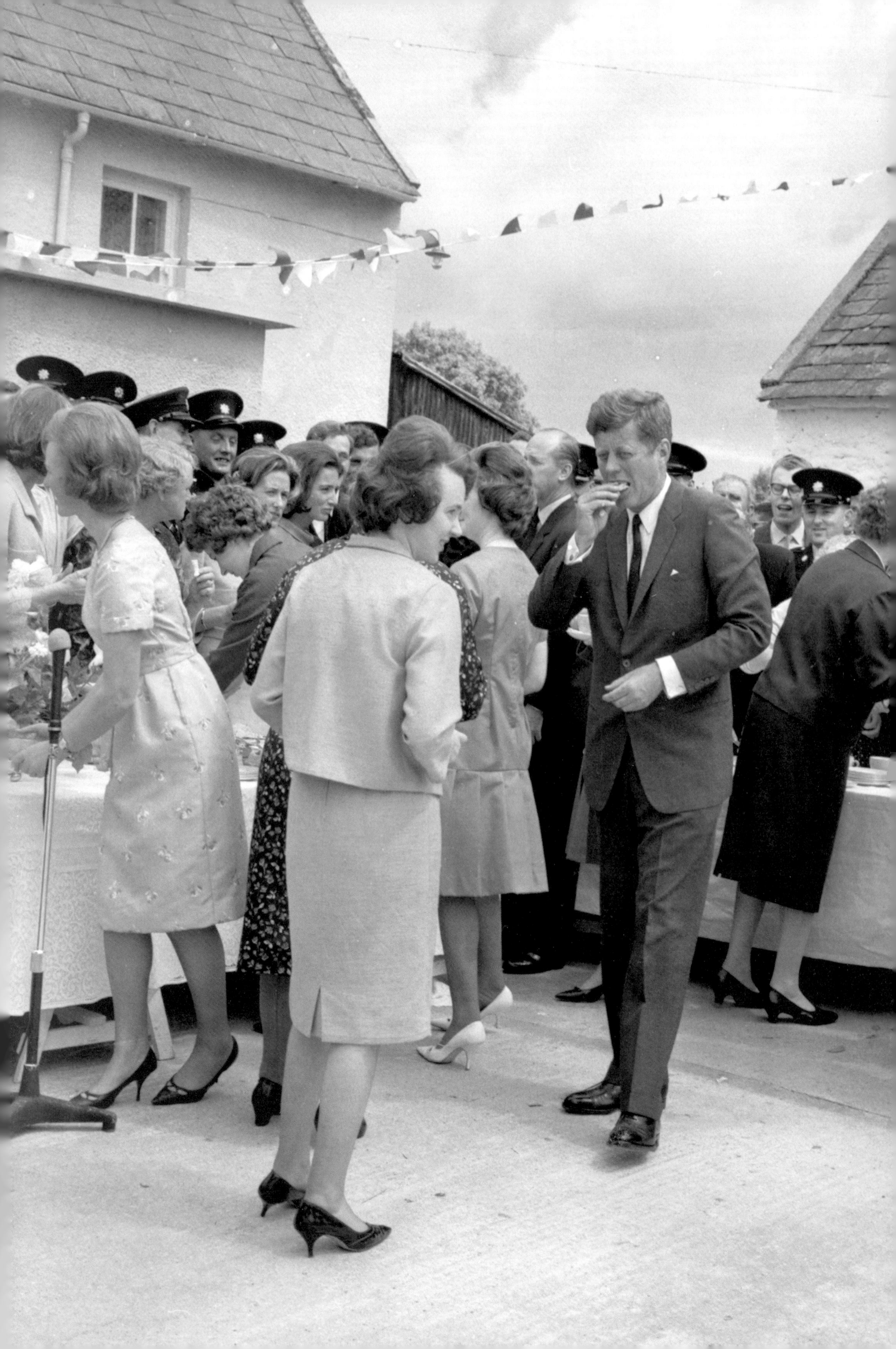

8 PRESIDENTIAL

Heads of State visits to County Wexford became a feature only in the twentieth century.

It is something of which we are now reasonably familiar with a record of official and private visits from all Ireland's Presidents, even the aged Dr. Douglas Hyde. He did not visit when he was in office but when forty years younger he was in the county to vigorously form branches of the Gaelic League.

It would however, be remiss were we not to stress the life-changing, morale-stimulating visit of County Wexford's own special, pride-inspiring President of the United States, John F. Kennedy, in June 1963.

> It is a party in a south County Wexford farmyard. The family, the relations, the neighbours are all there because the Kennedy cousins from Massachusetts are visiting the Dunganstown homestead of their grandfather. Josie and Mary Ryan are busy in the foreground managing the work of hospitality. There are friendly Gardai, detectives and other important people there. The focus of attention, protection and affection is gazing at everything in a moment of deep reflection while eating a sandwich. He is the great grandson of a Dunganstown Kennedy. He is also the President of the United States of America and the most powerful man in the world.
>
> Opposite: *Irish Times* photograph.

We thank RTÉ's Stills Library, Bride Rosney and Mary Creely who helped us lay hands on this great photograph.

THE GREATEST DAY

The day was in that sunny June of 1963 when the direct descendant of a County Wexford man, the President of the United States, John F. Kennedy, at the height of his world power, fame and popular affection, visited the county of his Dunganstown great-grandfather.

It is startling for all who saw the young man to realise that, had he not been murdered in cold blood in Dallas that same year, he would be in his nineties now, if still alive.

The photograph shows J.F.K. admiring the beautiful receptacle containing the Freedom of Wexford scroll.

The Gardaí, all seriously on the alert, were amongst hundreds of Gardaí in Wexford and New Ross that day. A train load of them disembarked at the South Station and it looked as if every Garda in Ireland was there. we cannot positively identify the men in this photograph. Perhaps someone will. We will do our best not to confuse with the identities.

Front row starting at extreme left: Wexford Corporation Accountant, Victor Merriman; John Howlin, Wexford Corporation; Dr. James Ryan, T.D., Minister for Finance at the time; John Byrne, Town Clerk; Lorcan Allen, T.D.; Brendan Corish, T.D., leader of the Labour Party; President Kennedy; Alderman T.F. Byrne, Mayor of Wexford.

Seated in foreground are the Minister for Foreign Affairs, Frank Aiken, T.D., and James Bowe, chairman Wexford County Council. On the row behind Mr. Aiken: Firstly, we have Dr. Anthony Esmonde, T.D.; the U.S. Ambassador to Ireland; Chief Superintendent Tom Collins; Séamus O'Gallachóir, Co. Council Secretary ; T.F. Broe, County Manager; Unidentified, Unidentified officer, John Flaherty, Wexford Corporation and Fr. Thomas Murphy, Adm, Wexford.

In the row behind Chief Superintendent Tom Collins: Eddie Hall, Wexford Corporation; a familiar but unidentified face; John Bierney, Wexford Corporation; Jim Morris, Wexford Corporation; Paddy Cullen, Wexford Corporation, Frank Cullimore, Wexford Corporation and William Kehoe, Town Sergeant and Mace Bearer.

Behind are: Jim Morris, Gearóid O'Broin, Sgoil na gCeard; teacher Eugene Curtin, Unidentified, Unidentified. To the left of the uniformed town sergeant is a Fianna Fáil member of the County Council who was also employed by the Sugar Company as their agent in North Wexford. At extreme left is Bill Esmonde.

The group standing with the C.I.E. notice board at their back starts with Myles Redmond,

Wexford Corporation official; Aidan Murphy with chain of office, probably Wexford Chamber of Commerce; the bold Captain John O'Leary; the applauding Paddy Fitzpatrick of the Talbot Hotel and South East Tourism interests; Unidentified; Leo Carthy, M.C.C.; Harry Doyle, Wexford Corporation official and Senator Seán Browne in front of the American officer.

We now move back to the left-hand side to the row behind Dr Ryan, starting at the window. First, Michael O'Brien, National Bank manager; P.J. McNally, Wexford Borough Council surveyor; Princess Lee Radziwill, sister of Mrs. Jacqueline Kennedy; Jean Kennedy Smith, and Fintan M. O'Connor, solicitor. Row behind Michael O'Brien: Jim Quirke of Wexford Steamships; a Franciscan, Fr. Barnabas, a fluent Irish speaker and preacher; another Franciscan; Dan Kavanagh, County Engineer and famed Kerry All-Ireland medal winner; Dr. Honoria Aughney, County Medical Officer of Health, and Dr. Toddy Pierce, highly respected and an All-Ireland senior football medal winner with Wexford in 1918 and again with Dublin.

Next row behind Jim Quirke is the ill-fated rector of Wexford, Eddie Shearer, tragically drowned along with his son off the Raven Point; Dick Elgee, immediately behind Dick Elgee is Fr. Thomas Rossiter, president, St. Peter's College; next is Thady O'Loughlin, M.C.C., Ballygarrett; Councillor Dunne, Caim; and Chief Executive Officer, P.B. Breathnach, Sgoil na gCeard.

Now for a stab at guesswork. Half hidden behind Jean Kennedy Smith, baldish, is another happily-remembered Friar, Fr. Humilis. He was a brilliant musician and organist. I'm not certain if he was American-born but he had spent part of his life, professionally, on an American band. He will be remembered because he used crutches. He had been badly injured in a motor car accident.

Snapshot taken from an upper window of a house on Common Quay, Wexford. J.F.K had just laid a wreath at the Commodore Barry statue and was on his way to Redmond Square for every civic honour possible.

Echo Files.

The crowds did not want to lose sight of him and kept running, trying to keep up with the motorcade. One local cameraman is standing on a barrel opposite for a better view.

John F. Kennedy has arrived at Redmond Square, Wexford. Comment would be superfluous.

1966. PRESIDENT DE VALERA at the Athenaeum where he reviews the veterans of the 1916 Enniscorthy garrison on the fiftieth anniversary of the rising of Easter Week.

The unveiling of the Commodore Barry statue presented to the people of Ireland by the U.S. government. It was unveiled by the President of Ireland, Seán.T. O'Kelly in 1956 at the Crescent Quay close to the point where young Barry embarked to seek his illustrious naval fortune.

Courtesy of A. Marsh, Monageer.

Irish Press.

THE CROWDS at the actual unveiling on an unpromising weather day crammed the Crescent Quay. The clever took to the boats. One of those was Dr. Peadar 'Pax' Sinnott, historian and 1919-1923 veteran who chose the third boat from right. He is without hat or coat. He had studied the life and times of Commodore John Barry and on the occasion gave the major lecture.

AN TAOISEACH ÉAMON DE VALERA inspects the Local Defence Force guard of honour in the Faythe, Wexford, early in World War II.

Courtesy of Kilmore Journal.

PRESIDENT ÉAMON DE VALERA on his last visit to County Wexford chatting with the venerable and inexhaustible Wexford hero patriot, Methodist missionary in war-torn China and world traveller, Dr George Hadden.

THE DAY of the official opening of the Irish Agricultural and Folk Museum in Johnstown Castle grounds, June 18th 1979, showed a culmination of ambitious planning. En route from the Castle to the Museum in a tub trap driven by Mr Joseph Breen of Wexford are the President of Ireland, Dr P. J. Hillery who performed the opening, Mr T. J. Maher, Chairman of the Museum Committee and Dr. Tom Walsh, Director of the Agricultural Institute.

In their own spheres the three guests were patriots of towering significance. The Museum has been of outstanding interest and intrinsic value for the nation and thousands of visitors annually. A large number of farm and rural artefacts have been collected including home, farm and rural items, machinery, home-made furniture and living quarters with utensils. Just in time.

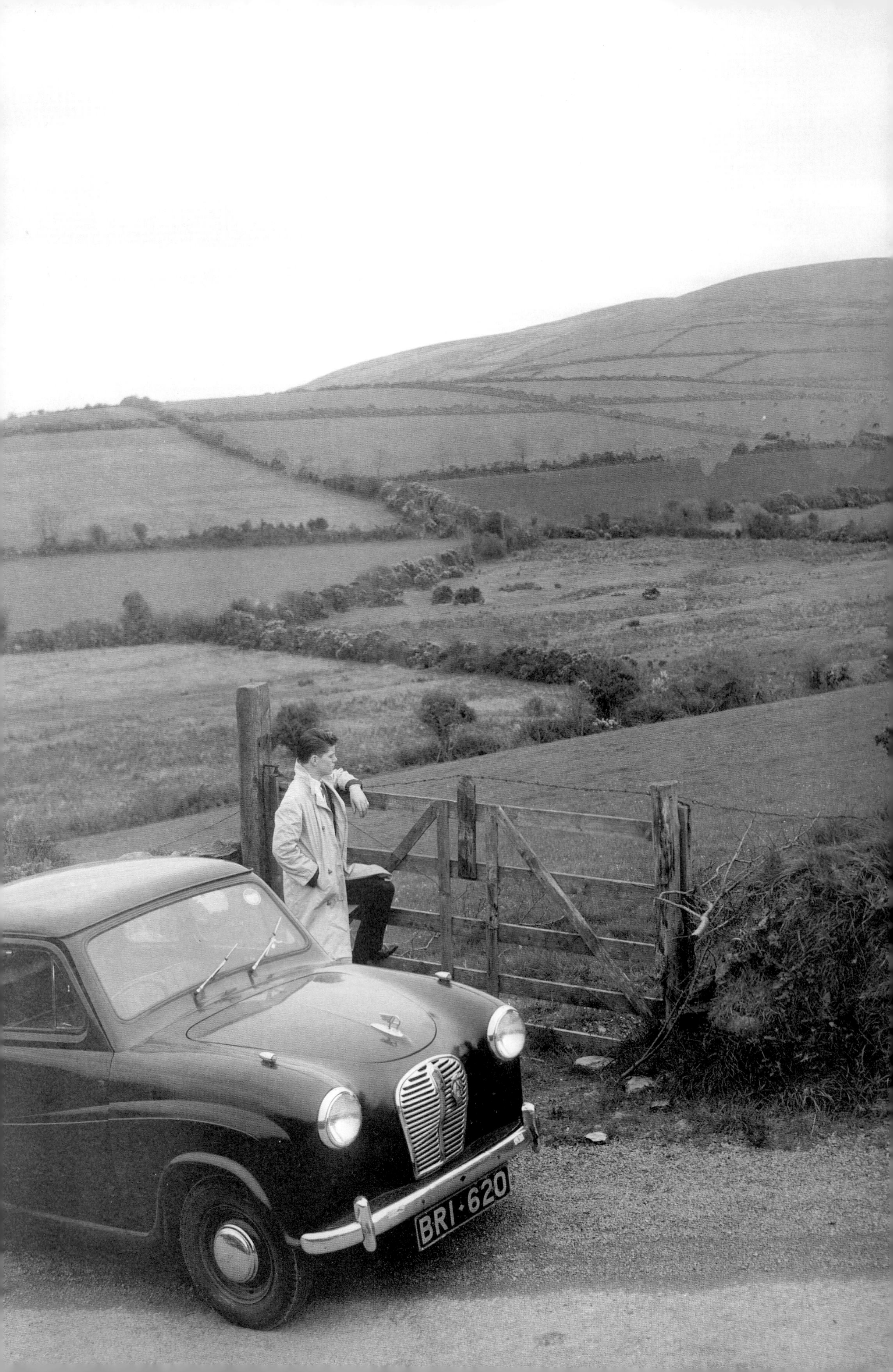
BRI 620

9 SIGHTS AND SCENES – A Miscellany

A Ferns viewer saw for the first time in his life, a photograph of his own father. The father had died in the viewer's infancy. No image of him was thought to exist.

In this chapter, we have a photographic assembly of separate but significant merit. The value depth may not be staring the viewer in the face, but to the families of those bearing a special connection with a single photograph, the experience can be riveting.

Take time. Look carefully.

Opposite: View near New Ross.

Photograph courtesy of Fáilte Ireland.

FERRYCARRIG'S OLD ROAD, C. 1880, when the picture had to be posed. Photographer unknown, but it may be Strangman Davis Goff of Horetown House who had taken the first ever photographs of this beautiful area.

ROSSLARE as the Nicholas Kelly lens caught it in 1929.

KILLINICK VILLAGE, 1929. *Photograph Nicholas Kelly.*

BEAUTIFUL BORODALE BRIDGE alongside the Fort of Gold – Dun an Óir. *Photograph by Nicholas Kelly 1930.*

KAVANAGHS' BREAD VAN doing the rounds in front of the Wexford Work House complex, later Wexford General Hospital, 1927. The building in the foreground was demolished in the early 1950s.

MARTIN HAYES. IN MEMORY

Martin Hayes of Clifford Street, Wexford, was a soils type researcher with An Foras Taluntais, later Teagasc, in Johnstown Castle. He had more strings to his bow. He was a skilled photographer at the service of Teagasc nationwide and was an enthusiastic, experienced flier. With these skills he was instrumental in supplying the Irish soils service with photographs from the air which were of enormous benefit to the service as well as geographers.

With thanks to Martin's brother Tomás Hayes, Whiterock and his colleague Alan Cuddihy, An Foras Taluntais.

He was tragically killed in an accident at Castlebridge Airfield on September 19, 1975. These photographs from the air are published in his memory.

Our photograph of Martin in action was taken near Navan, County Meath, during the streams sediment survey conducted by An Foras Talúntais all over Ireland under Garry Fleming. The Navan experience proved a first class sensation for Martin and his colleagues who discovered high levels of lead, zinc deposits which led to the development of the extensive mining industry there

1970. Wexford's yawning and empty industrial estate from the air. Wexford G.A.A. Park is at top of the left.

SIGHTS AND SCENES | 141

An aerial picture of the ESB oil fired generating station at Great Island, Co. Wexford. One of seven oil-fired stations on the ESB system. Great Island has capacity of 240Mw. In 1972-73 65% of Ireland's electricity needs were supplied from oil-fired generating stations.

Gorey from the air long before its dramatic 21st century expansion.

1963. Landlocked Lady's Island Lake indicating the herculean manual labour involving the neighbours to dig the water-releasing channel annually. It is now made by modern mechanical diggers. Hay was saved by hand, left lower corner.

Courtesy of Teagasc.

1970. St. Peter's College Wexford in centre, Mercy Sisters Convent Schools and laundry in foreground. The Bishop of Ferns's house (The Bishop's House) and former lands are on right of picture.

LEST WE FORGET

Our next batch of horror photographs is undoubtedly going to create a shock but on the other hand it has to be with considerable relief that the viewer will realise that they were of forty years ago. We have moved decisively forward: it must never be allowed to deteriorate or revert to such an extreme again.

These depressing sites were snapped unexpectedly by an executive appointed to Wexford town forty years ago. At the time Ireland was not yet in the European Union. The visitor was shocked at Wexford's derelict sites. He photographed them as memento of his first impressions. His impressions were certainly akin to the viewer's reaction 2010. In short he was thoroughly depressed.

Our thanks to the donor who naturally prefers to remain anonymous.

Talbot Street, Wexford 1973

Talbot Street, Wexford 2009.

Slippery Green.

Wexford's Talbot Street.

St John's Gate Street.

Cinema Lane, Wexford.

Maudlintown.

Peter's Street (" Gibson's Lane").

SIGHTS AND SCENES | 143

Unidentified.

Bride Street with crop growing on roof.

John Street.

Cornmarket!

John Street / Thomas Clarke Street.

John Street.

Thomas Clarke Street.

Mary Street.

Abbey Street.

Cot Safe View.

Unidentified.

Unidentified.

THE HEART OF VIKING WEISSFJORD. c. 1973 A.D. The discovery of consolidated remains of Wexford life as it was one thousand years ago was sensational at the time. It proved to be the precursor of an even greater settlement discovery. It took place at Oyster Lane, once famed for its shellfish food shops. The National Museum became intensely interested and following their notification they sent down a brilliant young scholar whose major studies were on the Norse. Dr. Patrick Wallace seen in front at centre is now internationally renowned as Director of The National Museum of Ireland.

In attendance with him on the site are the city fathers and notaries public with alert members of the Wexford Historical Society in 1973 A.D. From left, Gus Byrne, Dr Brendan Swan, William Igoe, Tom Roche, Brendan Culleton, Thos. Broe, County Manager, Jack Dunne, James Maguire, Dr Ned Culleton, John Flaherty, Seán McLoughlin, B.E., Desmond Corish, Mrs Wixted, Mai McElroy, Desmond Wixted, Town Clerk, and Nellie Walsh.

Echo Newspapers. Enniscorthy in flood 1947.

IN 1969 A NATIONAL SOCIAL STUDIES Conference was held in Wexford. It was in August during the holiday period so the facilities of St. Peter's College were put at the disposal of the conference. I recall it as a huge occasion with an attendance of academics, scholars, trade union chiefs, national commentators, university professors and all with a special interest in sociology. They were from every part of Ireland. The conference which was held over a three day period included many from the Six Counties and Queens University.

1969 was an unforgettable year when fury, revolt and counter revolt erupted from Derry to Belfast. The first indication of trouble brewing was made plain to us at a panel discussion when a highly qualified lady panellist from Belfast (later murdered) declared in ringing tones that "we" (the citizen nationalists) would not lie down and take "their" treatment one day longer. A Trinity College professor arose next and condemned in more than robust tones that "her sentiments were damnably wicked". The complacent southerners gripped their seats. Tension took over.

The Wexford coordinating committee for this fascinating extravaganza are photographed with Fr. William Gaul,P.P. Kilmore; Ms Coleman, St. John's Road; Mrs Gonda Collopy (a Dutch lady) and the college President, Fr. Sylvester O'Byrne.Second row, Robert (Robbie) Roche, William Collopy, John F. Byrne,Wexford Town Clerk. At back, Thomas P. Walsh, N.T. Duncannon, Fr Patrick Jordan, St. Peter's College Bursar and Patrick Sheridan, Sheridan Insurances.

HADDENS. Famous Name, Famous Staff. Although the famed and most generous workers for Wexford's progress in commerce and culture, the Haddens are no longer in Wexford, their reputation will never be diminished. The staff reunion or maybe Christmas party shows the boys and girls of Haddens staff before the old firm was amalgamated with Shaw's.

Our thanks to Eva Kelly, Farnogue.

Standing, Liam O'Shea, N. Hubert, Pat Browne, Nick Kane, Michael Hanrahan (New Ross), Pat Moran, Eamon Sweeney, Christy Darcy. Middle row: Ann Hill, Rose N, Liam Donoghue, Zilpah Jacob, Ms Shields, Muriel Armstrong, Ann Kavanagh, Ann Pollard, Elizabeth Taylor. Front, Madge Sweeney, Brema O'Byrne, Mairead Doran, Eva Byrne, D. Foxton, Siobhán Mahon

THE 1975 REUNION OF WALKERS' STAFF, North Main Street and Charlotte Street, Wexford, the Harrods Food Hall of the south east, exemplars of service to the old gentry, the new gentry, aspirants to the gentry classes, poseurs, the wealthy no less than the plain people as well as penniless gentry and merchants.

From left standing: Messrs Kiernan Ruttledge, Gerard O'Mahoney, Tom Walsh, Richard Rice, Denis Roche, Seán Walsh, Gerry Cleare, Gerard Roberts, Terry Murphy, Bernard Reville, James White, Patrick Donnelly, Patrick Murphy, Robert Murphy. Seated, the Misses Esther Bright, Anne Doyle, Betty Chambers, Mr Patrick Parle, Manager, Mrs Maureen Parle, the Misses Elsie Reville, Margaret Stamp, Mary Parle, Ann Chambers.

Enniscorthy in snowfall, firm date uncertain, possibly early 1980s (Anonymous donor)

SIGHTS AND SCENES | 147

Enniscorthy in 1953.

AT THE TIME of Smith Engineering's sale of Pierces, artefacts were removed to their H Q Dublin or Cavan – including the beautiful furniture and oak decorations in the boardroom of that world farm machinery company. Beryl Kinsella née Waters was secretary there in the writer's period as press officer 1966-73 approx. Beryl retrieved this remnant of the factory photographs and environs. Taken at a guess in Pierces in centenary year 1939.

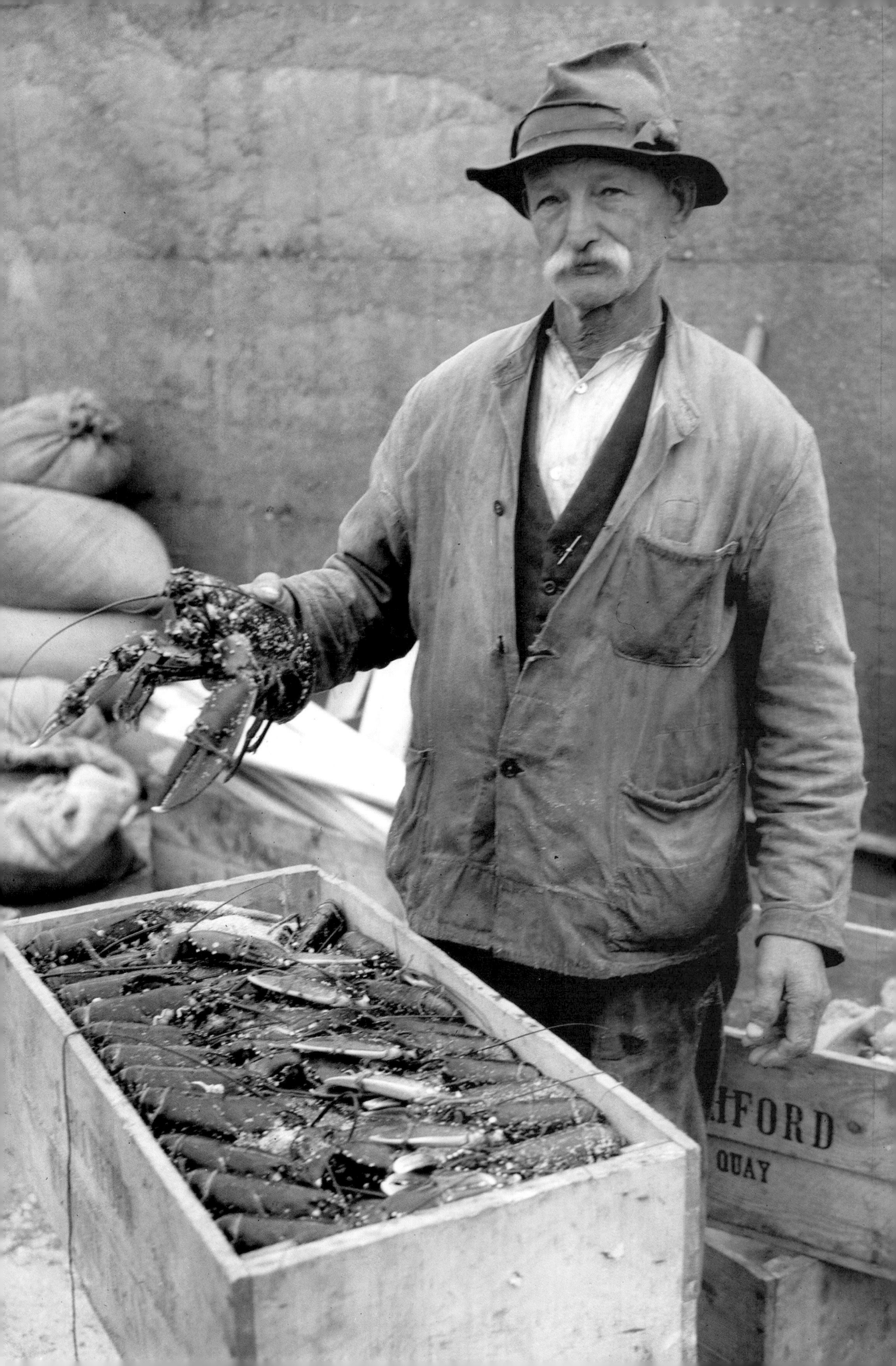
IFORD
QUAY

10 PEOPLE OF THE SEA

We are familiar, perhaps too familiar, with the sea and tidal rivers of our county, east, south and west, that we think nothing extraordinary about the position. It is no more unusual than the stairs in a house. Yet we are unique in Ireland with the Atlantic Ocean on our south coast and the Irish Sea on our East coast.

It has never been over-emphasised but the possession of our territory was deemed necessary to retain supreme power in the North Atlantic since the rediscovery of the Americas' potential over 500 years ago. To the three imperial tribes, England, Spain and France, the possession of Ireland's seaports and facilities was very desirable indeed. Still normal work went on. The sea was our friend and provider. Few, that is except military and naval experts, thought otherwise. We were blissfully unaware that we were not as secure in peace as Iceland.

The Kilmore Quay fisherman, no stranger to the gourmet potential of lobster and shellfish, spreads his catch before the exporters of eighty years ago.

Opposite: *Fáilte Ireland* photograph.

Photographer most likely Handcock.

GATHERING WORE at the Hamogue. Hamogue is in the parish of Bannow near Blackhall. The first Bishop of Ferns diocese, Saint Aidan, landed at the rough beach in the photograph, brought there by the prevailing winds. Travelling from his tutor Saint David's school in Menavia, Wales, he was probably, driven off course. The local chieftain 'offered himself his district and family to Aidan for ever'. Aidan in Irish is Mo aodh óg (Mogue), therefore the name Hamogue (acha Mhaodhóig) sounds as Hamogue. (Acha means field or ground)

Wore, our word for sea weed, is a proven top quality fertiliser especially for root crops. Of special significance is the crop of potatoes in the seaside districts of County Wexford. In the 19th century, as in previous centuries, wore was harvested off the beaches with vigour at low tide as our photograph shows. The date must be the 1880s because the photographer has every single man in still pose. I think there are at least 16 horses and cars at the Hamogue.

KILMORE, WEXFORD, Rosslare Harbour? Another daunting mystery. It's County Wexford in origin but we have no positive facts. The occasion was auspicious. Apart from the crew the gentlemen on board are in their formal best. In fact the venerable figure in silk topper, frock coat, striped pants and holding a cigar closely resembles the Lord Lieutenant of Ireland, Lord Aberdeen, who opened the cross-channel ferry service on July 2 1906. The gentleman facing the camera in centre with white beard, bowler hat and thumb in lapel is Patrick Parle, owner and resident farmer of the Great Saltee Island.

One could speculate for hours on the identities of the gentlemen on the top deck. Apart from crewmen they appear to have stepped straight out of the board room. Is it Kilmore or is it Rosslare Harbour? I have examined comparable photographs of the Lord Lieutenant on that opening day and am now of the belief it is Rosslare Harbour. It could be a harbour viewing of work in progress. Other views and identities will be welcomed by the editor.

BUILDING ROSSLARE Harbour bridge and facilities. There had been a pier at Ballygeary (the port's townland) in 1864. This pier and infrastructure were under construction to facilitate the railway and cross channel ferry service as envisaged. It was carried out in stages. The photograph was taken from the cliff by Handcock or Strangman Davis Goff c. 1880.

THE WHALE

A whale was washed up in Ballyhealy in December 1941, but due to uneven reporting and publication problems during the war it does not appear to be mentioned in any newspaper. P.J. Purcell, the Garda sergeant in Kilmore Quay at the time, wrote to the Natural History Museum in Dublin to report officially. The museum authorities wrote back asking him for certain details. He replied that he couldn't provide these details as the whale had been covered with sand.

It appears that Wexford County Council employed a man to bury the remains but no information on this can be traced in the Council's records. Willie Doyle, Neamstown, says that the man who got the task of burying the whale was the late Dan Cullen, Neamestown.

The jaw bones were brought to "The Elms", Bridgetown, and were used by Dr. Doyle to make an ornamental archway in his garden. They are now in the grounds of Latimerstown House.

The snapshots are from the Eamon Doyle Collection. Our thanks for additional information to Jim Hurley and Hilary Murphy.

Dan Keegan and Erdie Murphy. The whale was 62 feet long. The Jaw bones were 12 feet across. The question remains if it was a war casualty or was beached and died.

The whale was investigated by Maureen Murphy (Mrs Hickey, William Street), Dan Keegan (cabinet maker and musical instrument maker, Francis Street), Eamon Doyle, Erdie Murphy, Waterloo Road, Wexford.

Eamon Doyle Collection.

NEW ROSS from the old bridge, c. 1890, possibly by Wm. Cavanagh. The sign warns "Speed 3 Miles".

Wm. Cavanagh. TWO THREEMASTERS ON THE CALM RIVER BARROW at New Ross. Year and photographer uncertain. It may be c. 1890.

The *barque Saltee* (centre) arriving simultaneously off the Wexford coast c. 1885 with *The May Queen* and *The Hantoon*, all three Wexford bound having taken part in the most memorable race in the port's maritime history. They left Galatz (Galati in Romania) down the Danube together and arrived off Wexford together. It was the period of the great trade in County Wexford grain to the Mediterranean and the Black Sea.

The brig *Industry* (Captain James Murphy) icebound at Galatz, Winter 1877. The *Industry* was trapped at Galatz for a year because of the Russian-Turkish war. The barque *Hantoon* and the brig *Alert* were also at Galatz when the war began, but just managed to get away.

The S.S. Irish Larch on independent passage in the North Atlantic in 1943. She was managed by The Wexford Steam Ships Company.

Staffords of Wexford M.V. *Menapia* in the Atlantic with the obligatory wartime markings indicating neutrality.

Paintings by Ken King.

THIS IS HOW machine-private first class (engine room artificer) Franz Stor looked in 1943. During his career he served on the T 26. He was one of those saved by the Kerlogue and particularly by crewman Tom O'Neill, following the battle in Biscay, Christmas week, 1943. He attended the torpedo boat survivors reunion with the Kerlogue survivors in the Maritime Institute, Dun Laoghaire, in 1994.

TONY JACOB

In 1951 two exceptional events in Ireland grabbed Irish and certainly Wexford's attention. One was the steamrolling emergence of the Wexford senior hurling team. The second was the daring attempt, indeed successful attempt, to cross the Atlantic Ocean from Wexford to New York in a small sailing boat with what one heard was a 'sick' auxiliary engine. At the time it was as adventurous as a Moon exploration. A popular and prominent young man, Tony Jacob of Rathdowney, Rosslare, was one of the dominant seafarers deemed crazy, a chum named Dalton and a Tipperary architect and hurler, Seán Kenny.

Tony was one of the finest specimens of manhood, tall, broad, blonde, regular featured. He was an only son, and a cheerful daredevil also addicted to motorbikes. Kenny's career later claimed international heights in stage set design. His most famous was that for the world-famous musical 'Oliver', London. This writer was present at a Kenny design exhibition in Dublin in the late '60s. Amongst the famous at the exhibition was John Huston, the great film director, who opened it. Kenny was rather young when he died. The great tragedy was Tony Jacob's. Shortly after their triumph and hero's acclaim he contracted polio in New York and died with shocking rapidity.

Our photograph shows The Ituna being lowered into the water following its sick auxiliary engine being fixed by 'Nyko' Scallan.

Tony Jacob, Rathdowney. *Courtesy of Helen Skrine.*

HOPELANDS

The first recorded Notice required by Admiralty of an attempt to reclaim land from Wexford harbour was in 1813- fifteen years after the Rebellion of 1798.

The notice was given by and on behalf of the following, the majority of whom were residents of the locality: James Boyd, Esq., Captain in the King's Dragoons Guards; The Right Hon. Henry, Lord Viscount Monk;John Knox Grogan, Esq., Johnstown; Vigers Harvey- a minor, by the Rev. Roger Owen, his guardian;The Rev. John Jacob, Killowen Cottage; Parsons Frayne, Bormount; Henry and John Cooper, Birchgrove; Walter Hore, Harperstown; Richard Neville, Furness, Co.Kildare; Wm. and Archie O'Toole (Both then in Spain with British Army); Mary O'Toole, spinster and Elizabeth O'Toole, widow (both of Wexford); Louis B.V. Williamsdorf Richards, Esq., Rathaspeck; John and Henry Bruen, both of Painstown, Carlow; Percival Swan Esq., Summerseat; Sir Francis Loftus,

1935. The last breach of the Hopelands dam, South Slob at Rosslare.

Attempting to fill the Breach as the Hopelands dam collapsed.

Photographs donated by Peter Maguire, B.L.

Mount Loftus, Kilkenny; Lt. Col. Nicholas Loftus, Richfield, Wexford.

To make application to the Parliament for a Bill to enable them to reclaim the Mudlands in the Harbour of Wexford. The Bill was obtained and the work commenced with enthusiasm near Rosslare.

But in the fall of the year an easterly storm of great ferocity arose, accompanied by an extraordinarily high tide and swept away the embankment in one night. However, one of the villains of the 1798 rebellion, by great perseverance and industry, Major Boyd of Rosslare had reclaimed 240 acres from the harbour adjoining his demesne, and in the summer of 1847 - the year of the great Famine - oats was seen growing on part of this land, the straw of which was 7ft long! This was called Hopelands.

The reclamations of two polders, or slobs as we call them, were by 1860 successfully reclaimed, totalling, north and south, approximately 5000 statute acres. The Boyd family successfully farmed Hopelands but eventually the property was in the possession of Mr. Nicholas Furlong of the Iona Hotel, Rosslare.

In 1935, peril from the sea arrived which could have lost every acre ten feet under highwater level, all protected by dams. The polder known as the South Slob had as its south eastern bulwark the Hopelands intake. In September 1935, the Hopelands dam was breached during a long and ferocious storm.

The Dublin to Rosslare Harbour and the Waterford to Rosslare Harbour railway lines were now in imminent and certain danger as well. The battle to save the Slobs was joined but Mr. Furlong, a lone farmer, concerned himself, workmen and helpers with filling the Hopeland bank breaches. Fanaticism was required, but filling with cart loads of marl, cement blocks, sods, stones and bushes gave the raging high tide no problem. As soon as one breach was sealed, another opened. Hopeland was lost.

The major Slob Company was faced with either building a new bank to protect their Hopeland flank or being inundated. And so a new embankment of 900 yards long was made. Granite slabs were bought from Aughrim, Co. Wicklow and the entire job cost £1,700.

Our two photographs of the Hopelands breach in 1935 are enough to strike terror in any heart. They were snapped by an excited schoolboy on holidays with his parents and probably about to be lodged shortly in school. His name was Peter Maguire, second son of Chief Justice Conor Maguire and Cathleen Maguire, née Whelan, Drinagh House. His presentation of these heart-breaking sights to us, hitherto unknown and as far as we know the only ones, has been one of the greatest acquisitions for the edition of this publication.

The sponsors for the first Kilmore Festival in 1986, with associates.

Front row (l to r): John Keane, auctioneer; Tommy Howlin, council chairman; John Power, Festival chairman; Fr. Jim Cogley, Jim Symons, Slaneyside Dairies. Middle row: Des Whelan, Beamish and Crawford; Peter Kelly, Heineken; Eamonn Doyle, grocer; George Stafford, Heineken; Frank Boxwell, tiling contractor; Noel Whelan, contractor; Peadar Raftery, tiling contractor; Willie Furlong, builder, Pat Bates, central-heating contractor. Back row: Eugene Kehoe, Patrick Leguay, Sofrimar; Hugh Crosbie, PMPA; Tom Hynes, Animal Health; Eben Stewart, Drover Meats; Paddy Murphy, Kilmore P.O.; Michael Cunningham, Irish Distillers.

Building Wexford's New Bridge, 1958-1959.

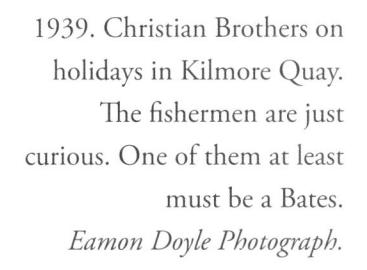

1939. Christian Brothers on holidays in Kilmore Quay. The fishermen are just curious. One of them at least must be a Bates.
Eamon Doyle Photograph.

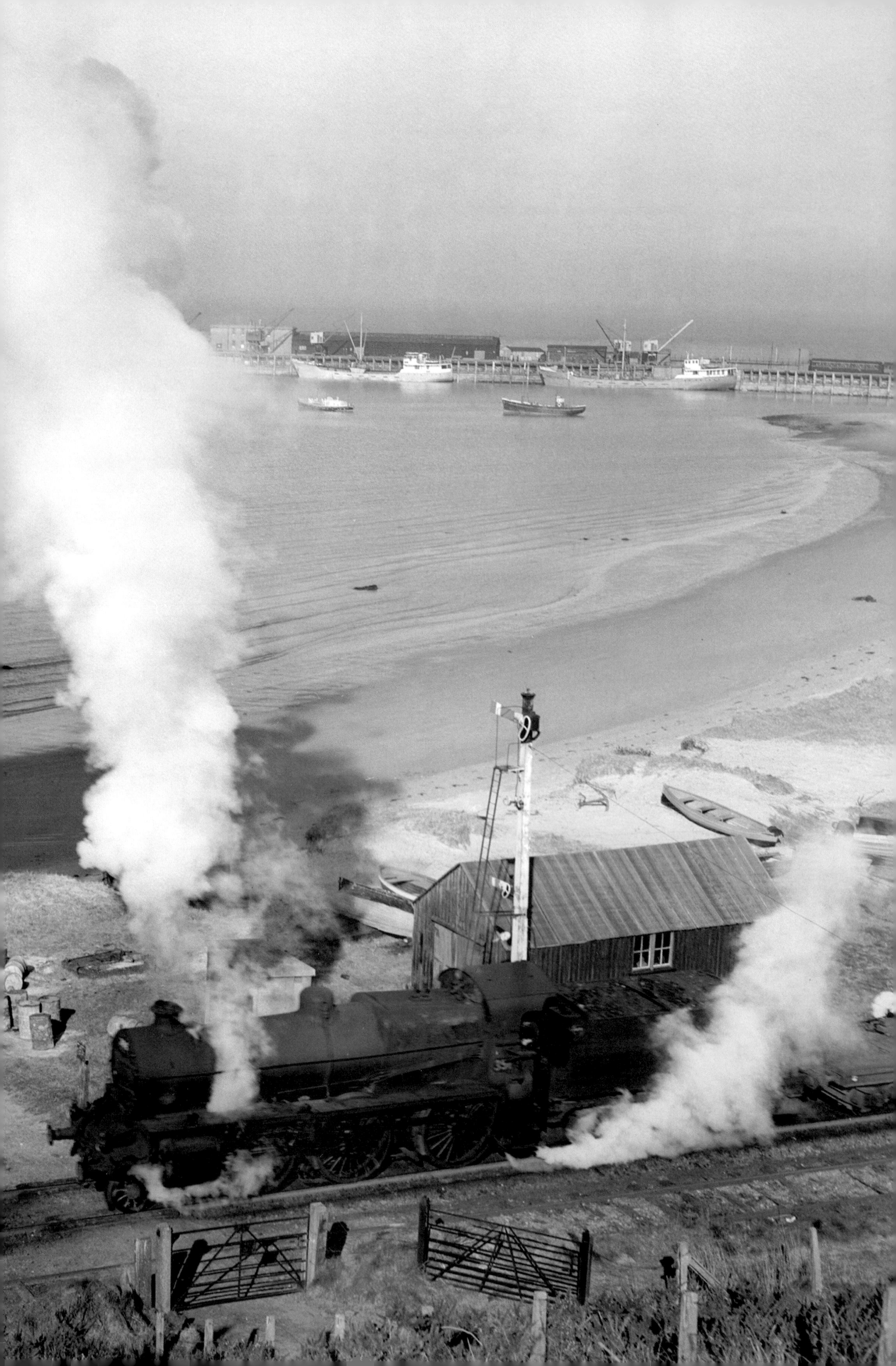

11 TRANSPORT

At the time of writing in Summer 2010, County Wexford is going through a spasm of citizen alarm due to the publication of major but potential routes linking Rosslare Europort with the greater road system in Ireland, its vital commercial links with Europe and the landmass beyond.

It is no longer relevant to the controversies or the several defence committees that it was transport which first opened County Wexford through its geographical boundaries of harbour, river and mountain range. Apart from seafarers and horse travellers, few County Wexford citizens travelled outside their geographical province. The arrival of the railways dramatically charged all that. Today the facilities at Ballygeary or Rosslare Europort enjoy an urgency for development and progress which constitutes a pre-eminent dynamic.

Opposite: Rosslare Harbour

Fáilte Ireland

Photo by Strangman Davis Gough.

EARLY REPLACE TRAIN AT ROSSLARE HARBOUR, 1886. The absence of buildings, apart from the tiny signal box, shows how primitive the area known as Ballygeary was at that period.

A posed photograph taken by the pioneer County Wexford photographer, Augustus Handock of Colebrook House, Wellingtonbridge in 1880, of in all likelihood his mother.
Jack Handcock Collection.

Mr Jack Walker of Ballybrennan's pre-railway, pre-Slob reclamation port on the south of Wexford Harbour near Killinick.

Gorey workmen, quarry stones for road making, circa 1930. From left to right are: Peter Hughes, A.N.Other, Ml. Lawlor, engine driver; Johnny Doyle, P. Grannell, Jim Kinch, Jim Daly, Johnny Kinsella, A.Kinsella, Jack Finn, Willie Kenny, Lar Kinsella and Ben Gordon with horse.

Outside the Bank of Ireland, in Gorey, c. 1915.

A very important photograph appeared in 2004 which attracted much curiosity. Lent by Nadine Murphy it shows a lorry halted in the commercial sector of Taghmon's monastic city. Nadine tells us that the house on the left is still owned by the Cullen family who carried on a saddlery business. The three thatched houses on the right-hand side were owned and occupied by the Condon, Walsh and Daly families. Initially it was thought that this was a photograph of Royal Irish Constabulary officers on duty with their armoured car in Main Street Taghmon. It was not. It was on a commercial mission of peace in 1927. The lorry delivering supplies was owned by Messrs Walkers and Sons, Ltd., 78 North Main St. Wexford, licensed for commercial goods. The make is difficult to make out but it looks like 'GUY'. It was manufactured in 1923 but the previous owners are not recorded. Its colour was red and blue. Its unloaded weight was 2 tons 15 ¼ cwts. The annual rate of duty was 45 pounds sterling.

A well-known old friend on the local County Wexford railways in the 30s, No 183 was distinctive because unlike other steam engines she had a flatter roof.

Ml. Fitzpatrick Collection.

From rail expert Michael Curran.

MATTHEW BOGGAN'S pioneer bus services from Wexford town. It was private enterprise at its best. This snapshot may be mischievous. It has all the appearance of a "comfort stop" on the way to a match or races, 1930s. McCormack and Hegarty's, builders and timber importers, fill the roof space on the first bus. Boggan's bus colours were light blue and cream.

BREAD DELIVERIES at Phillips, South Main Street, Wexford, 1930. Buckland's had two shops at the time. One was opposite the other on either side of the street.

THE BILLY MALONE EXPRESS, 1944. The Emergency was it? A monumental inconvenience more like. Thirsty souls, seaside travellers, firms and friends on outings were greatly inconvenienced we insist. The brave entrepreneurs raised themselves above such trifles, particularly Mr Billy Malone of Selskar, businessman, horse-lover with shining turn-outs and top class trotters, transport arranger, particularly outside the three mile limit where refreshments and stimulants were legally supplied to proven travellers.

Our photograph (camera manipulator unknown) shows Mr Malone in foreground having delivered paying guests to O'Connors' Strand Hotel, Curracloe. One can but admire his comprehensive skill in recycling what may have been (we must assume) an abandoned 1930s motor car.

Proprietor, photographer Nicholas Kelly, Rosslare Strand Hotel, photographs the latest 1920s model and its proud, well-clothed owners.

MEN OF STEAM. We have a vital photograph for the records of steam and rail transport in County Wexford. It is vital because it's a photograph the like of which will never be seen again. There are 30 faces in this photograph. There were so many again working on and out of Wexford town's stations, North and South. There were five steam train crews.

Aidan Cogley of Drinagh who joined C.I.E in 1963 tells me that more than sixty persons were employed at Wexford's stations. The South Station is now gone. The former North station is named O'Hanrahan Station in honour of the executed 1916 leader, County Wexford born Michael O'Hanrahan from New Ross.

The North Station at Redmond Square was so busy that Eason's of Dublin, the book sellers, had a movable shop on the platform which employed one lady permanently. They had the usual magazines and newspapers on sale as well as books. Eason's of Dublin did not invest in such outlets unless there was a profit making source there. That situation obtained up to the 1950s.

Seated in front is the station master, Patrick Lawlor whose rank was certified in uniform and gold braid on the cap; Jack Grant, War of Independence veteran, whose travel instincts are emulated by his photographer grandson, Padraig Grant; Mr Lynch, Maud Murphy, Miss Roberts of Eason's outlet on the North Station; Leo Goodison of the famed sporting dynasty; Mr Lynch from Cork; Owen Conway of another hereditary railway family and lastly Jimmy Allen.

Middle Row: First is Michael Kelly of Enniscorthy, now an executive with Wexford's Credit Union. The next resembles Ned Franey in a cap; then another Lynch; Pat Leacy, patriot and calm bookkeeper; Willie Carley of Park; Jim Cousins, of Mannix Place, then the golden tenor John Hackett; Jim Brennan, Nicky Sinnott, son of Alderman James Sinnott, Labour Mayor of Wexford, and lastly Jack Kelly who much later became a priest. Back row: Stephen Mernagh with whom I once travelled in the guard's van from New Ross to Wexford and listened as best I could while he proved the Young Irelands were better than Volunteers; Joe Walsh of Castlebridge; Denny O'Brien of Carcur; Mick Culleton and Jim Heffernan of High Street, reckoned by John Hackett to have more railway management brains than Dr Todd Andrews himself; young Carthy of Maudlintown; Mick Sutherland who never changed in appearance; Joe O'Donoghue of Castlebridge; and one of the Brennans of John's Road. We are grateful to John Hackett and Aidan Cogley for their help with identities and background information.

1959. THE FIRST CARS ACROSS WEXFORD BRIDGE. The opening of Wexford Bridge alongside the site of the Ferry crossing point, used for thousands of years before long span bridges, was an historic day by any standard. It was a day of much emotion as well, for the abutments of the 1795 Lemuel Cox bridge were incorporated into the 1959 pre-stressed concrete structure.

This very abutment where our photograph was posed was the exact site of the great many executions of loyalists and United Irishmen which took place during and after the insurrection of 1798.

The faces in the photograph, of which only three belong to women, are the faces of the dominant personalities in County Wexford politics and local government from the twenties to the sixties. More of the faces are of those who became headline makers in national affairs, political and ecclesiastical. The great political upheaval survivor was Neil Blaney, T.D., Donegal, Minister for Local Government. We cannot identify all the faces but we name those following.

Our first identified face is the man with the stick, Tom Fardy, Michael Darcy, Thomas Hayes, Larry Kinsella, Paddy Kinsella, Mrs Evelyn Nolan (née O'Leary); Tommy Howlin; County Manager Thomas Broe; James J. Bowe, Neil Blaney, T.D., Minister for Local Government; John J. Byrne, Town Clerk; Dr James Ryan, T.D. Tanaiste; John Flaherty Mayor of Wexford; James Kennedy, William O'Connell, Consultant Architect, Dr Honoria Aughney, County Medical Officer of Health; Tom Funge; Tom Redmond; Richard Elgee, solr.; Kevin C. Morris, Séamus Gallagher, Fr. Henry Sinnott, County Engineer Joseph Doris; Thomas F. Byrne; Fr. Ned Murphy; Brendan Corish, T.D.; Fr. Tommy Murphy, R.C.A.; Fr Barnabas McGahan, OFM.; County Secretary, Pat O'Halloran; Frank Cullimore; Ciaran McNally, Borough Surveyor; Eugene Curtin; Seán Browne, T.D. Leaning on the railings, Tom Kennedy, B.E.; Dr Thomas Esmonde, T.D.; Edward Conroy, manager, National Bank; Garda Inspector; Ray Corish, Ted O'Loughlin; Jack Dunne; Jim Morris; John Howlin: Michael Flusk, Andy Minihan; Martin Kennedy; Harry Doyle, Seán McCarthy, Tommy Browne and Fr. Matty Doyle, John Sinnott of Garrywilliam, Gearoid O Broin, C.E.O.; Cyril Roche, Consultant Engineer; Gerry Forde, Chief Superintendent Tom Collins and Maurice Foley.

BILL WHITTY mans the signals at Rosslare Strand Junction.
Murphy Collection.

Wexford Veteran, No 461, Dungarvan, 1961.

PIERCES ENGINEERING
Pierces of Wexford, 1969 -1970.

The final voyage of the last and familiar old battery lorry which clanked from factory to station with a tram bell. At the steering handles is expert Nick Roche. At extreme right is the purchaser and researcher, Manus Coffey, Crossabeg.

Manus Coffey taking to his home the last of the Pierces battery driven low lorries at the end of the Con Smith era in or about 1969. While staff may think Coffey to be mad or the lorry to be scrap, one suspects that Pierces design engineer may yet have turned it into gold.

MI 1 MYSTERY. Colonel J.R. Magrath of Ferrybank in his Benz car numbered MI 1 when car registrations began in 1903.

The registered owner of MI 8 in 1912 was Frank. B. Jacob, Rathdowney, Killinick. However, the man behind the wheel in this picture, date unknown, has been identified as James J. Kirwan, cattle dealer, John's Street, Wexford.

The vehicle currently bearing the registration number MI 1 is this Dion Bouton owned by Osmond Bennett, Johnstown, Co. Kilkenny.

The registered owner of MI 1, c.1912, was Colonel J. R. Magrath, Bann-a- Boo, Wexford. In 1897, Colonel Magrath owned an Arnold which he had imported from England. A list of seventeen cars in County Wexford in 1904 describes the vehicle owned by Colonel Magrath as a 7hp Turrell. However, it is not clear which if any, of these vehicles was first registered as MI 1.

In 1922, according to the Council's vehicle registration book, the registration number MI 1 was assigned to an18 Hp dark green Ford owned by J C Beauchamp Doran of Ely House, Wexford. The council also issued garage plates and the first one, MI 0001, was by 1922, owned by R.H.Nixon, Gorey, Co. Wexford.

(With thanks to editor of The Bridge, Fr. Walter Forde).

The vehicle bearing the registration number MI.1. is the Dion Bouton owned by Osmond Bennett, Johnstown, Co. Kilkenny.

(With thanks to Bill Creedon, editor, Exemplar Hibernae).

JUNIOR TRAFFIC WARDENS GRADUATE. A team of beautiful junior traffic wardens, winners of their competition, from Gorey Loreto Schools, receive their certificates to save the south east in 1970. The donor of our photograph is Tom O'Connor, identified in greying hair at centre back, Town Clerk of Gorey. At extreme left is Richard Molloy, National Road Safety Officer; two of the girls' teachers, unidentified Sister and Mrs Mannion née O'Leary, Ballyduff; Inspector Dan Kenny, Garda Síochána; Niall O'Gorman, managing director, Volvo who sponsored the important schools competition, and the meticulous Jim Kelly of Ballycogley, then National Director of Road Safety.

Courtesy of Tom O'Connor.

BESIDE the Corbett-Wilson monument at the entrance to the Murphy farm at Crane, Monageer, where the famed pilot crash-landed during the history-making first flight from Britain to Ireland are from left to right: Mr Colin O'Connor, Siúicre Éireann; Mr Jim Murphy, Mrs Bernie Murphy, Mr John Murphy, secretary, Corbett-Wilson Committee; Mr John Murphy Snr., and Mrs Sarah Murphy with children in foreground, John, Stephen and Fiona Murphy, all, with the exception of Mr O'Connor, from the Crane area.

JAMES BREEN (the "horse whisperer") at the pinnacle of his career taking distinguished guests to the Wexford Opera Festival in the old Theatre Royal. The guest who is seen in the cab window was one of the most influential writers internationally attending. He brought a party from London with him yearly. He was Bernard Levin, now deceased. His writings, books and wit acquainted thousands with Wexford Opera Festival, particularly his Times of London diaries and reviews. His very annual attendance was in itself a huge recognition of the Festival's reputation.

THIS PHOTOGRAPH of zealous men with steam, petrol and diesel in their blood was taken at what was once known as Wexford's North Station. Their influence of course was felt throughout the national transport system not to mention folk music and sport.

We are pleased to honour, standing: Andy Ellis, Ned Frayney, Jimmy Cousins, Paddy Culleton and Matt Carthy, and kneeling, Ted Kelly, motorised division, nationally famous as one of the greatest exponents of the folk dance art of Mumming (As we write, he is still "King of the Mummers"), John Roche, Paddy "Whacker" McCormack, whose interest in tourism continued long after he retired from the railway, and Billy Sinnott.

Appropriately, the backdrop to this photograph, taken I suspect by Michael Murray, is Mr Ted Kelly's lorry.

Our thanks to Aidan Cogley.

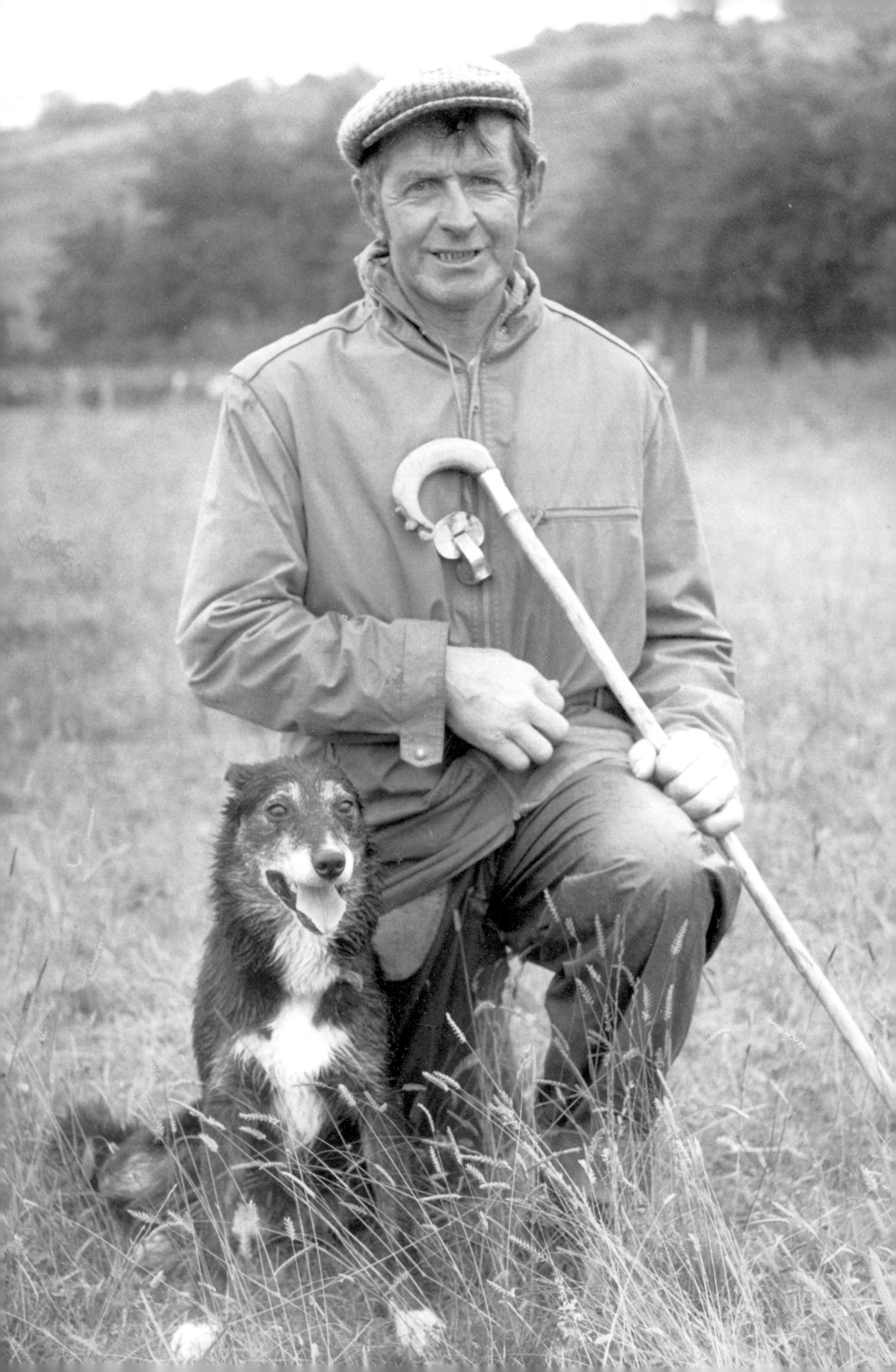

12 SPORT

Sport in County Wexford has employed the talents of youth since evidence of those pastimes have been produced. In early Norman tombslabs, hurlies in the hands of a dead knight, have been etched on their tombs in stone. The term 'Yellow Bellies' to Wexford teams was bestowed early in the 17th Century. Hurling, various forms of football, sometimes called caid, have flourished with inter-parish and inter-landlord rivalry. Today, sport in Co. Wexford is not as in Kilkenny confined to one specialisation. It has many codes and many followers. It could be said that 'twere a pity we do not concentrate on one sport. However, the vast numbers of young people who are given a wonderful healthy outlet on the field of play as are their mentors and voluntary helpers, make County Wexford a dynamic arena for the greatest possible amount of athletic endeavour.

Opposite: One Man and his Dog. Tim Flood of Cloughbawn, mercurial forward, "The successor to Christy Ring" (Mitchel V. Cogley), three times All-Ireland senior medal winner, interprovincial and national leagues in the 50s and 60s, showed in retirement additional, even equal skills in traditional music and championship-winning sheepdog trials.

THE SUMMER street leagues in football and hurling kept the towns at fever pitch in the pre-television era. The inter-street rivalry along with the fun spectacle of next door neighbours making up fifteen was accompanied by serious intent. Our street league selection for 1925 is that of the John Street Volunteers who would not be shaking in their boots when facing the "Counter Jumpers" of Wexford town's main street shops. The mentors standing are Jim O'Neill, Ned Mahon and Tom McGrath. Back row: N.Kehoe, Paddy Roice, N, Goodison, James O'Leary, Nick O'Brien, Pat McDonald. Front row: B O'Neill, Tom Kinsella, N. Doyle, Mattie Morris, Dick Kelly, N. Gaul, Jack Jones. Reclining in confidence are Willie Roberts and Willie Morris. The fearless infant mascot is our donor, Ned Roice.

THE WEXFORD CYCLING CLUB photographed by the firm of pioneer professionals, Andrews and McCabe, High Street, Wexford.

A smudged clue suggests 1908. But it may be earlier. Cycle fans will find the make of bikes interesting (Pierce's perhaps?). The venue is a puzzle. The sheet and type of rock should give a clue. Could it be a quarry?

NEW ROSS CYCLING CLUB. A fine cycling club photograph comes to us via Dr. Billy Colfer of Slade port on the Hook Peninsula. It has attached to it a clip stating it to be the New Ross Cycling Club with a 'suggested' date of 1900.

It's a brilliant photograph which almost screams the name of the great New Ross pioneer photographer William Cavanagh as the cameraman, but to the best of my knowledge it is not from the Cavanagh Collection. Jimmy Fitzgibbon, custodian and scholar confirms that it is not a Cavanagh photograph so we must be content with what we have for the moment. It may be a Poole of Waterford photograph.

Dom Williams Collection.

BLACKWATER 1903. Wexford's Blackwater selection fought their way through to the All - Ireland Final of 1901. Due to unfortunate circumstances this final was delayed by long and protracted inter county matches until 1903!

Cork won when the final was eventually played in Carrig-on-Suir, Co. Tipperary. Back row: Pat Rath, Michael Brien, Pat Kinsella, Mike Cummins, Denis Whelan, Sim Donoghue, Con Dempsey, Pat Murphy.. Middle Row: Barney Murphy, Mogue Brien, Willie Crean, Jimmy Furlong, Aidan Dempsey, Simon Kehoe. In front: Denny Corrigan, John Corrigan, Jack Murphy, Jack Shiel, Jack Sinnott. These same names keep cropping up in the great games records to the present day.

PRIVATE TENNIS parties are not new but between 1917 and 1919 American Naval officers from the US Naval Airbase at Ferrybank were invited guests to every ambitious social function. Our tennis garden party snapshot was taken at the Westlands' home of Michael J. O'Connor seen second from right with his son, Fintan M.

The O'Connor girls are enjoying the company as are the gallant airmen. At the time they would be comparable to today's space aces.

F.M.O'Connor Collection.

SARSFIELDS F.C. 1925. This year 2010, the Sarsfields G.A.A. football club of Carrigeen and other geographic associations celebrate the centenary of their inauguration. For many years a prized possession has been an upmarket cardboard-backed, posed photograph of the Sarsfield men and mentors who competed in the street leagues of 1925. It was framed. It was a golden possession of a close relative whose request to have it buried with him, I resisted. From this electrifying squad grew the teams which became terrors of the land and a pain to the St. John's Volunteers from the water-productive end of the capital town.

Pay careful attention to the names. Those not sharing the DNA of these gentlemen would not be of the right sort. I speak as an infant rescued from a riot in Wexford Park by a Mulgannon Harrier. Back row: Mr Pat Parle, co-founder of the Holy Family Confraternity Band and other virtues; Will Donohoe, Tom Morris, Edward Kehoe, E.McGrath, J. Murphy, Stephen Lewis, Phil Barnwell, D. Cullimore and P. McGrath. Seated: Peter Kehoe, George Walsh, Ibar Murphy (captain), Michael Collopy, Willie Morris and James Quirke. Front: the pint-sized dynamo Mike Morris, P. Murphy, Pat Morris, the mascot became one of the best football forwards in Ireland, Davy Morris, Willie Hore, Willie Roche and Fran Rossiter.

BALLYMURN HURLING TEAM. Winners Co Wexford Feis Shield 1931. Back row: Owen Gordon, Ml Cummins, Thos. Middleton, Jas. Redmond, Patk. Grady, Liam Gordon, Martin Cummins. Centre: Stephen Hayes (Co. Sec., G.A.A.), Jas Donohoe (Co. Chairman); Ml. Doyle, Lce. Doyle, Jas. Redmond, Thomas Crosgrove, Jas. Doyle, Phil Doyle, Ml. Kehoe, N.T. (Sec.Shield Committee); Watt Cummins. Front Row: Very Rev.

J. Murphy, P.P. (Ballymurn); Patrick Murphy, John Murphy, Lce. Roche, John Cummins (Capt), John Grannell, John Grady, John Roche, Rev. L. Allen, C.C. (Wexford), Chairman, Shield Committee. On ground: Wm Cummins, Patrick Roche.

ADAMSTOWN has a long and successful hurling tradition, so it is hardly surprising that the 1934 junior football championship winning team is given prominence in *A History of Newbawn*.

The team in this photograph shows back row from left: Leo Tector, Stephen Curtis, Jim Doyle, Ben Nugent, P. Whelan, Tom Furlong, Dave Power, and John McDonald. Second row: Paddy Foley, Tom Cadogan, Ger O'Leary, Jim Power, Fred Curtis, Pat Doyle, Patsy Moloney, Tom Quigley, Matty O'Neill, Joe Cadogan (Sec), Front row: John Butler N.T. (chairman), Lar Furlong, Canon James O'Brien, P.P. (1902-1939); Tom Doyle, Fr. J. Nolan, Paddy Leacy.

MULGANNON HARRIERS MINOR COUNTY FOOTBALL CHAMPIONS 1931. We publish this photograph while an unbidden tear trickled down our rough cheek. These were the Mulgannon Harriers when Mulgannon was a paradise for hunting with dogs and the working man's terriers. The name 'Faythe' Harriers was introduced after the 1940's. The rivalry between the south seafaring and Viking end of Wexford town and the north end team, the St. John's Volunteers was legendary (or perhaps acute) although our photograph contains a few expensive transfers. This team of lads with potential were the county minor champions of 1931, 1932. Standing are mentor Richie Pierce, Jim 'Sacker' Furlong, Nick Scallan, Harry Doyle, Paul Nolan, Jimmy Browne, Tommy Murphy, John 'Dough' Murphy, and mentor Nicky White. Seated: John Myrtle, A.N. Other, N. O'Connor, N. Lawlor, Johnny Hackett, James Dowdall and Jimmy Roche. In front: Wally Sinnott, Willie Martin, brave mascot Michael Lawlor, N. Walsh, Jack O'Rourke and mentor, Mr. O'Brien.

Dom Williams Collection.

FOLLOWING the end of the War of Independence and the debilitating Civil War 1922-23, the playing fields flourished again. This press photograph from the drawn Leinster Senior football final against Dublin in Croke Park, 1924, indicates a mixture of 1913 to 1918 veterans with up and coming youth.

Dominick Williams Collection.

One of the most mercurial, dextrous young showmen was Dentist Willie Doyle at extreme left kneeling. It may also have been the first year to show the footballing genius of Martin O'Neill of Ferns, standing at left. The meticulous may want to know where Dr. Toddy Pierce is. Since he was also a star in 'the foreign games' he may have been shy. He was accustomed to appear on team lists as 'Pierce Todd'. During this game he was replaced by Jack Crowley. Big John Doran, a veteran, was brought on to replace Francie Meyler. Back row left to right: Martin O'Neill, Ferns; Paddy Kilroy, New Ross; John Murphy, Starlights; Stephen Hayes, Starlights, Seán O'Kennedy, Selector, Francie Meyler, Gusserane; John Doran, Moneyhore; Pat Byrne, New Ross; Jim Dempsey, Tom McGrath, Blue and Whites; Dick Walsh, Ballyhogue; Nick Walsh, Ballyhogue. Front row left to right: Willie Doyle, Murrintown, Martin Howlett, New Ross, Jim Byrne, Capt, New Ross, Michael O'Connor, Starlights, Tom Howlett, New Ross, Jack Crowley, Wexford, Willie Newport.

ENNISCORTHY'S inspirational sports athletic club of the early 1930s. It spurred the interest and participation in field athletics which encouraged the foundation of other clubs 1930 – 1950.

P. Nolan, T. McDonald, Wm Cullen, A. Kehoe, Jnr, M. Murphy, T. Hare, F. D'Arcy, M. O'Connor, P. Larkin, P. Cullen, M. Driscoll, A. Kehoe, Snr, Wm Leacy, J. Murphy, A. Mythen, P. Murphy, W. Sutton, P. Murphy, P. Doyle, M. Whelan, Rev. P. Quaid. J. Mythen, J. Murphy, J. Doyle, W. Mullally, M. Doyle, J. Whelan, S. Fitzpatrick, J.J. Murray, F. Doran. S. Larkin, P. Franklin, T. Mahon.

THE LEGENDARY O'ROURKES. County Wexford Orme Billiards League. St. Iberius Club Teams 1932-33. Back row, left to right: M O'Rourke, T. O'Rourke, M. O'Rourke (Senr.), Front: E. O'Rourke, M. O'Rourke (Junr), S. O'Rourke.

IN BUSINESS, SPORT, EDUCATION AND POLITICS this group, each individual in it remained a character in public focus, some up to the sixties. County Wexford Orme Billiards League. St. Iberius Club Teams 1932-33 Other victories are recalled for 1924, '25, '26, '30 and '31. Back row, left to right: J. Kehoe, J. Keane, N.P. Corish, (Hon Sec.) M. Kennedy Second row: J. Byrne, P. O'Connor, M. O'Rourke, (Senr) M. O'Rourke, W. Hynes, Front row: J. Busher, J. McMorrough.

Eamon Doyle Collection.

Charles Vize photograph. Eamon Doyle Collection.

CARNESORE shooting party under the command of solicitor, Fintan M. O'Connor (second from left).

At left elegantly dressed is clay pigeon shooting and rugby international cattle dealer Barney Mullen, 1930.

Nicholas Kelly Collection.

THE WEXFORD team which defeated Offaly (4.10 to 2.0) in the Leinster Gaelic League football tournament final at Croke Park, December 2, 1945.

Back row, l. to r.: S. Roche, Rosslare Harbour (Co. Secretary); J O'Connor, Volunteers; J.J. Culleton, Camross; T. Doyle, Starlights; P. Kehoe, Gusserane; J Leacy, Gusserane, P. Stafford, Gusserane (sub), J. Morris, Volunteers; W. Goodison, Volunteers, Rev. W. Mernagh C.C. Screen (Chairman C.B.), Front row: M Kehoe, Gusserane (goal); N. Rackard, Killanne; S. O'Neill, Ferns, T. Somers, Gusserane, J. Coady, Emmets, J. Foley, Emmets, P. Banville, Camross, T. O'Leary, Volunteers.

THE WEXFORD UNITEDS were a team which boasted nothing more substantial than a set of jerseys, maroon and white bands, but they were brave. Their very existence was evidence of hurling's absence in the capital town. Most of Wexford town knew football only. Men who did love hurling, mostly non-natives of the town, came together and formed the hurling Wexford Uniteds. They entered one junior hurling team in the championships. This snapshot shows that plucky mixum-gatherum that was the Wexford United team in the 1947 junior hurling championships.

Dominick Williams Collection.

Standing: Ned Roice, Jimmy Goodison, Andy Kehoe, Johnny Murphy (Goal Bar), A.N. Other, Tony Connolly, A.N. Other, A.N. Other, Billie Ireland (Haddens). Kneeling: Davy Morris, Tom McGuinness, Cyril Sutton (Godkins), Jack Hayes, Dermot Redmond, Pat Browne and Mick Heffernan. Seated: Aidan Kelly (photograph donor) and A. N. Other. We feel that Paddy Hynes, the Bullring draper should be in the vicinity.

1945-1946 Hurling.

Ned Roice Collection.

Cute viewers of sport may well detect a cross pollination of names who may be styled perhaps triple club players especially in the pre-hurling revolution years. We make no aspersions. In order to keep the show on the road, the footballing St John's Volunteers gallantly entered a junior hurling team in the 1945 -1946 county championships. Back row: John Howlin, mentor, Joe Bolger, Niall Kennedy, Jimmy Goodison, Frannie Walsh, Mylie Morris, John Morris, Gerry Hayes, Brendan Corish, a hurling consultant from Killurin (Club, Glynn). Mr Bobby Randall with permanent secretary John Howlin. Front row: Jimmy Doyle, consultant, Clonard, Johnny Murphy, Martin Hanlon, Pat Browne, Kevin Roche, Willie Goodison, Séamus McGrath, Ned Roice and Tom Walsh, Coolcotts.

In the Dark Ages

These are stories of brave men, outstanding individual athletes, who to use a modern show business phrase, could not "get their act together". It was a dark age for Wexford in inter-county hurling but although these optimistic players did not know it, it preceded the greatest light to shine on Wexford sport in the fifties and sixties.

Despite disappointments it is only right and proper that these men who kept club hurling and football at top level excitement in the county championships should be honoured as well as those who were saturated in later glory and national fame. So while some may shudder at past misfortune, historians know that such developments are merely a phase in an ever evolving process where hope, heart and determination play a vital role .

On next page is the loneliest championship hurling photograph we have ever seen. It was Dublin versus Wexford in Aughrim, Co. Wicklow, on May 1st 1938. At the time Dublin had an all-Ireland selection from the commercial sector where top players from the traditional hurling areas were induced to take positions in Dublin.

The Dublin team in our photograph won the All-Ireland Senior Championship later in September. It was Dublin's last time to claim the McCarthy trophy. On the day this Irish Press photograph was taken Dublin won by 6-1 (19) to 3-7(16). It was a creditable performance watched from the far sideline by about thirty or so human beings. There is no dog to be seen. The only Wexford player we can identify is Tom Boggan of the Saint Fintans at extreme right.

Wexford's hurling progress continued at inter-county level when the team enjoyed a great run in the 1938-39 National Hurling League. They were narrowly defeated in the League semi-final by the 1938 All-Ireland finalists, Waterford, at New Ross. The team members on that day were:

Back row Left to Right, John Foley, Tom Furlong, Ned Colfer-in cap, Willie Duggan, Paddy Foley in cap, Denny Cloney, Ben Nugent, Peter Cullen, Bobbie Randall, Andy Holden in cap, Joe Duggan, Patsy Boggan. Front row, left to right: Tony Boggan, Tom Boggan, Tom Butler, Michael Foley, Matt O'Neill, John Doran, Aidan Kealy, Bill Murphy, Tom Rowe. This was the last occasion when the woollen jerseys pattern had the purple on the shoulders and the yellow on the stomachs. It's a mystery to this day how or why the pattern was reversed – as our next photographs show.

Dom Williams Collection.

The Throw In, 1939

The 1939 championships attracted interest. This grew to enthusiasm when Wexford hurlers met Offaly in the first round at Kilkenny. They had a resounding victory, Wexford 4-7, Offaly 1-4. The senior footballers were also doing very well indeed. The County Wexford newspapers, all three, went into overdrive. Wexford's hurlers were scheduled to meet the All-Ireland champions Dublin in the Leinster senior hurling semi-final on home ground, Wexford Park. The Dublin national newspapers joined in the fray. Spotlights were beamed on the players.

This writer was to be taken by his father to his first major inter-county game. It was a day I will not forget. There was a programme which cost two pennies. It cost one shilling to get into the park and another shilling to get on to the sidelines. The pre-match atmosphere was palpable, alive, sickening with excitement.

Bishop Codd had died so it was decided to ask the respected parish administrator of Wexford, Fr. John Sinnott, (Later P.P. Blackwater) to throw in the ball. The parade was led by the Confraternity Brass Band on a perfect summer day for hurling, 18 June. What an occasion it was for the county town!

We now have the big time experience to understand what in fact happened after the throw-in. It appears that an injury or illness beset the selected goalie and a substitute was compelled to replace him. To that disaster was added the pressure and publicity of previous weeks. As later happened in the All-Ireland finals of 1949 (Laois) and 1951 (Wexford) and many other occasions the nerve of the back line and the goalie was shattered. A terrible rout stunned Wexford Park, Dublin 10 goals and 7 points; Wexford 2 goals and 3 points. Denis Cloney of Curracloe who donated the photograph of the throw-in many years ago told me that one ball went over the Wexford goal line and never even got as far as the net!

An unmitigated disaster? Purely temporary! Meanwhile, the junior hurling county team was motoring through Leinster, winning their Leinster championship. On that team was a gangly awkward schoolboy from Rathnure, Nicholas Rackard, as well as 14 other triers including the Brownes of Crossabeg, Paddy O'Connor of Fardystown and Paddy O'Connor of Garryhubbock.

The players in clear new Wexford jerseys are Bill Murphy, Ferns, Denis Cloney, then playing with Ballyhogue, Kevin Whelan, Adamstown and Patsy Boggan, St. Fintans.

Photograph Patrick Kinsella Collection.

NEW COUNTY JERSEYS

In modern times, traditionalists have been alarmed by the Walt Disney kaleidoscope of colours and designs imposed on the county's time-honoured pattern. In 1951, a change was viewed with shock. To illustrate this we are fortunate to reproduce what could be described as a forgotten photograph and a forgotten team.

Following the long and overpowering senior football and particularly senior hurling championships tournaments and National League campaigns of 1950-1951, the one good set of county jerseys was in bits. The county board did not anticipate such simultaneous fame and fortune. In April 1951, the senior hurlers played in their first National Hurling League final ever in Croke Park. It was played against Galway with borrowed Gusserane club jerseys,' before the eyes of the world'.

It was too much for the Dublin Wexfordmen's Association to bear. The 1951 championships were opening so they generously set about to purchase a new set of jerseys. There was one technical lack. It was impossible to get the dye required for the colour purple and the colour purple was unique to Wexford as the black and amber stripes are to Kilkenny. The result was a brave effort; clean and well numbered jerseys with white collars, but with a light blue and yellow bands design.

The new set still had to be shared between hurlers and footballers senior county teams. So we see a much changed senior football selection about to face Laois in the 1951-52 National league or challenge in Carlow.

Standing: Bill 'Spider' Kelly, Ballymitty; Dan Spillane, Kilmore, A.N. Other, John Morris, Volunteers; Martin Codd, Rathnure; A.N. Other, John Fardy, Gusserane, and Joe O'Neill, Ferns. Kneeling: Willie Goodison, Volunteers; Billy Rackard, Rathnure; Paddy Kehoe, Gusserane; John Joe Culleton, A.N.Other, Nickey Rackard, Rathnure, Padge Kehoe, Enniscorthy.

Our photograph of a great Wexford senior hurling team serves two purposes. One is to honour the men in transition. They came second best to a really great Tipperary team in the All-Ireland Senior Hurling Final of 1965.

Secondly, it illustrates the return of the Wexford purple and gold pattern which was efficiently organised by Billy Rackard in the summer of 1951. He was in the cloth business, had done his apprenticeship in Dublin, knew the channels through which to go, but above all where to make permanent the purple dye. By 1952, the colours and design which dazzled our hearts were restored.

The 1965 hurling championship runners up are, standing: John Nolan, Oylegate-Glenbrien; Joe Foley, Ballyhogue; Martin Codd, Rathnure, Phil Willson, Ballyhogue; Martin Byrne, Rathnure; Dan Quigley, Rathnure; Willie O'Neill, Kilmore; Ned Colfer, Gers O'Hanrahans. Kneeling: Pat Quigley, Rathnure; Willie Murphy, Faythe Harriers; Jimmy O'Brien, Gers O'Hanrahans; Vincent Staples, St. Martin's; Tom Neville, Gers O'Hanrahans (captain); Pat Nolan, Oylegate-Glenbrien and Dick Shannon, Horeswood.

THE SACRED SELSKAR YOUNG IRELANDS. The team which brought All-Ireland Championships glory to County Wexford for the first time in history, senior football, 1893. Our photograph was taken when the club, even though in its declining years, dazzled in the minor football ranks. This is the team with mentors of experience and genius who won the 1948 minor football championship.

Standing from left: Mr. Charles Fitzhenry, who because of deafness was wise of comment and impervious to abuse, impudence or dispute; M. McClean, Seán Clancy, Bernard McGuinness, Ml. Healy, Brendan Duggan, Cyril Nolan, Hugh Latimer, Edward Morrissey, the greatest tenor to recite the ballad of Pat O'Leary, from New Ross; Lar O'Connor and Wally Keane (Trainers). Kneeling: Tommy Hynes, Pat Kearney, John Connors, John Malone, Paud McDonald, Billy McCabe, Paddy Parle and Dick McCabe. Note the jerseys please.

The jerseys photographed were on loan to the Young Irelands while new green jerseys were being knitted. So you are looking at the battered, exhausted, worn out, blood stained county jerseys in non-glittering purple and gold.

RESPECTABLE JERSEYS early in 1950 with Wexford versus All-Ireland champions Meath, Leinster Senior Football semi-final in Croke Park. Standing: Paddy Mythen, Enniscorthy; Paddy Waters, Ballymitty; Joe O'Neill, Ferns; Nicky Rackard, Rathnure; Bill 'Spider' Kelly, Ballymitty; Séamus Kelly, Young Irelands; Jim Rogers, Blackwater; Dan Spillane, Kilmore; Joe Nolan, Enniscorthy; D. Fitzgerald, Rathnure; Martin Comerford, Volunteers; Rory Deane, Bunclody; L. Quinn, Enniscorthy; Des O'Neill, Ferns; Seán Browne, T.D., County Chairman.

Kneeling: Tom Kehoe, County Secretary; Seán Eustace, Sam 'Wilkie' Thorpe, Enniscorthy; Pat Nolan, Enniscorthy; Nick Redmond, Young Irelands; Willie Goodison, Volunteers; Junior is the mascot – you'd never guess, Seánie Sinnott, Young Irelands; Tim O'Leary, Volunteers; John Morris, Volunteers, Result: Meath 1-5; Wexford 0-6.

While this is a jersey illustration story, the players in the jerseys had an incredible hour of superiority on the field. This was the team that should have and would have won the 1950 All Ireland title. That is except for a defect which horrified their followers. They could not score either from placed balls or from the hand. It was unbelievable, outrageous and nationally recognised.

Photograph by courtesy of Eamon Doyle.

'MEANWHILE' AS THE WESTERNS HAVE IT, 'back at the ranch,' a thoroughly unexpected development was gathering momentum. The County Wexford senior hurlers were sweeping through Leinster undetected to such an extent that no press photographers were sent to the Leinster semi-final against Leinster S. H. champions, Laois in Kilkenny. Neither did the County Board anticipate fame on two fronts. There was only one clean and decent set of jerseys (photographed) for everybody.

1955 ST. JAMES BOYS NATIONAL SCHOOL, Ramsgrange, winners of South Wexford schoolboy's football league, at Tomcoole, Taghmon. The football league was organised by the schoolteachers whose school participated, led by Peadar Byrne, NT, Mulrankin and spanned over a decade or so, to be followed by the Nicky Rackard league encompassing the whole county in the 1960's. Back row, l. to r. James McDonald, Seánie Dalton, Bob Howlett, Michael Banville, Peter McDonald (Capt), Matty O'Connor, Paddy Nash. Front, l. to. r : Liam Ryan, Walter Hayes, Nickey Butler, Dicky Butler, Stephen Howlett, Eddie Ryan.

THE TABLE TENNIS whirlwinds of CYMS. The club over decades had an extraordinary record in Table Tennis tournaments, interclub and provincial championships, well attested to in Michael A O'Rourke's splendid, illustrated *History of the C.Y.M.S.* Nos 1 and 2. One of the proudest members of the CYMS donated this photograph of an honours-laden squad in the early 1950s)

Standing: the senior influence (a hereditary position) John O'Rourke, Paddy McCormack, Tom Kelly, Seán Kelly, Sim Hore, Unidentified, Jack Breen and Tommy Kelly. Seated: Victor Bridges, Billy Turner, Seán O'Rourke, Gerry Foley, Tom McGuinness, Pat Roice and Bernard McGuinness.

Patrick Kinsella Collection.

THE EXHIBITION PRESS PHOTOGRAPH from Murphy's Newsagents was saved for posterity to give us a goodly chunk of County Wexford faces. It was taken at the 1956 All Ireland Final against Cork on September 23.

It's the sideline personnel under the Cusack Stand who witnessed the greatest victory imaginable against Christy Ring's Cork. There are several recognisable faces as well as names that no longer trip from our lips. The ones that do are Mr and Mrs Scallan, lower right side, row two. In row four at left under the Wexford flag is Pat Moran of The Gem confectionery shop Abbey Street, Wexford; George Roche of Drinagh; Kevin Ruttledge, The Faythe; Paddy Duggan, James Maguire of Barrack Street, and Paddy Kinsella of Carrigeen.

DYNAMIC PURPLE AND GOLD, All-Ireland Champions of 1968. Is it really 42 years since once more Wexford shocked the hurling world? The team is Dan Quigley, captain, Paul Lynch, St. Aidan's; Willie Murphy, Faythe Harriers; Jack Berry, St. Annes; Eddie Kelly, St. Aidan's; Phil Wilson, Ballyhogue; Vincent Staples, St. Martin's; David Bernie, Ferns; Christy Jacob, Oulart; Séamus Whelan, St. Martin's; Ned Colfer, Gers O'Hanrahans; Jimmy O'Brien, Gers O'Hanrahans; Tony Doran, Buffers Alley; Pat Nolan, Oylegate; Tom Neville, Fethard-on-Sea.

GOOD COUNSEL COLLEGE, New Ross. Dungarvan Cup winners Senior Football 1958/59.

Back: Tiger Lyons, Tom Williams, Larry Rochford, 'Jampot' O'Leary, Jose Garcia, Nickey Kavanagh.

Middle: A.N. Other, Declan Staunton, Seán English, Larry Rochford, Tom Dennehy, Pat Feehan, Donal Kavanagh, Bob Howlett, Fr. Whelton, OSA.

Front: A. Feehan, Frank Bresnihan, Stephen Howlett, Brendan O'Rourke (with cup), Jack O'Hara, Arthur Kavanagh, A.N. Other.

YES WE DID! 1975 Wexford Team- All Ireland Camogie Champions. Back row (l to r) Dorothy Walsh, Elsie Walsh, Joan Murphy, Bernie Murphy, Margaret O'Leary Leacy, Eileen Hawkins, Mary Furlong, Gretta Kehoe, Breda Murphy. Front row (l to r): Kit Codd, Peg Moore, Kathleen Tonks, Mary Shannon, Bridie Doran, Maggie Hearne, Mairead Darcy, Bridie Fox, Bridget Doyle.

Look at that beautiful child with her Teddy bear, chewing the butt of the hurley. That's Wexford's mascot Sinéad Codd. The famous hurler Tom Dempsey paid attention later and the girl agreed to marry him.

M. QUINN, winner of the Cusack Cycling Club road Race on the 27th April 1952. Pictured in Island Road, Enniscorthy.

THE FIRST DECADE of the new Millennium has been dominated by the utter brilliance of our neighbour Kilkenny's hurling. Hearty good wishes are appropriate despite intense rivalry (for centuries!) It is however apt that we now remember in our comfort zone of proud recall of one of the greatest sensations of the 70's which looked once more as if Kilkenny would without difficulty continue on their fifth in a row (albeit close and tactical) defeat of Wexford.

In 1976, Kilkenny, massive favourites, played what the media regarded as 'weary Wexford'. The game itself and the result of that Leinster Final in Croke Park shocked every single follower and media commentator of the game - Wexford 2-20, Kilkenny 1-6. Our press photograph donated by Paddy Kinsella shows the Wexford captain, Tony Doran of Buffers Alley receiving the Bob O'Keeffe cup from fellow Wexford man and Leinster Council chairman, Jimmy Roche. At extreme left, the great Bobby Rackard is seen enjoying the drama.

IN MY SIRELAND parish, dedicated to Saint Martin who gave his rich maroon cloak to a beggar, there are still murmurs (dark) about this team. They, St. Dympna's, were able to afford a press officer, Billy Quirke, who camouflaged all cross territory complaints. It was held that the boundaries of this team's area were elastic. Its reputed headquarters was St. Senan's Psychiatric Hospital but it will be seen that both side of the Slaney's water are represented.

Further, the gilt of medals from another code made them hungrier still. Despite their skill, wealth and comfort zone, a team so rurally poor that they togged out behind furze bushes and washed the blood off themselves in a farmyard pump, namely St. Martin's, beat them in the 1957 County Junior Football final played in a New Ross blizzard of rain and gale. St. Martin's won by double scores - 0-2 to 0-1.

ST. DYMPNA'S TEAM, County Junior Champions 1958, when they beat Our Lady's Island in the final. Back l to r.: Ml (Doc) Doyle, Charlie Cullen, Liam Swan, Bill Murphy, Nick O'Donnell, Billy Quirke, Ml. Donegan, Joe Nolan, Patsy Canavan. Front, l. to r.: Harry Goff, Eddie Kelly, Ted Morrissey, Harry O'Connor, Nick Harpur, Billy Kelly, Pat Lawler, Tom Ryan.

Dan Walsh Collection.

A MUCH UNDERRATED TEAM OF TRIERS. GALBALLY UNITED, 1976. Back: Sonny Sheil, Pat Shannon, Míchael Shannon, Lar Rochford, Ned Swan, Donie O'Brien and Noel Sheil. Front: Phillie Rochford, Frank Rochford, Tony Berney, Henry Rochford and Charlie Rochford.

MICHAEL HICKEY OF GARRYRICHARD, hereditary horseman and breeder, with reinforced tables holding about forty or more silver trophies for comprehensive distinction in the Sport of Kings.

BREE HUNT meet at IFA H.Q in Enniscorthy with Master Geoffrey Deacon, Matt Roche and the next generation

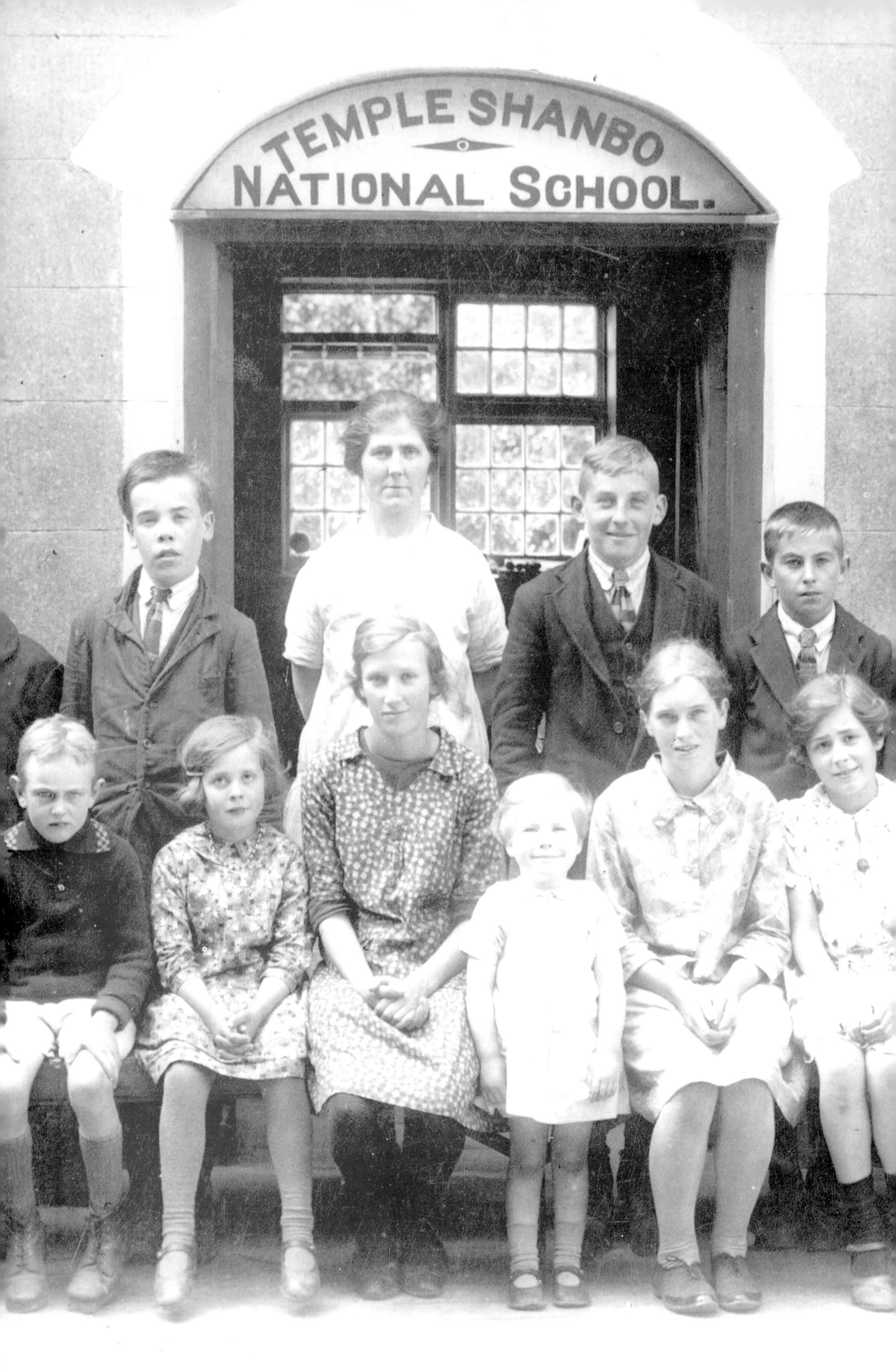
TEMPLE SHANBO
NATIONAL SCHOOL.

13 EDUCATION

It is not necessary to stress the urgent importance of education. Everyone who has been to school is a primary source of evidence for their experience, the encouragement or otherwise received, the skill and commitment of teachers. Everyone has a favourite teacher in mind, one who maintains an influence to old age. It is an obligation to remember that sacrifices willingly made by parents and teachers in the last and previous century formed the building blocks of the standard we are at today. A gigantic debt is owed to those who nourished the potential.

TARA HILL NATIONAL SCHOOL SCHOLARS with the mistress standing at the right c. 1900.

Courtesy of H. Murphy.

Courtesy of Shay Doyle.

1900. THE HOUSE OF THE SCHOOLMASTER and his family, Mr Morgan Nolan, Ballyroebuck, Kiltealy.

Peter McDonald Collection.

SHIELBAGGAN NATIONAL SCHOOL, c 1926, as the 20th century dawned. We have been unsuccessful in identifying every scholar but we present our best effort following countless hours of research. We are told that in the back row are five Sleator brothers of Shielbaggan and Joe Kent, and that fourth from left is Jimmy Sleator. Next are Peg Murphy, Brigid Murphy, Mary Cadogan, and seventh from right is a Power of Winningtown. On left corner is Jim Culleton, Haggard, and Sonny, Martin and Maureen Culleton of Haggard. In the third row are an O'Rourke, a Kennedy, Nellie Cadogan, Mary Cadogan, Maggie Howlett, and a Power from Winningtown. In the fourth row are Statia Stafford, Peg Murphy, Bridget Murphy, and Annie Dalton.

The original building built in the mid 1800s operated as a Famine soup kitchen. In the 1870s it is known a primary school was in existence under Miss Budd who is said to have arrived every morning on her ass and cart from Arthurstown, two miles away.

From around 1890, the St. Louis Sisters, Ramsgrange took charge of the school and they arrived in a pony and trap until the 1950s when a motor car was provided.

Sinn Féin held Court sittings there during the War of Independence under Judge Philip Kennedy (father of the late James J. Kennedy T.D. and grandfather of Simon W. Kennedy, solicitor, New Ross) for a short time. From the early 1980s, the National Primary school continued under principal Martin Kennedy, New Ross. The present principal is Ms Teenie Murphy assisted by Ms Catherine Breen. (Thank you to Mary Cadogan, Millbrook Nursing Home, New Ross and Mary Anne Maher, née Sutton, Calford Nursing Home, for their help with identities.)

By courtesy of Stephen Maloney, Kerlogue.

1924. THE INDEPENDENT Wexford students of the Christian Brothers Schools, "The Boker" (a modern pronunciation of An Bothar, the Irish for the road, the main road from the south to Wexford's markets)

Courtesy of Ken Hemmingway.

TEMPLESHANBO NATIONAL SCHOOL, 1929. Back row (standing), left to right: Joe Dormer, Kiltealy; Robert Moulton, Tomona; John Moulton, Tomona; Mrs. Constance Attridge, N.T., George Dormer, Kiltealy; George Copeland, Coolree; Jimmy Sheil, Tomona; Fred Hatton, Monalee; Sam Jacob, Shroughmore. Front row (seated), left to right are: Ivan Jacob, Shroughmore; Sidney Griffin, Rossard; Ethel Sheil, Tomona; Hannah Copeland, Tomona; Beryl Attridge, Mary Jane Copeland, Coolree; Molly Attridge, Alfie Hatton, Monalee; Robert Hatton, Monalee.

Donor, A. C. Nolan.

GOLDEN YEARS Miss Greta Irwin is the lady in the photograph. She was the teacher in a school which specialised in learning up to Holy Communion age back in the thirties. The school was situated at Wexford's Westgate. Her pupils had nothing but praise for her methods of teaching.

Standing at the back is Miss Irwin and the pupils from left to right are: Beryl Quaid and Teresa Quaid, two sisters from Park and Niall Corcoran, Spawell Road, a member of the Corcoran Family who published the old Wexford Free Press newspaper. Ann McCabe, Westgate; Junior Staunton, Michael Kavanagh, St. John's Road; Carol Kavanagh, "Weston"; Alan Hore of the musical and entertainment family; Sinéad Dennehy and her sister Sheila, Spawell Road; Billy McCabe, Selskar; Hugh Latimer, Hill Street; James Cunningham, Auburn Terrace; Cyril Nolan, Fort View; and Dick McCabe, Selskar. The catchment area of this private school might be described as Wexford 4.

VERY LITTLE IS KNOWN of the Tara Hill school once located in the farmyard of Mr. P. Byrne adjoining the present school. This was a mud-walled structure with a thatched roof, a type of hedge school perhaps. A teacher, Mr. Cullen is remembered. After subsequent use as a shop and later as an outbuilding, the structure was demolished in the late 1950s.

GALBALLY NATIONAL SCHOOL which has consistently maintained the highest standards (c.1933). Back: Dolly Doyle, Nan Millar, Peg Rochford, Molly Barnes, Kitty Byrne, Kathy Sullivan, Mary Doyle, Nellie Byrne. 4th row: Phil Jackman, Pat Dempsey, Jim Dempsey, Larry Murphy, Paddy Noctor, John Cogley, Jim Foley, Mosie Barnes, Jackie Donohoe.

Kevin Spenser.

3rd row: Maggie Walsh, Nancy Walsh, Ciss Foley, Liz Murphy, Kitt Doyle, Liz Rochford, Nan Murphy, Maggie Murphy, Alice Foley, Peg Brennan, Biddy Murphy, Annie Roche, Nell Rochford, Katie Murphy, Peggy Murphy

2nd row: Peter Shannon, Mick Murphy, Mickey Fenlon, John Jackman, Matty Kennedy, Johnny Brien, Joe Banville, Pat Cogley, John Foley, Joe Quirke, Jerry Donohoe

Front: Jimmy Johnson, Ted Brien, George Quirke, Mike Quirke, Tommy Donohoe, Tom Brien, Jack Rochford, Tom Cogley, John Roche, Paddy Fenlon.

Bree Journal No 2.

ST LOUIS COLLEGE, Ramsgrange, which specialised in Domestic Economy, had pupils from a wide area of the south east, Wexford, Kilkenny and Waterford. It was under the teaching sisters of the Order of St. Louis. First year students of the 1962 – 63 class of St. Louis Rural College of Domestic Science Ramsgrange. Front:Breda Kehoe, (Carlow). Ann Harney, (Wexford). Peggy Doyle (Wexford). Ann O'Connor (Wexford). Mary Weddick (Wexford). - ? – (Kilkenny). Mary Cahill, (Kilkenny).2nd Row – Dorothy Stamp (Wexford). - ? – (Kilkenny). - ? – (Kilkenny). - ? - (Kilkenny). Joan Waters (Kilkenny). - ? – (Kilkenny). - ? ? ? 3rd Row – Mary Hanton (Wexford). Eileen Crosby (Wexford). Bridget Sinnott (Wexford) - ? – Maura Fitzpatrick (Kilkenny). Mary ? (Kilkenny). - ? – Maura Ryan (Tipperary). - ? - Ann Walsh (Waterford). - ? – (Kilkenny).

Sr. Mary Clancy, S.S.L.

The Sisters of St. Louis were founded in Paris, France in 1841 by French philosopher and educator, Albe Bautain, with the assistance of Baroness de Vaux who became, as Mere Therese de la Croix, the foundress of the Sisters in France. The main focus of the new congregation was the education of the young girls and boys, especially the children of poorer families,

On the 6th January 1859, three Sisters from the new congregation came to Monaghan town. From there on the 4th May 1871 one of these three with two other Sisters came to Ramsgrange at the invitation of the Very Reverend Thomas Canon Doyle, the Land League leader, who was Parish Priest of Ramsgrange.

OUR VINTAGE PHOTOGRAPH is indicative of Wexford's music tradition. It is also a memento of a majestic lady who almost singlehandedly made the highest quality of music live in Wexford as Grattan-Flood did in Enniscorthy. The photograph was taken by the Vize Dean Art studio of Wexford and Enniscorthy. Ned Roice, inter-county footballer and St. John's Volunteer is our donor. It shows the Christian Brothers Schools, The Boker, Wexford, Junior entry for the Feis Ceoil in Dublin, 1933.

The descendants of these lyrical prodigies are legion, and their later characters explosive and electrifying. Back row from left to right: Dom Sinnott, Tom Bell, Ned Roice, Pt Leacy, Nick Hayes, L Edwards, Eddie Dwyer and John Barnes. Middle row: Tom Devereux, John Taylor, Pat Carroll, Dick Edwards, Unidentified, Willie Robinson, Unidentified, Tommy Rush. Seated in the centre: the genius Miss Mary Codd. Kneeling: Séamus Cummins, John Edwards, Jimmy Nolan, Unidentified, Seán Donoghue and A. Dempsey. In front: Tim O'Leary and Joe Mythen.

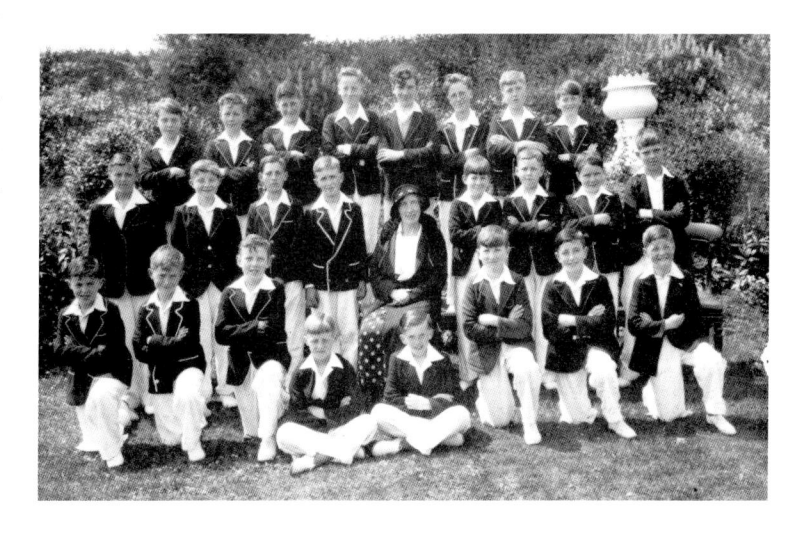

Photograph by Charles Vize, Dean Art Studios.

Photograph by Fr. Tim Nolan.

LEAVING CERT 1946. In view of the increase in numbers of those sitting for secondary schools exams in 2010, our photograph of a group of students taken in the cloisters of St. Peter's College will shock. With possible absentees, these are the Leaving Certificate students of 1946.

From left: Paddy Moore Brookfield; Jim Cullen, Brownscastle, Taghmon; Martin McDonald, Saunderscourt; Pat Doyle, Enniscorthy; Tony Scallan, Maudlintown; Aidan Brennan, Davidstown; Paddy Burke, Enniscorthy; Charlie Kehoe, Wexford; Michael Butler, St. Ivers, Lady's Island; Albert Lennon, Wexford and Joe O'Neill, Ferns.

THIS SCHOOL PHOTOGRAPH IS an historic link with the past for it is one of the last photographs taken of the Church of Ireland parish school classes of Wexford in St. Patrick's Square. That itself is a long link because it is quite likely that there was a school on the site alongside St. Patrick's Church for centuries in a pattern which survives to this day. The photograph was taken on November 14th 1961. Starting with the back row, the line-up of scintillating stars is as follows (from left to right): George King, (now in Zimbabwe); John Randall of the hurling craftsmanship dynasty; James Boyd of Tagoat; John Reilly of Millknock; Addie Burrell of Murrintown; sunburnt Johanna Phillips of Barntown House; Wilfrid Jones of Park, and then Sammy Hawkins of Killinick, and Angus Lee (junr.) Middle Row is George Coe, then Philip Shearer of sad memory, lost in the appalling drowning tragedy off Curracloe; Richard Reilly of Millknock; Eileen Jones of Park; Violet Hornick of Killurin; Olive Shudall and Mary King. Next is George Whitehead of Ballyell, Tagoat; William Goold of Carlow and George Rhynhart.

Seated alongside the second row is the pretty new arrival and junior teacher, Miss Irene Honner from Co. Meath. Seated next to her are the Reilly twins from Millknock, Kathleen and Mary; then Olive Whitney and Elizabeth Wood of Coolballow whose English parents, Dave and Mrs Woods, kept a shop at the top of The Faythe, and a pig farm in Coolballow. Next is Betsy Walker of Rathaspeck, Olive King, Elaine Rhodes of Avenue de Flandres whose father was with Pierces, and Vera Hemingway of Cottage, Tagoat, still on the staff of Kelly's Resort Hotel, Rosslare.

Seated is the veteran and distinguished Wexford educationalist, the Principal, Miss Victoria Mary Sherwood of Parnell Street,. David Watchorn, Taghmon; Peter Shearer, Ian Shearer, Christopher Bodenstab, Jim Burrell of Staplestown and Frank Burrell.

One of the smallest boys in the school, four years of age, was Christopher Bodenstab, son of Gunther, one of the German cheese manufacturers from Kempton, Allgau in Bavaria, the pioneers of the great Wexford cheese industry. Chrisopher hadn't a word of English and certainly had no Irish. One fatal day, Miss Honner heard a scream, a yell and crying out in the yard so out she rushed to find Christopher Bodenstab doing a jig of rage and crying tears of temper in a loud voice. She forgot that he knew 'no English' and pleaded with him: 'What's wrong with you, Christopher?' The reply which yelled forth at her in fluent Wexford – Irish – English was 'I was swingin' out of the clothes line and that bloody divil there knocked me down!'

The clue to the whole performance was the cheese factory's indefatigable gardener, John Kelly. In addition to fluent Wexford-English, John taught him a whole range of Irish and Wexford songs which the German mite rendered for the school perched on a high stool. Still remembered are the songs with impeccable Irish accent, taught by John Kelly, "Kelly from Killanne", "The Boys of Wexford", "Boolavogue", and "The Mountains of Mourne".

By courtesy of Ken Hemmingway.

THE BRIGHT CHILDREN OF MODERN TIMES from Templeshanbo National School, 1965/66. Back row from left to right: Bertie Gethings, Monart; Eddie Warren, Gurteen; Fred Gethings, Monart. Middle row (Standing) from left to right are: Sam Griffin, Rossard; Austin Griffin, Rossard; Joan Hemmingway, Tomona; Martha Wilson, Tomatee; Ruth Hatton, Monalee; Heather Sheil, Coolree; Vera Warren, Boarmona; Desmond Jacob, Shroughmore.

Front row from left to right: Pamela Jacob, Shroughmore; Alice Gethings, Monart; John Farrar, Kilcullen; Geraldine Leech, Ballyhamilton; Jennifer Leech, Ballyhamilton; Lorna Jacob, Shroughtmore.

1985, BEGERIN ISLAND, now surrounded by the reclaimed North Sloblands, a site of ancient, sacred importance and neglect had a FIFTH century monastery and school. It presented a formidable challenge but the young helpers of 1985 for a while at least brought life, blood and active restoration to the place where Ibar brought Christianity before St. Patrick. His monastic settlement lasted until 1160.

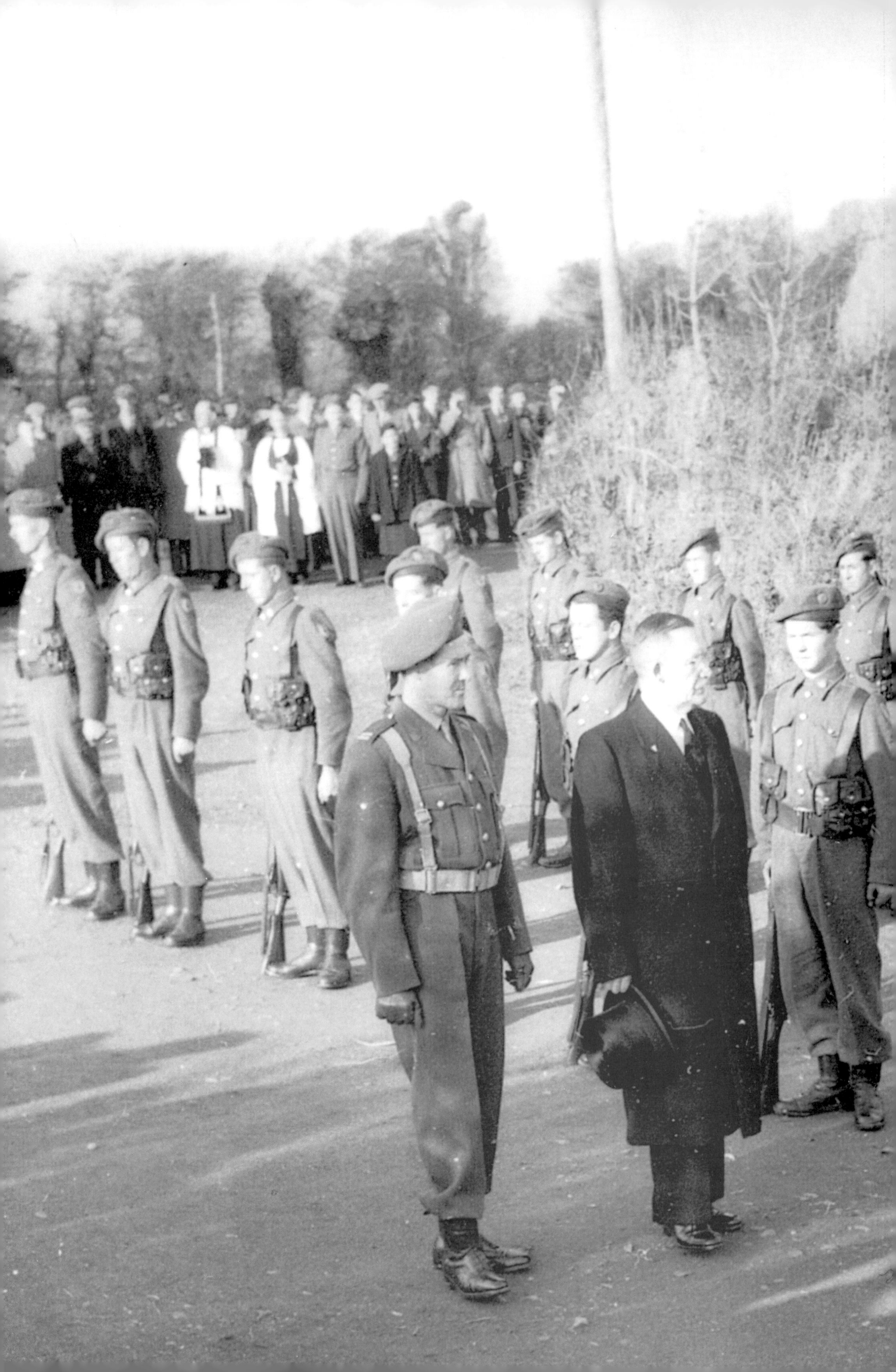

14 ARMIES AND WAR

The First World War 1914-1918 was one in which the greed and expansionist determination of European and Asian colonising empires found excuse to create catastrophic war against one another. The conditions which the narrow victors imposed on the defeated central European powers created ample fuel for an even greater awfulness just twenty years later. Populations and vast territories had been torn from their native lands. Colonisations and occupations had continued unabated. New political systems were introduced from Moscow to Lisbon.

It was fortunate that newly-independent Ireland was in a position to unanimously declare its neutrality in 1939 or Ireland, positioned strategically in the north Atlantic Ocean war zone would have been rendered as Coventry, Caen or Dresden were. The effects were, however, felt everywhere. It is comprehensively documented. This section continues, as in other numbers, to give an indication of the military effects on life here in the south-east corner of Ireland bordered by the Irish Sea and the Atlantic.

The ambassador, Dr Herman Katzenberger.

THE IRISH NATIONAL FORESTERS CONVENTION in Court Street, Enniscorthy, 1920. The Devonshire Regiment raided or rushed the procession and broke up the parade. The Devons were stationed in the courtroom opposite.

WILLIAM ST., WEXFORD, during the Second World War photographed by the great cameraman John Scanlon. The emptiness tells its own story but the most dramatic artefact might escape attention. Of course the Gas Works have gone but the large, long, dark-roofed building in the right centre was a hanger from the United States Naval Air Base at Ferrybank, 1917-1919. When the First World War ended an auction was held of everything that could move. Several businesses made use of the hangers. The last still employed is auctioneer Ray Corish's Showroom at Crescent Quay.

Photographer John Scanlon. Dominic Kiernan Collection.

CIVIL WAR 1922 – 23

On November 11th 1922 outside Killurin station the rails were pulled out of the embankment edge and broken just before the arrival of the night goods train from Dublin. The anti-Treaty column stopped the train by signal and took off the crew before wrecking the engine, number 18. It was a powerful engine built in the Great Southern Railway's own works. She rolled down the bank into the Slaney River 'like a boulder, rolling over and over'.

By courtesy of Ken Hemingway. Photograph by J.J. O'Brien.

Taylorstown viaduct was blown up by the IRA. By breaking the rail connection between Rosslare Harbour and Cork, Waterford was militarily isolated and remained so until 1924. The first scaffolding is erected in winter 1923 after the Civil War's end.

Robert Brennan, the Dominant Presence

The national resurgence from the 1798 Rebellion centenary commemorations to the conclusion of the War of Independence brought to the forefront men and women of intellectual brilliance and physical bravery. Some did the nation's work quietly and undetected. When their role was over, many just faded into craft, business or normal civilian occupations. Their names never made headlines and may only be recorded, if at all, in the confidential Irish Army archives at Cathal Brugha Barracks, Dublin.

Such a contrast exists with Wexford brother and sister Robert and Nan Brennan, born in John's Gate Street, Wexford, later living most of their formative years at the corner of Abbey Street and George's Street.

Beyond question while Nan remained camouflaged, Robert became a colossus in the resurgence of cultural and political Irish Ireland. Like many, despite a career defiantly continued even though sentenced to death in 1916, his personality and enormous contribution has subsided. He must shoulder some of the blame. He was the thorough, skilled diplomat, the quiet mover, the trained writer-reporter in *The Echo* newspaper, the intellectual planner, and determined revolutionary. It's perhaps enough to declare that Robert Brennan was the man chosen by Éamon de Valera to head Ireland's diplomatic mission in Washington in the World War II period of awfulness.

His memory in Wexford is not that of the revolutionary at all, but as a popular young fellow of normal pursuits - dances, concerts, and girls. His return to Wexford in 1947 as I recall it made my mother's generation excited, and led to at least a week of nostalgic tales of fun, mostly centred around the AOH club premises in Mary Street.

We cannot do justice here to this neglected patriot and statesman when a full biography is needed. It must suffice to select quotations from his substantial attention in the Dictionary of Irish National Biography by Michael Kennedy.

He was born on 22 July 1881, second child and eldest son amongst four children of Robert Brennan (d. 1919), cattle dealer, and Bridget Brennan (née Kearney; d.1938), Selskar, dressmaker. He was educated at the CBS in Wexford and subsequently studied for an RUI qualification. An employee of Wexford County Council as assistant County Surveyor, he left in 1909 to join the staff of the *Enniscorthy Echo* as a reporter. Brennan was also Wexford correspondent of the *Irish Times*.

Brennan was a founder member of the Wexford branch of the Gaelic League, teaching the Irish language to local League members. He became county secretary of Sinn Féin and organised the IRB in Wexford.

As one of the leaders of the 1916 rising in Enniscorthy, he narrowly escaped execution, his

Seymour Berkson, Hon. Robert Brennnan, Hon. James A. Farley, 'Bugs' Boer.

Robert Brennan listens intently at a conference with diplomats who include at extreme right the young Dr Conor Cruise O'Brien.

death sentence being commuted to penal servitude. Brennan spent much of 1916 and 1917 interned in English prisons including Dartmoor, Lewes (where he wrote two full-length mystery novels), and *Parkhurst*. On release in June 1917 he returned to the staff of the Enniscorthy Echo and was involved with the reorganisation of the Irish Volunteers. Arrested again, he was sent to Cork prison, where he went on hunger strike. He was released in November 1917. By January 1918, he was in charge of the Sinn Féin publicity bureau.

After the May 1918 'German plot' Brennan was appointed director of elections for Sinn Féin for the 1918 general election, but was arrested before the election in November and imprisoned at Gloucester until March 1919. Later in 1919, on his return to Dublin, Brennan briefed the American delegates selected at the Irish Race Convention in Philadelphia to attempt to secure a hearing for Ireland at the Paris peace conference. Brennan produced the Irish Bulletin during the Anglo-Irish war. From February 1921 to January 1922, Brennan served as the first secretary of the Dáil Éireann Department of Foreign Affairs, with the title 'under-secretary for foreign affairs'.

He travelled to London with the Irish delegation to the treaty negotiations in October 1921 and then began a tour of various European capital cities, meeting Irish envoys stationed on the Continent. Brennan was in Berlin when he heard of the conclusion of the London negotiations. He did not support the 1921 Anglo-Irish treaty and resigned in early 1922.

In 1921 his first novel, *The False Fingertip*, was published under the pen name 'R. Selskar Kearney'. Through his life Brennan was a prolific writer of stories for magazines and various newspapers. In 1926, his second novel, *The Toledo Dagger*, was published. In the 1930s, his play about the life of convicts in an English prison, *The Bystander*, was performed in the Abbey, and later in the decade, his comedy on the disappearance of the Irish crown jewels, *Goodnight Mr. O'Donnell*, was performed in the Olympia theatre in Dublin. It was later translated into Irish as *'Oidhche Mhait agat, a Mhic Ui Dhomhnaill'*.

In 1950 he returned to the public service as director of the Irish News Agency. A further novel, set in Washington, *The Man who Walked like a Dancer*, was published in 1951. Through 1956 and 1957, Brennan published a weekly column of reminiscences in the Irish Press. In 1958, his valuable memoir and study of de Valera were published in serial form in The Irish Press. Robert Brennan died 12 November, 1964, at his home at Dodder Park Road, Dublin and was buried at Mount Jerome cemetery, Dublin.

He married, 6 July 1909, Una (Anastasia) Bolger, Coolamain, Oylegate (1888-1958). They had five children: Emer (b. 1910), Manus (1911 -12), Maeve who later wrote for the New Yorker, Deirdre (b. 1918), and Robert Patrick (b. 1928). Brennan's Ireland standing firm (1958) and *Eamon de Valera: a memoir* (1958) were republished by the UCD Press as a joint edition in 2002.

Into captivity: Volunteer leaders are marched away from the Enniscorthy Athenaeum under armed guard after the surrender on 1 May 1916. Bob Brennan is at the front wearing a grey cap and on his left is Head Constable Collins, RIC. Immediately behind Brennan is Seán Etchingham, wearing a long overcoat and Volunteer slouch hat and behind him are Richard King, Michael de Lacy, Séamus Doyle and Séamus Rafter.

1916 LEADERSHIP. The leading figures in a determination to rise in arms in the middle of World War I were photographed in Enniscorthy. The formal photographs followed the March 1916 tour of inspection by Padraig Pearse when the plans were formed, a date fixed and future developments estimated. Robert Brennan was clear that national honour demanded an armed uprising. Seated: Vice-Commandant Séamus Rafter; Robert Brennan, Brigade Quartermaster and standing, Robert Brennan's wife Úna, née Bolger.

Robert Brennan, convict, England, 1916-1917.

Robert Brennan, following his return to Wexford after his war-time diplomatic posting in Washington (1934-1947), with his SISTER NAN.

The photograph was taken at the rear of their old home in Abbey Street, Wexford, with the 13th century town wall in the background. This is a unique record because Nan refused to have her photo taken at all times. This may be because of her intelligence service during the War of Independence. She was very well acquainted with the major figures but remained rigidly unobtrusive.

By courtesy of Robert's granddaughter, Yvonne Jerrold.

Courtesy of the Nance Cahill Collection.

This photograph by Miss N. Curtis of Hibernian House, Georges Street, Enniscorthy, (Bolger's Drapery and now Dunnes Stores) was taken on the firm's annual outing to Courtown Harbour on May 28th, 1911.

While undoubtedly the photograph boasts of a great staff and great characters few on that day could conceivably imagine the developing role in Irish history of the young man with the girl second from the right in the front row. He was then an *Echo* newspaper reporter in Enniscorthy and was brought along on many such outings to record the day. He was Robert Brennan of Wexford town who in four years time was to be sentenced to death by firing squad for his leadership in the 1916 Rebellion in Enniscorthy. He became a founder director of the daily Irish Press, and then the head of neutral Ireland's Diplomatic Mission in Washington during the delicate years of World War Two. He was Director General of Radio Éireann and finally the author of one of the great source works of the War of Independence and subsequently. His memoirs, titled *Allegiance* with other works on the period, are essential records particularly for County Wexford.

W.J. BRENNAN WHITMORE GOREY T.C..

Brennan-Whitmore, a British army Boer War veteran, joined the Irish Volunteers and took part in the 1916 Rising in Dublin where he was promoted commandant. He was an advocate of guerrilla warfare on a national scale rather than a last stand defensive gesture as took place in Easter week, even though it was an unequivocal success politically.

LEADERS IN THE LOCAL UNIT OF THE SOUTH WEXFORD BRIGADE of the Irish Republican Army. Photograph taken at Ballytory in 1920.

Back: Nick Devereux, The Trap; Jim Gaul, Bennettstown; Paddy Parle, Tacumshane; Jim Pettitt, Ballycushlane; Pat Keating, Yoletown; Phil Furlong, Loughtown, P.A.Corry, Ballyfane. Front: Jim Devereux, The Trap; Paddy Cullen, Lady's Island; Officer Unknown; Jack Devereux, The Grange (Captain of Battalion); Tommy Marley, Broadway.

CAMPILE BOMBED

During the Luftwaffe campaign over England and Wales especially Pembroke Docks and Bristol in 1940 many German planes were driven off course. The RAF had discovered how to bend the radar beam directing the German bombers. Several Luftwaffe planes crashed in County Wexford or off our coast. On August 26, 1940 a Heinkel III bombed Campile railway station and the Shelburne Co-op, killing three women and inflicting heavy damage.

The Irish Embassy head in Berlin protested the Campile bombing with the authorities in Berlin. In October 1940, the then Irish Department of External Affairs issued a statement in which it noted that the German government "because of their desire to act in the spirit of their friendly relations with Ireland, are prepared to admit the possibility the bombs had been dropped by a German aircraft, the pilot of which had lost his way owing to bad visibility".

The statement added that the German foreign office had expressed its "regret" for the incident, offered "sincere sympathy" to those who suffered and expressed its willingness to "pay compensation for the loss and damage sustained".

Our photograph shows Irish soldiers with gasmasks working in the Co-op ruins near the refrigerators. See *County Wexford in the Rare Oul Times, Vol. 4, 2005)*. Editorial committee of *The Campile Bombing- August 26th, 1940*, by the Horeswood Historical Society.

Photograph by courtesy of John Flynn.

Wexford Air Raid Precaution volunteers march in early 1940 before there was time to issue anything else but helmets.

ENNISCORTHY COMPANY, L.D.F. – SEPT. 1942.

Front row: T. Stringer, Coy. Adjt; S. Browne, Coy. Q.-M; P. Pierce; P-L E. Carty, P.L.; M. Kelly, Asist, Coy. Ldr.; S. Carty, Instructor; Sergt. J. Brady; S.-L; P Scully (with cup); Coy. Ldr. Wm. Quirke; Dist. Adjt. M. Murphy; Dist. I.O P. Tobin; P.-L. D. Butler; P.-L. S. Jordan; P.L. J. Kelly; P.-L. D. Doran; P.L. J. Breen.

Second row: P.J. Maguire; T. Pierce; J. Bradley; Assist. P.L. J. Cardiff; T. Leacy, S.L. T. Askins; O. Carty; P.J. Doyle; S.L. T. Byrne; P. Reid; J. Connors; J. Sheehan; S.L. H. Ringwood; S. Pender; T. Kavanagh; P. Browne; D. O'Donohoe.

Third row: J.J. Doyle, W. Gleeson, Assist. P.L. P. O'Neill; N. Hendrick, W. Martin, J. Ringwood, W. Enright, H. Ryan, J.J. Doyle; S. Murphy; S.L. T. Doyle.

Fourth row: S.L. J. Tully, J. Morrissey, P. Murphy, R. Murphy, Assist. P.-L. W. Moore; S.-L. P. Kiernan; M. Tobin, M Kehoe, P. Doyle, R. Hogan, W. Jordan, W. Murphy, J. Dwyer, E. Devereux, J. Hyland.

Fifth row: T. Nolan, W. Roche, P. Breen, L. Foley, T. McGrath, R. Roche, W. Moore, J. O'Brien, R. Whitney, K. Carty, S.-L. P. Darcy; M. Nolan, J. Courtney, S.L. L.Cowman; E. Hudson, W. Peare.

Sixth row: L. Healy, M. O'Neill, S.-L. M. O'Connor; E. Carley, O. Murphy, E. Byrne, S. Devereux.

Ned Roice Collection.

THERE ARE FEW PHOTOGRAPHS remaining in private hands showing the first uniforms of the army's Local Defence Force. They were brown in colour and introduced early in 1940. Sometimes the units in the unusual uniforms were called "the chocolate soldiers". These light uniforms were later replaced by the army's green.

Snapped at Hill Street, Wexford before their 'fall-in' order, summer 1940, are standing, Ned Roice, Nick Scallan, Pat Hore, Jimmy Hogan, Billy Hendrick, John Flaherty, Mike Egan, John O'Neill. Kneeling are: Johnny Hore, Willie Tierney.

War Time Garda Wexford District

This photograph is lent to us by Garda archivist, Dick Conway. It is certainly sixty years old, some have dated it at 1947. I wonder how many of that Boker generation or girls in all the national schools will remember Garda Gerry Corcoran, the school's attendance officer. He came into classes with a big black book going through the names with our teacher, Donal (Dan) Twomey, from Rathlurk in Co. Cork.

In our photograph one particular Garda is of interest. He, Garda Edward Mulhall, is in the exact centre of the second row, In the critical urgency of The Emergency, Ned, as he was known, was selected to train the hundreds of volunteers who joined the Defence Forces. He was seconded to the army, given the rank of Captain, based in Wexford.

At the end of The Emergency he returned to normal Garda life as a rank Garda. He did not, as one might have expected, return to the officer rank or presumably salary he may have had in the army. The first Bean Gardaí were appointed in 1959.

We thank the houses of Armstrong, Nolan and Conway for their identification help. Back row: John McCaffrey, Pat Fogarty, Jim Smith, Pat McCarthy, John Treanor and David Stenson. Middle row: Joe Lynch, Barney Forde, Jim Corcoran, Ned Mulhall, Martin Bond, Frank O'Connor and Pat Lawlor. Front row: Barney Reilly, Detective Mick Medlar, Sergeant C. Armstrong, Sergeant Jack Spillane, Superintendent Farrell, (we think) Detective Sergeant Diffley and Gerry Corcoran.

Dick Conway Collection.

ENNISCORTHY'S IRISH RED CROSS UNIT, 1964-65. Back row: Tom Kelly, St Michael's Road, Dave Curran, Esmonde St., Dr. Conlan, St. Senan's Psychiatric Hospital; Dr. Dunphy, Monamolin, Murt Sullivan, Cluainin; Willie Redmond, Coiscuinne. Seated: Angie Martin, Upper Shannon; Heather Kerr, Mill Park Road, M. dal Bysartem, Mill Park Road; Ethel Tector, Ballinure; Miss Lueqte, Enniscorthy and Bridget Moran, St John's Villas.

Dick Conway Collection.

TOM O'KEEFFE
Veteran Honoured by the Republic of Korea

On the 25th of June 2010 at the Embassy of the Republic of Korea, Irish veterans of the Korean War were conferred with medals on behalf of the Korean people. Among them were three Wexford men, John Hawkins of Enniscorthy, formerly of the Australian Army and two Royal Navy veterans Michael Kehoe of Ballycullane and Tom O'Keeffe of Bernadette Place, Wexford town.

Tom O'Keeffe comes from a seafaring background. His mother was Anna Mary Stafford of Carigeen and his father was Paddy O'Keeffe of The Faythe, a brother of Eddie O'Keeffe, the well-known newspaper reporter. His maternal grandfather was at sea in sail and steam before joining Irish Lights in 1910. His uncle Martin Stafford was a Royal Navy man and served in World Ward II as did his father's brother Raymond O'Keeffe who was killed on board the Aircraft Carrier H.M.S. Ark Royal.

Maritime affairs writer Jack O'Leary succeeded in getting a reluctant Tom O'Keeffe to tell his story in the County Wexford Free Press. " My twin brother and I joined the Royal Navy as boys. We were just 16. Two years later in 1949, I was on my way to the Far East on H.M.S. Cockade, a wartime destroyer. In June the following year the Korean War broke out and as part of the United Nations Task Force we were diverted to Sasebo, a Japanese seaport."

"We were part of the U.N. blockade and escort force. The British and Commonwealth ships were formed into The West Korean Support Group.

"I came home on the troop ship in '52. My abiding memories of Korea are, apart from the engagements, the sub-zero temperatures that thick underwear and duffle coats couldn't keep out. That biting cold on an open gun deck. Ranging up and down the coast for weeks on end. Wartime complement meant that we had almost double our crew. You slept in your clothes, on tables, under tables, space was at a premium. There was a scarcity of food. And yet we were well off compared to the land forces. They really had it tough.

"I arrived in Wexford on the 9 o'clock bus one night after two and half years. The town was quiet and dark, very little lights and the smell of turf fires which I've always loved, lifted my heart and I felt I had never been away.

Boy seaman, 1949, Tom O'Keeffe of The Faythe, Wexford, on the left, before embarking for the war in Korea. Was it to be World War III?

He served as Able Seaman throughout that threatening conflict. He was later decorated by the Government of South Korea.

H.M.S. Cockade, able seaman Tom O'Keeffe's ship and complement in the Korean War, 1950

WAR GRAVES

In 1941, Luftwaffe crash landings and crew deaths increased in County Wexford. Proximity to Wales and Cornwall, damage from anti-aircraft fire overflying, were probable causes. Three German airmen crash-landed into the Blackstair mountains in early October 1941. All were killed in this particular crash and were buried with full military honours in Rathnure.

Since November is the month when all the combatant nations honour their dead, perhaps not on the same date, the German Ambassador came to Rathnure to lay a wreath on the Luftwaffe graves. The date was 14 November 1954. THE AMBASSADOR, DR HERMAN KATZENBERGER, who as the photograph shows lost his left arm in the war, reviewed the F.C.A. guard of honour and laid a wreath on behalf of the German Government. Draped in the national colours of black, red and gold, the legend read "Our Dead Soldiers" On the grave crosses were written the names and ranks with the addition of "Fallen for Germany" and the dates.

In the funeral service the parish priest of Rathnure, Fr. John Doyle, officiated for the Catholics and the Rector of Killanne, Rev. Joseph Ruddell officiated on behalf of the Lutherans. The ceremony concluded with the ambassador giving an address at the graves.

Bundesarchiv Militararchiv, Freiburg, Wiesentalstr 10, Deutschland 79115.

Diarmuid O'Leary.

NEW ROSS FCA contingent probably after Easter Sunday parade on the steps of their HQ in Maher's Yard, South Street. Back L to R - Capt. Jim Bailey, Commdt. Andy Minihan, Commdt. Paddy Barry, Capt Dick O'Grady, Lt Jim Sutton, Seán Doyle NT. (Retd. OC Commdt.). Front Row, Lt. Jim Murphy, Lt. Tom Dunne (Caim), Lt. Danny Jevens (Wexford)

CAPT DICK O'GRADY AND COMMDT. ANDY MINIHAN stand to attention outside wooden huts in Maher's Yard, South Street, which were used as a headquarters. In 1968 the huts were burned and new HQ were established in the annex of Delare House.

Diarmuid O'Leary.

RECEPTION for FCA Commdt. Rtd. Tom O'Hanlon, Horeswood who commanded the New Ross district Forsa Cosanta Áitiúil during the Emergency 1939- 1945.

Back row: Tom Howlett, Tom Conway, Sgt Tobin, Duncannon, Richard Rowe.

3rd row: Tom Shannon. Dr. Jack Hickey, Bob Flynn, Garda Gerard Dowling,Terry Dalton, Dick O'Grady.

Seated: Michael Egan, Seán Doyle NT, Tom O' Hanlon, Jimmy Kennedy. AndyMinihan. Front kneeling: Jerry Ryan, Peter Cummins, Mersheen, Christy Hall, Principal, New Ross Vocational School, Jimmy Coughlan, Solicitor.

Diarmuid O'Leary.

NEW ROSS FCA PIPE BAND parade to St. Stephen's Graveyard on EasterSunday 1979 for annual wreath-laying ceremony in memory of the veterans of the Old IRA. On the bottom left is PDF QM Sergt. John (Johno) O'Brien based in New Ross who was MC on many occasions. In the sixties, Johno was one of the first Irish soldiers to set foot in the Congo to organise supplies and accommodation for the main UN Irish Peace force contingent to follow.

NEW ROSS FCA PARTY taken about 1982 in Albatross Recreation Hall, Front l. to r.: Lt Pascal Bolger, John Sweeney (Commdt.), Andy Minihan (Rtd. Commdt), Commdt. Michael A. (Sam) McDonald, Sgt Tom Bolger, O.C. of 10th Battalion, Seán Doyle NT (Rtd Commdt), Jim Murphy (Rtd. Capt.),Lt. Bobby Reck. 2nd row: Jim Sutton (Rtd. Lt.) Alan Bailey, Michael Griffin, Sue Furlong. Bernard McGarr, Ronnie Whelan, Michael Ryan, Anthony Flynn, James Hennebry.

3rd row : A.N.Other, Sgt. Michael Ryan, Mark Minihan, Tom MacDonald, Johnny O'Leary, Larry Shannon,

Back row:Jimmy Allen, John Ryan, Aidan Dwyer, Brendan Wafer.

FIRST FEMALE SOLDIERS. A new development, one that was long overdue, was publicly demonstrated thirty years ago in Enniscorthy. It was the first occasion that female soldiers of the F.C.A. were seen on public parade.

L. to r., Corporal Stephen Byrne, Corporal Frank Murphy, Private Sara Carty, Corporal Dick Martin, Private Patrick Burke, Private Keith O'Connor, Private Paul O'Sullivan, Private Collette Murphy, Private Paul Murphy, Private Ed Brosnan, Lieutenant Gerard Whelan, Private James Doyle.

VETERANS from the reduced ranks of 1919–21. L. to r.: Tom Hearne, Felix O'Connor, Ml Maher, Matty Kinnard, "Wee" Joe O'Brien, Tom Doyle, sentenced to death in 1916, and Pat Keegan.

REVIEWING STAND on the 50th Anniversary of the Rising in 1916. Eddie Breen, grandson of veteran Jack Breen, reads the Proclamation of 1916. The veteran Brigade Adjutant, Séamus Doyle, stands alongside him. On the platform, l to r: Seán Browne, T.D., Dr Anthony Esmonde, T.D., Brendan Corish, T.D., Lorcan Allen T.D., Paddy Tobin with the Cumann na mBan veterans Mrs S. Doyle, Miss M. Stokes, Mrs L. Shortall, Miss M.E. Doyle, Miss P. King, Councillor Paddy Doran on left of platform. The guard of honour in foreground consists of veterans of the Enniscorthy Irish Volunteers Garrison 1916.

Courtesy of Echo Newspapers.

1916 Rising Enniscorthy leader, Séamus Rafter commemoration in Ballindaggin on 12th Sept 1950.

The last surviving eleven of Enniscorthy's 1916 garrison with the veterans of Cumann na mBan. Mrs Pat Doyle, Pat Doyle, Templeshannon, Mike Nolan of John Street; Denis Doyle, Munster Hill; Jack Kelly, Pearse Road; J. Carley, Old Church, (formerly Station Master, Camolin), Jack Murphy, Ross Road ; Paddy Pierce, St. John's Villas; Mrs Tom Hearne, Ross Road; Padruig Toibin, Bohreen Hill and Mrs James Whelan, Pearse Road.

Old Soldiers. As the lights went down over the 1970s, the ranks of the Forsa Cosanta Áitiúil were gradually being reduced and replenished by younger faces. A reunion of the men who volunteered and soldiered during The Emergency 1939 to 1945 and longer, assembled for a last parade and reunion in Wexford Military Barracks. It took place in 1981.

The gallant veterans, now with medals and arm insignia, whose identity we can confirm are: Larry O'Neill, Ned Burke, Nick Kavanagh, Jim Reck, Tom Kelly, Mal Donohoe, Jim Morris, Dom Sinnott, Johnny Hore, Dan Maher, Jack Burke, A.N.Other, Nick Scallan, Ray Whelan, Nicky Rossiter, Seán Murphy, A.N.Other, Richie Mahoney, Johnny Murphy,

Echo Newspapers.

Ned Roche Collection. N. Malone, Jack Sharkey, Seán Kelly, John Murphy and Tom Beale. Seated: N. Fortune, John Ruttledge, Mark Roche, N. Furlong, N. Carley, Tom Cleary, Tommy Howlin, Arthur Lewis, John Codd, Christy Hanton, Wally Doyle, Mosie O'Leary, Pat Carr, Jimmy Dempsey, Pierce Walsh, Ned Roice, A.N. Other, N. Rossiter, Paddy Kelly.

OFFICERS OF THE 25TH BATTALION relaxing after lunch outside their headquarters, Bawnjames House, New Ross, 7 June 1942. The Emergency brought together not alone those who had fought in 1916 and the War of Independence but also those who had fought on opposing sides during the Civil War.

'STEP TOGETHER' WEEK, New Ross–2 May, 1943. Many large towns organised special weeks involving parades, concerts and sports events in which military and civilians participated.

AN IMPROVISED ALTAR at Castle Annagh Camp outside New Ross, 5 July 1942. The Army fought a long battle with the Hierarchy to have chaplains appointed to units so that they could accompany the troops on exercise. The Bishops were not initially in favour of the idea of priests travelling outside their dioceses.

By courtesy of F.C.A. Officer James Sutton.

SKINHEADS are not a new phenomenon! NCOs and men of the 25th Battalion showing off their haircuts while on brigade manoeuvres, Castle Annagh Camp, New Ross, 6 July 1942. *(With thanks to Military Archives, Cathal Bruga Barracks, Dublin 6, publishers of The Nation, The Irish Defence Forces 1939-1946, printed by Defence Forces Printing Press, Defence Forces Headquarters, Parkgate, Dublin 8)*

Camp Guard awaiting the arrival of the Orderly Officer, 25th Battalion lines, Bawnjames Military Camp, New Ross, Co. Wexford, 16 August, 1942

THE HOOK

The Hook Peninsula has an underlying utilisation known to archaeologists, naval and military strategists since the Iron Age. On either side of the peninsula stabbing into the Atlantic there are found dúns, promontory forts of substantial dimensions, and up to the modern period a major fortress, Duncannon, on the Waterford Harbour side. The reason remains the deep water harbour of Waterford City in which today huge cruise liners can navigate with facility, and its minor river routes to the hinterland. These facilities were of vital importance to every imperialist wanting to control the north Atlantic routes to America and all three were at war against each other intermittently, France, England, Spain.

The two world wars and the "Cold War" produced ample evidence of that. The U Boat warfare and mine laying on the nearby Atlantic sea routes are indicated graphically by our photograph thanks to P.H. Hickey. The Irish army were on alert 24/7 as the phrase has it in World War II.

Billy Colfer Collection.

Coast watching unit of the Irish Army at Hook Head. Tourist priest with binoculars is not a German or British spy. The army unit on the Hook comprised Matt and Patrick Murphy, John White, Patrick Banville, Tom Colfer, William Colfer, Richard Fortune, Thomas Colfer and Jack Colfer.

The submarine and mine laying warfare in the Atlantic waters off the County Wexford coast in both world wars was extensive because of the shipping lanes to and from the U.K. Submarine warfare reached ferocity levels. Our photograph by P.J. Hickey shows British Navy mine sweepers who were clearing German mines in 1946 sheltering in the lee of Baginbun Head.

Photograph by P.J. Hickey. By courtesy of Billy Colfer, *The Hook Peninsula* 2004.

Hook Light house, environs.    The Head Keeper, 1960.    Saint Dubhans Medieval Church.

PREPARED FOR ANYTHING, The Wexford Boy Scouts, Second Wexford Troop, 1941, with senior officers, in *loco parentis*, we hope. Seated, Peter Clarke, Manager, National Bank, Edmund Hassett, M.P.S.I., Fr. John Butler, chaplain, Joseph Scallan, Celtic Laundry Ltd., Harry Murray, Scout Master and Kevin Kehoe, chief scout.

THE GOLDEN JUBILEE PARADE of the Easter Rising took place in Enniscorthy in 1966 and was led by veterans of the rising. The Colour Party seen here crossing Slaney Bridge included from left to right, Patrick Pierce, James Whelan, William Quirke and John Carroll.

Courtesy of Eamon Doyle.

LOCH GARMAN FEIS: Presentation Convent's entry 1941 had a decidedly military flavour. Front: (with hurleys), Kieran Flynn, Aidan Ffrench. Middle: (Musicians), Tom Kelly, Jack Carty, Eddie O'Connor, A.N. Other, Georgie Murphy (with plane), Eamon Doyle, Oliver Byrne, A.N. Other, Jimmy Rossiter, Jim Bond, A. N. Other, young Rossiter and Morris. The missing names are known but to the Lord.

ACKNOWLEDGEMENTS CONTRIBUTORS, DONORS

We are extremely grateful to the following generous contributors without whom this publication would not have been possible.

Alan Aherne

Helen Ashdown

T.J. Barrett

Eileen Berry (née Dillon)

Bernard Browne

Paddy Browne and Mary Browne

Richard Browne

Denis Cadogan

Nance Cahill

Tommy Carr

Ger Carty

Ibar Carty

Tom and Mai Carty

Pat, Nicky and Rosaleen Cleary

Eileen Cloney-Kehoe

Pat Codd

Aidan Cogley

Billy Colfer

Bill Creedon

Co. Wexford Library Service

County Museum, Enniscorthy Castle

Alan Cuddihy

Evelyn Cullen

Noel Culleton

Eamon Doyle

Echo Newspapers

Irene Elgee

Michael Fitzpatrick

Gráinne Doran

Jimmy FitzGibbon

Ray Flynn

Mairéad Furlong (for Research)

Garda Síochána Archives

Jarlath Glynn

Liam Griffin

Fionnuala Hanrahan

Pat Hayes

Tomás Hayes

Ken Hemingway

P.J. Hickey

Ted Howlin

Irish Press

Irish Army Archives

Cathal Brugha Barracks, Dublin, The Irish Railway Record Society

Yvonne Jarrold

Christina Jordan

Dominic Kiernan

Breda Kelly

Eva Kelly

Simon W. Kennedy

Patrick Kinsella

Patricia Kinsella (née Sinnott)

Kenneth King

Beryl Kinsella

Joan Kirwin

Liam Lahiff

Robert Lambert,

John Lee

Ann Marsh

Peter Maguire

Muriel McCarthy

Peter McDonald

Tom Mooney

James G. Murphy

Paddy Murphy

Philip Murphy

William Murphy

Danny Neville

A.C. Nolan

Lar and Cis O'Brien

Jimmy and Sylvia O'Connor

Pat O'Connor

Denise O'Connor-Murphy

M. O'Keeffe

Séamus O'Keeffe

Jack O'Leary

Austin O'Sullivan

OPW

David Parle Furniture Ltd.

James Parle

People Newspapers

John Power

Celestine Rafferty

Niall and Sarah Reck, Graphedia

Mrs Billie Ringwood

Harry Ringwood

Ned Roice

Jean Ruddock

Michael Ryan

Vincent and Ann Staples

J. Stott

Jim Sutton

Teagasc

Hugh Tunney

Catherine Walsh

Dan Walsh

Dermot Walsh

Nancy Walshe

Des Waters

James Whelan

Seán Whelan

Dominic Williams

Tomás Williams

Valerie Willoughby

Donors of Photographs and Images

Anonymous

Eileen Berry, née Dillon

E. Breen

Bree Journal

Patrick Browne and Mary Browne

Ger Busher

Mary Cadogan

Nance Cahill

Ibar Carty, P.A. Crane Collection

Tom and Mai Carty

Sr. Mary Clancy. S.S.L.

Paddy, Nicky and Rosaleen Cleary

Cloney Collection

Pat Codd, M.C.C.

Aidan Cogley

Nan Cogley Collection

Billy Colfer Collection

Bill Creedon

Michael Curran

Eamon Doyle

Shay Doyle

Echo Newspapers

Irene Elgee

Fáilte Ireland

Lt John Fitzpatrick, *Fethard on Sea*

Michael Fitzpatrick,

Ray Flynn

John Flynn and Editorial Committee, *The Campile Bombing August 26th 1940*

Fr. Walter Forde

Michael Freeman

Jack Handcock

Pat Hayes- Eamon Doyle Collection

Tomás Hayes

Brendan Hearne

Ken Hemingway

P.J. Hickey

Gerard Hore

Irish Press

Yvonne Jerrold

Christina Jordan

Eva Kelly

Nicholas Kelly Collection

Simon W. Kennedy

Dominic Kiernan

Kilmore Journal

Joan Kirwan, Vinegar Hill

Ken King

Patrick Kinsella

Pat Langan, *Irish Times*

John Lee

Peter Maguire. B.L.

Mary Ann Maher

Stephen Maloney

Ann Marsh,

Military Archives, Cathal Brugha Barracks, Dublin 6

Paddy and Sheila Mulligan

J.G. Murphy

Hilary Murphy
Patrick Murphy
William Murphy
A.C. Nolan
Bernard Nolan
J.B. Nolan
Richard Nolan, IT manager, *Echo* Newspapers
Fr. Tim Nolan
National Agricultural Museum, Johnstown Castle
New Ross History and Archaeological Society
Office of Public Works
Dan O'Brien
J.J. O'Brien
Denise O'Connor-Murphy
Denis O'Connor Photographic Archive
F.M. O'Connor Collection
Pat O'Connor
Tom O'Connor
M. O'Keeffe
Séamus O'Keeffe
Diarmuid O'Leary
Austin O'Sullivan
James Parle
Poole of Waterford
Edward Prendergast

Mrs. Billy Ringwood
Ned Roche
Marion Rackard
Richard and May Reville Collection
Ned Roice
Ryan Collection
Jean Ruddock, Family Collection
John Scanlon
Sinnott Collection
Helen Skrine
Kevin Spenser
J. Stott
Vincent Staples
Strangman Davis Goff
Taghmon Historical Society
Teagasc
Hugh Tunney
Charles Vize
Catherine Walsh
Dermot Walsh
Des Waters
Wexford Festival Opera
Dominic Williams
Tom Williams
J.W. Whelan, M.P.S.I.
Valerie Willoughby, Bishop Willoughby Collection

CASTLEBRIDGE, 1949, with the mill which was pivotal in the jealously guarded grain industry.

BOOKS
by Nicholas Furlong

Dermot King of Leinster and The Foreigners
Diarmait Mac Murchada (Dermot MacMurrough), King of Leinster, the man credited with inflicting 800 years of strife on Ireland.

The Mighty Wave (with Dr. Daire Kehoe)
This collection of essays offers a new interpretation of the Rebellion in Wexford where ordinary people, goaded into ferocity, 'swept o'er the land like a mighty wave'.

Fr. John Murphy of Boolavogue 1753-1798
The remarkable first and only biography of a major, if unexpected, 1798 Rebellion leader.

The Women of 1798 (with Dr. Daire Keogh)
No aspect of the 1798 rebellion has been so neglected as that of women's role in the events of that year. It is the intention in this work to redress this neglect, to bring a new light to bear on the subject and create an accurate assessment of the role of women in that year of devastation.

A History of County Wexford
Furlong traces the story of the county from its earliest settlements through its Gaelic, Christian, Norse and Norman phases of life to the turbulence of the Elizabethan and Cromwellian regimes. He brings the reader through the great upheaval of 1798 and the institutional revival of Catholicism in the 19th century, its sporting and cultural revival, the Wexford Opera Festival and modern Wexford which has built itself into the nation's holiday playground and a vital European transport hub."

County Wexford In The Rare Oul' Times, Volume IV, 2005
The fourth edition theme is County Wexford in War, 1910 – 1924. It is a wide spectrum, period photograph issue covering the political and military build-up to World War One; the World War on land and sea particularly off Wexford's Irish Sea and Atlantic coasts; the 1916 Rising in Enniscorthy, the War of Independence, The Civil War and the aftermath in the strategically important south-east. It includes sensational photographs from private collections and photographs never before published. It will in short be essential, not merely for the general public, but scholars and researchers, particularly as we approach the centenary commemorations of a monumental decade in Irish and world history.

County Wexford In The Rare Oul' Times, Volume I – Out of Print

County Wexford In The Rare Oul' Times, Volume II - Out of Print

County Wexford In The Rare Oul' Times, Volume III – Out of Print

Young Farmer Seeks Wife- a novel
"The mother told me to avoid the company of girls until I was thirty five or so and then marry a good sensible match, a respectable girl with a farm and money. 'Take your time, Nicholas,' the mother said, 'there are thousands of farmers' daughters with their tongues hanging out to be married, and don't worry about a thing, for after my day you'll have this place free of rent forever, and your uncle Dick's place as well"

- "The greatest comic novel of the century." (Dr. Gerry Dukes)

A Foster Son for a King, (1986), - a novel for schoolchildren.
A castle in Wales... an Irish King fighting for his kingdom... a Norman earl in disgrace... From the meeting of Dermot MacMurrough and Strongbow are born the Norman landings in Ireland. Gwyn, the Welsh boy who becomes Dermot's foster son, sees it all - the siege of Wexford, the sack of Waterford, the taking of Dublin. Tiernan O'Rourke is Dermot's mortal enemy. Can he prevent him becoming High King.? A marvellously exciting story!

The Greatest Hurling Decade
In the 1950s one team dominated all others. Wexford was the possessor of only one national title – won in 1910 – when, at the end of the Forties, it gathered together a band of warriors that was to swashbuckle its way through the next ten years.

By Bishop's Rath and Norman Fort, (Wexford 1994) with Dr Edward Culleton and Patrick Sills. A history of Piercestown - Murrintown parish, Co. Wexford: an interdisciplinary compilation.

FESTSCHRIFT

The Wexford Man Ed. Bernard Browne.
This collection contains twenty-two essays addressed to Nicholas Furlong. The various contributions, written by distinguished scholars, colleagues and friends, focus mainly on matters pertaining to the county of Wexford. The volume is intended to serve as a befitting and long standing tribute to Furlong for outstanding service to his native county.

STAGE PRODUCTIONS
by Nicholas Furlong

Insurrection '98 Wexford Opera Festival, 1965, Dun Mhuire Theatre:
Directed by Tomas Mac Anna
Revived 1998, Directed by Harry and Billy Ringwood

The Lunatic Fringe, Wexford Opera Festival 1966, Dun Mhuire Theatre: Directed by Tomás Mac Anna

Purple and Gold, GAA Centenary, 1984, Dun Mhuire Theatre: Directed by Tomás Mac Anna

Storm the Bastille, Abbey Square, Enniscorthy – July, 1989: Directed by Harry Ringwood for the bicentenary commemoration of the French Revolution.

Harvest-time in the Haggard field, Mulgannon.